THE LITERARY AFTERLIVES OF SIMONE WEIL

GENDER, THEORY, AND RELIGION

GENDER, THEORY, AND RELIGION

AMY HOLLYWOOD, EDITOR

The Gender, Theory, and Religion series provides a forum for interdisciplinary scholarship at the intersection of the study of gender, sexuality, and religion.

THE LITERARY AFTERLIVES OF SIMONE WEIL

FEMINISM, JUSTICE, AND THE CHALLENGE OF RELIGION

CYNTHIA R. WALLACE

Columbia University Press   *New York*

Columbia University Press
Publishers Since 1893
New York   Chichester, West Sussex
cup.columbia.edu
Copyright © 2024 Columbia University Press

Library of Congress Cataloging-in-Publication Data
Names: Wallace, Cynthia (Cynthia R.), author.
Title: The literary afterlives of Simone Weil : feminism, justice,
and the challenge of religion / Cynthia R. Wallace.
Description: New York : Columbia University Press, [2024] |
Series: Gender, theory, and religion | Includes bibliographical references.
Identifiers: LCCN 2023035307 (print) | LCCN 2023035308 (ebook) |
ISBN 9780231214186 (hardback) | ISBN 9780231214193 (trade paperback) |
ISBN 9780231560238 (ebook)
Subjects: LCSH: Weil, Simone, 1909–1943—Influence.
Classification: LCC PQ2645.E24 W35 2024 (print) | LCC PQ2645.E24 (ebook) |
DDC 848/.91209—dc23/eng/20231220
LC record available at https://lccn.loc.gov/2023035307
LC ebook record available at https://lccn.loc.gov/2023035308

Add cover/jacket credit information

COVER DESIGN: Chang Jae Lee
COVER IMAGE: © Hee Seung Chung, *Untitled*, 2011, from the series Still Life

For Josh

God is the supreme poet.

—Simone Weil, *First and Last Notebooks*

CONTENTS

THE LITERARY AFTERLIVES OF SIMONE WEIL

INTRODUCTION

Art. It is the triumph of art to lead to something other than itself: to a life which is fully conscious of the pact between the mind and the world.

—Simone Weil, *First and Last Notebooks*

T here is," the philosopher Simone Weil once insisted, "a way of waiting, when we are writing, for the right word to come of itself at the end of our pen, while we merely reject all inadequate words."[1] The right words present themselves of their own accord, a creation taking shape in the light of our patient openness. When the writer works in this way, she fades into the background, leaving room for the work to flourish in its own right.

Since her death in 1943, Weil has lived to be lauded—and castigated, and at points willfully ignored—in the words she left behind, voluminous notebooks and essays carefully preserved, curated, and published by friends and scholars. These life texts have also provoked perhaps more literary writing than any other twentieth-century philosopher: stories, essays, and especially poems given over to her thought and person. The poet Peggy Rosenthal goes so far as to "doubt there is a twentieth-century figure who has inspired more poetry."[2] Such literary texts are traces of traces, as the writers encounter Weil through her own writings and biographers' accounts, then wait for the right words to come to their pens or fingertips and bring her into being yet again, a perhaps ironic literary re-creation of a figure who famously sought to disappear into her work.

The list of poets, novelists, and nonfiction writers who attend to Weil is extraordinary, including Sharon Cameron, Albert Camus, Michelle Cliff, Robert Cording, T. S. Eliot, André Gide, Jorie Graham, Elizabeth Hardwick, Seamus Heaney, Geoffrey Hill, Edward Hirsch, Jane Hirshfield, Elizabeth Jennings, Mary Karr, Denise Levertov, Czesław Miłosz, Flannery O'Connor, Michael Symmons Roberts, Gjertrud Schnackenberg, Susan Sontag, Cornel West, Rowan Williams, Christian Wiman, and Jan Zwicky, to name just a few who write in or are translated into English. The scope of Weil's influence extends to philosophers and popes, theologians and politicians, but as Joan Dargan notes in *Simone Weil: Thinking Poetically*, Weil had a special appreciation for literature, a deep love of the classics. Her own prose is wonderfully readable, even lovely, as many of her commentators have noted. "Refreshingly, mystifyingly, her words are rarely predictable," Dargan writes. "Weil's cast of mind is the sort that ponders, lingers, amplifies, races ahead, cuts through forests of impressions with aphoristic sweep; one comes across elaborations of insight and equally abrupt silences. Such writing is never far from poetry."[3] Weil wrote poetry herself—although in Dargan's estimation it doesn't compare to her prose—and left behind an unfinished play since published as *Venice Saved*.[4] She taught the classics at any opportunity, to working men and even children on a ship as she crossed the Atlantic. Given her love of literature (Platonic suspicion of imagination notwithstanding), one wonders what Weil would have thought to find herself so frequently immortalized—and at points argued with—in imaginative writing.

One also wonders what, precisely, has motivated so much literary engagement. Is it deep calling to deep, Weil's limpid prose inviting more of the same? Is it her brief and intense life, its perplexing paradoxes? As Robert Zaretsky notes in *The Subversive Simone Weil*,

> It has become a ritual among Weil biographers to sum up her life with a series of contradictions. An anarchist who espoused conservative ideals, a pacifist who fought in the Spanish Civil War, a saint who refused baptism, a mystic who was a labor militant, a French Jew who was buried in the Catholic section of an English cemetery, a teacher who dismissed the importance of solving a problem, the most willful of individuals who advocated the extinction of the self.

Zaretsky reads these paradoxes as "invitations to reflect on both one and the other," comparing this practice to Weil's own insistence on thinking persistently through opposing ideas.[5] Indeed, even apart from the paradoxes of her life, Weil's writing refuses easy categorization, encompassing political philosophy, ethics, aesthetics, epistemology, and metaphysics while theorizing power and suffering, the interpersonal and structural obligations for a healthy and just society and humanity. But Weil's work is also difficult to classify because, as A. Rebecca Rozelle-Stone and Benjamin P. Davis articulate, "she is a philosopher of margins and paradoxes" who "philosophized on thresholds and across borders."[6] Is this what inspires literature to and with and about Weil—the compelling pull of contradictions and the refusal of common boundaries?

Whatever its source, surprisingly little has been written *about* Weil's presence in literary texts, although a cheering trend of attention to Weil's influence on literary writers is appearing in scholarly journal articles, usually focused on just one or a handful of writers.[7] Lists of public thinkers Weil has influenced are commonplace in discussions of her, but apart from the philosophers Hannah Arendt and Iris Murdoch, these lists usually emphasize famous men. Yet while Weil's influence certainly exceeds gender categories, as evidenced by own my partial list, her most devoted literary interlocutors have tended to be women, a fact that is particularly intriguing given her fraught relationship to gender, religion, and sacrifice.

In this book I focus on a group of anglophone literary writers who have shown some of the most sustained engagements with Weil's thought and life in their published work, engagements that have yet to receive much scholarly attention. These writers include Adrienne Rich, the radical feminist poet; Annie Dillard, famous for her metaphysically rich nonfiction; Mary Gordon, the feminist Catholic novelist; and a series of poets who have written either poetic sequences or full books devoted to Weil, namely, Maggie Helwig, Stephanie Strickland, Kate Daniels, Sarah Klassen, Anne Carson, and Lorri Neilsen Glenn. This gathering, which encompasses poetry, fiction, and literary nonfiction, allows me to interrogate the wide-ranging literary fascination with Weil's thought and life. These texts learn from Weil's philosophy and biography and also at points problematize them, especially their intersections of embodiment and Christianity. To varying degrees and in sometimes radically different ways, these literary texts both celebrate Weil and resist her, rendering her present in words that seek, in the way of literature, to be adequate to the task of enlivening their subject. Beyond what these texts can teach us about Weil herself—present to us in their poetry and prose, again, as the trace of a trace—they raise questions about feminism and secularity, literature and philosophy, commemoration and refusal. Three intersecting trends become clear when we read these texts in concert. The first of these is a fascination, whether troubled or sympathetic, with Weil's turn toward a Christian God. The second is a fascination, usually but not always alarmed, with Weil's self-sacrificial theory and practice. The third is a fascination, more typically admiring, with her call to a practice of attention that manifests what we might call aesthetic and moral seriousness. These fascinations are not unrelated dynamics within Weil's thought and life, and in all three cases, the writers often struggle because they find something of value within the tangle—some pearl of great price buried in the field of Weil's difficulty.

In seeking to trace Weil's appeal, this book contributes to a growing but far from finished project documenting Weil's reception history in North America. It highlights Weil's importance—and challenge—to several generations of writers across the genres, with varying commitments to feminism, religion, and political action. More broadly, it enriches discussion not just of these writers, whose engagements with Weil have so far been mostly overlooked, but also about the very topics that draw these writers to Weil: the deficits, surpluses, and urgent need for certain modes of attention in the modern world; the risky possibilities of self-sacrificial care for others in the face of growing inequities and horrifying injustices; and the tension between Christian institutions' capacity to harm and their vision of justice, love, and human flourishing.

SKETCHING WEIL'S LIFE AND THOUGHT

More than a dozen book-length biographies of Simone Weil have been written in or translated into English in the less than a century since her death. Of these, Weil's schoolmate Simone Pétrement's *Simone Weil: A Life* (1976) is perhaps the most authoritative and most detailed, but it was proceeded and followed by many different approaches to the philosopher's life.[8] These are joined by influential magazine and newspaper profiles, as well as introductions to Weil's own writing, that have shaped popular understandings of her personality and motivations.

Weil's biography, however, presents particular challenges. Weil lived as a woman philosopher in a male-dominated world, and in her lifetime, she experienced ad hominem attacks based on her gender and personality, given names like "the Red Virgin" and "the categorical imperative in skirts." In her writing, she makes clear that she wants attention not for her person but her ideas, her work as a philosopher: indeed, the very impersonal yet specific nature of her prose manifests this approach. Yet even after her death, Weil's brief and unconventional life often overshadowed her writings. As Deborah Nelson notes, midcentury reviewers perplexed by the popularity of her posthumously published work often resorted to discussions of her biography as an explanation for her writing's surprisingly wide appeal.[9] Weil would doubtless have been frustrated at the way her life story at points superseded the work itself. As Rozelle-Stone and Davis write, Weil worried "that her person would be considered more than her thought."[10] Yet scholars like E. Jane Doering and Eric Springsted argue for an approach to Weil that doesn't erase Weil the person quite so fully as she may have wished, pointing out that her life illuminates her writings, just as her writings illuminate her life. "For Weil," Doering writes in *Simone Weil and the Specter of Self-Perpetuating Force*, "theory was never separate from action."[11] Zaretsky further insists, "To a degree rare in the modern age—or, indeed, *any* age—Simone Weil fully *inhabited* her philosophy."[12] The literary writers I read in this book often approach Weil in this integrated fashion, explicating her life through her writings and her writings through her life.

With these challenges in mind, I offer here a very brief biographical sketch for readers less familiar with Weil's life story, followed by a sketch of some of her key ideas that have sparked creative writers' imaginations. Any such sketch inevitably contributes to the textual construction of Weil and her legacy, and so I tread carefully and encourage anyone interested in Weil's life to seek out fuller biographies (note the plural). Our words can only begin to do justice to a singular human story, a limitation of language Weil herself repeat-edly highlighted.

Simone Adolphine Weil was born in 1909 to Bernard and Selma Weil in Paris, France. Her father was a doctor, and the family lived a comfortable bourgeois life, although Simone was often sick as a child, and World War I disrupted the family's stability when Bernard was compelled to serve. Simone was a sensitive child from early on, both in her compassion for others and in her sensory experiences of touch and food, in particular. Biographers often trace anecdotes about her childhood passions—giving up sugar in solidarity with soldiers, avoiding physical contact—to her adult moral and personal sensibili-ties, finding a coherence in her character from the earliest years onward.

Weil was close with her older brother André, a mathematical genius: in adolescence, she also compared herself to him and found herself wanting. But Simone Weil was brilliant in her own right, studying at the Lycée Henri IV with the philosopher Émile Chart-ier (who went by the name Alain) before going on to study philoso-phy at the esteemed École Normale Supérieur, where she was the only woman in her entering class. Simone de Beauvoir and Jean Paul Sar-tre were at the school at the same time: indeed, the two Simones earned first and second place in the "General Philosophy and Logic" exam, with Weil in first. Her dissertation focused on knowledge and perception in Descartes, and after receiving her *agrégation* diploma in 1931, she went on to teach philosophy in girls' lycées.

During her schooling and working years, though, Weil was also active in labor movements, marching with, advocating for, and teach-ing workers. These activities brought her notoriety both at school and in the communities where she taught. In 1934 she took a leave of absence from teaching to work at factories and more deeply under-stand working-class concerns: she found the experience physically and mentally demoralizing, a turning point in her understanding of human suffering. Over the years, Weil wasn't afraid to alter other positions, nuancing her early approach to Marx, trading pacificism for action as an anarchist volunteer in the Spanish Civil War, and eventually embracing Christianity after a series of surprising mystical encounters in the mid- to late 1930s, when Weil was in her twenties.

These religious experiences were surprising, given Weil's formation in French philosophy and her parents' agnosticism—Weil and her brother reportedly didn't realize they were Jewish until they began to attend school. But as she went on to write about in notebooks, essays, and letters, Weil found herself attracted to Christianity starting in 1935, when she witnessed Portuguese villagers singing hymns in a procession and recognized Christianity as the "religion of slaves." In 1937 she found herself "compelled" to pray in Assisi, in the church where St. Francis had prayed, and in 1938, already deeply moved by the Holy Week Services at the Benedictine Solesmes Abbey, she had a mystical experience of Christ's presence while she recited George Herbert's poem "Love III."[13] These experiences incontrovertibly changed her vision of the world, but they did not change her commitment to political thinking and action. Indeed, Springsted writes, "Her mystical experience in 1938 did nothing to lessen her practical concern, but if anything intensified it."[14] Françoise Meltzer goes so far as to claim, "Weil is the only writer I can think of, in what Derrida calls the Tradition (that is, Western metaphysics), for whom the mystery of the sacred is inextricable, not only from the idea of responsibility (as in Lévinas), but from political activism. 'Action is the affirmation of God,' she writes."[15] Weil's practical and ethical concerns contributed in large part to her refusal to be baptized and confirmed into the Roman Catholic Church—the primary Christian institution in France—for she could not bring herself to align herself fully with an institution that had wrought such historical harm as the Crusades and Inquisition, and such contemporary harm as excluding from redemption those in other world traditions. So she resigned herself to remain at the "threshold" of the Church, even as she longed for full communion.[16]

Weil's life was brief. In 1942 she traveled with her parents to the United States to escape Hitler's threat: while her family had not practiced the Jewish faith, they could not escape their ancestry, which had already debarred Weil from continuing as a teacher. Weil didn't want to leave France. She longed to put her life on the line to contribute to the French Resistance. But she knew her parents wouldn't leave her, so she accompanied them to New York City and then worked tirelessly to find a way back to Europe to participate in the resistance efforts, ideally as a secret agent or in a scheme she developed to parachute nurses to the front lines. Eventually she found her way to London, where she was put to work writing, but in 1943 she was diagnosed with tuberculosis. At the time, the primary treatment was rest and nutrition, but Weil refused to eat more than she believed those at the front lines had—ostensibly in solidarity. To the shock of her family and close friends, in August 1943 her heart gave out. Weil was only thirty-four years old.

Simone Weil's death has been cause for interpretive struggle, just as much as the life that preceded it. Did she take her own life by refusing food, as the coroner's report suggested? Was she baptized by a friend in the last days, as some have claimed? The early and tragic death doubtless contributed to her mystique, although to her family it caused only grief.

Weil published a little during her lifetime, mostly essays in periodicals. But she wrote voluminously, and she left some of her writings with friends. These essays, notebooks, and excerpts thereof began to be published in French and translated into English, among other languages, after her death. In 1945 the American journal *politics* began to publish Weil's translated work, beginning with the piece "Reflections on War."[17] Mary McCarthy translated "The *Iliad*, or the Poem

of Force," the second essay *politics* published, at editor Dwight Macdonald's urging, and as Doering explains, "after the impact of the
atomic bomb, Weil's depiction of force in her essay on the *Iliad* struck
a profound chord with readers."[18] Elizabeth Hardwick reflected
decades later that the publication of Weil's *Iliad* essay in 1945 "was, it
is no exaggeration to say, an event of great importance to those of us
who read it. This is one of the most moving and original literary essays
ever written."[19]

Doering traces how Macdonald, along with Albert Camus and the
Italian humanist Nicola Chiaromonte, helped set off a wave of translations of Weil's work, including the English-language publication
in 1951 and 1952 of the books *Waiting for God*, *Gravity and Grace*, and
The Need for Roots. These books were widely reviewed and read, and
Deborah Nelson argues convincingly that Weil's appeal in postwar
America arose from her tragic sensibility, her critique of mastery, and
her insistence on "blind necessity" and "painful clarity," which stood
in stark and perhaps refreshing contrast to the 1950s emphasis on positive thinking, progress, and freedom from suffering.[20] Hardwick
makes clear that from the mid-1940s, Weil's work fascinated New
York intellectuals, and it also seems to have spread among East Coast
universities and seminaries: Weil biographer Robert Coles recalls first
encountering her work in 1950, in a Harvard undergraduate course
with Perry Miller focused on "classics of the Christian tradition." Just
a few years later he heard theologian Reinhold Niebuhr lecture on
Weil at Union Theological Seminary, and a few years after that he
was encouraged by Paul Tillich to write a paper on Weil for a course
at the Harvard Divinity School.[21] Popularized in intellectual and
scholarly circles, Weil's work continued to be translated into English,
with books like *Seventy Letters*; *Selected Essays, 1934–1943*; and *First
and Last Notebooks* published starting in the 1960s, which seems to
have set off another wave of interest in Weil, including an influential
review of her work by Susan Sontag in the inaugural issue of the *New*

York Review of Books in 1963.[22] New editions, translations, and anthologies continued to emerge throughout the second half of the twentieth century.[23]

Weil's reception is complicated by the fact that her writings are so shaped by editorial decisions and paratextual materials. While she wrote *The Need for Roots* as one long-form project during her time in London, *Waiting for God* is an editor's very purposeful collection of letters and essays focused on Weil's religious musings, and *Gravity and Grace* is an aphoristic series of short thematic entries extracted from other writings. Published in France in 1947 as *La Pesanteur et la grâce*, the book was curated by Weil's friend Gustave Thibon, who drew from the eleven notebooks she left in his care when she departed with her parents for New York. Thibon's editorial selections, doubtless shaped by his own leanings as a devout Catholic and self-taught philosopher, construct Weil as a religious philosopher of the void; they introduced her work to many in a very different light than, say, *The Need for Roots* or "The *Iliad*, or the Poem of Force." This leads in part to what Nelson calls the "bifurcation" of Weil's reception, which allows scholars to make frankly opposing claims about the nature of Weil's influence.[24] So David McLellan can argue in *Utopian Pessimist* that Weil was popularized primarily as a mystic, while Jerry White can call *The Need for Roots* "probably her best-known work" and trace Weil's original North American importance to her influence on the journal *politics*.[25]

Yet whether one first encountered Weil as a rigorous political philosopher or a modern mystic, her reception was still incontrovertibly shaped by her editors, not just their selections but also their prefatory materials. Thibon's introduction to *Gravity and Grace* directed understandings of Weil, as did T. S. Eliot's introduction to *The Need for Roots* and Leslie Fiedler's to *Waiting for God*, presenting Weil as a sort of modern saint.[26] Fiedler famously opens his introduction, for example, "Since her death, Simone Weil has come to seem more and more a special exemplar of sanctity for our time—the Outsider as Saint in an age of alienation, our kind of saint."²⁷ These editorial decisions and paratextual materials in some senses create the Weil we can know; they undeniably and at points quite obviously shape the Weil with whom literary writers interact. And the ongoing publication and remixing of Weil's work—in anthologies like Siân Miles's from 1986 and Springsted's *Late Philosophical Writings* (2015)—continue to complexify the textual picture of Weil's writing and person.

Within these publications, key concepts emerge to be taken up by literary writers. These include the ideas of *force, attention, affliction,* and *decreation.* Weil conceptualizes the world as shaped by *force,* the impersonal functioning of power and violence that reduces people to "things"—objects of ownership in the form of slavery, or literal corpses through death. Force is an aspect of *necessity* and *gravity,* the functioning of the universe that inevitably includes pain and violence. Those who are subjected to force are *afflicted*—Weil's term for a particular mode of suffering that is physical, psychological, and social, rendering those who experience affliction (or *malheur*) voiceless and powerless. The answer to affliction is *attention,* a difficult, patient, and passive openness to the world and the afflicted other that, in truly seeing things as they are, makes space for the other to return to fuller existence. Attention truly practiced is risky because it consents to self-diminishment, prioritizing the other over the self, whether the other be a human or a creative work. In this sense, it requires the *decreation* of the self, the emptying of ego or self-protection in order to allow for otherness to be.

This sketch dramatically oversimplifies a complex series of thoughts for Weil and also gives the impression of a coherent system that is much less obvious in Weil's wide-ranging and paradoxical prose.²⁸ It also renders the concepts in an areligious ethical frame. But for Weil, these thoughts reached their height in her later work and are inseparable from her religious imagination: *attention* is most fully practiced in prayer; *decreation* is most fully exemplified by Christ, who "emptied himself and took on the form of a slave," as in the ancient Christian hymn records in Philippians 2:7. Weil's later ethical paradigms are Christ-haunted, cross-haunted, a fact that various readers and writers approach in different ways. And in a secular age, Weil's religious turn and decreative impulses—both theorized and embodied—raise particular challenges.

SECULAR AND POSTSECULAR

To write about Simone Weil in the third decade of the twenty-first century is to raise the specter of the "secular" and even the "postsecular," terms that have provoked increasing debate over the past twenty years. In popular use, of course, the word "secular" means nonreligious or worldly, and secularization is the movement of a culture, institution, or individual away from or out of religion. This is the sense in play when Adrienne Rich says, "I'm not a religious Jew. I'm a secular person."[29] Rich's vocabulary here highlights the presumption, common in both popular and scholarly conversation, that religious and secular are oppositional terms.

Such an opposition undergirds what scholars call the "secularization thesis," a widely assumed metanarrative of religion's decline. In this oft-retold story, the Peace of Westphalia in 1648, which ended the Wars of Religion in Europe and initiated the modern nation-state, works together with a growing Enlightenment emphasis on reason, the scientific method, and progress, moving Europe (and its colonial holdings) out of hegemonic religiosity into the liberal values of freedom, equality, individuality, and an increasing separation of church and state. Tracing this trajectory in broad strokes, Tracy Fessenden writes that "the secularization narrative moves always in the direction of freedom, experimentation, and progress, with each step forward an implicit moral, political, and intellectual advance over the corresponding limitations ascribed to religion."[30] These associations are true both for those who reject all religion as nonsense or oppression and for religious adherents seeking to resist the dreaded encroachments of the secular they see housed in liberal and progressive public policy and cultural slippery slopes.

But starting as early as the 1960s, and with renewed vigor after 9/11, scholars have been pointing to weaknesses of the secularization thesis. While, as Lori Branch notes in "The Rituals of Our Re-Secularization: Literature Between Faith and Knowledge," the secular is so central to the discipline of literary studies as to provoke anxious repetitions of secularization, other spheres are far from done with religion.[31] Sociologically, we are faced with ongoing religious affiliation in countries long termed post-Christian as well as the rise of global fundamentalisms in the twentieth and twenty-first centuries. Khaled Furani points to the Islamic revolution in Iran in the late 1970s, the 1980s rise of the Moral Majority in the United States, and ongoing conflicts among variously affiliated South Asian communities.[32] Further, it's impossible to look at twenty-first-century U.S. politics and claim that religion has played no role in public and political life. For these and other reasons—including an increasing discomfort with the religious/secular binary itself—many scholars have named the inadequacy of the secularization thesis. Influential projects like Talal Asad's *Formations of the Secular: Christianity, Islam, Modernity* (2003) and Charles Taylor's *A Secular Age* (2007) complicate the secularization thesis's broad strokes, offering more nuanced narratives of what is at work and at stake in the secular, not as a narrative of progress but as a complexifying and at points ambivalent movement.[33] Peter Coviello and Jared Hickman go so far as to begin their introduction to a 2014 issue of *American Literature*, "The secularization thesis is dead."[34]

Simone Weil's own biography corroborates these critiques of the secularization thesis. Despite being raised in early twentieth-century France by parents who ostensibly followed its metanarrative by turning away from their parents' Jewish religious observance, Weil herself turned toward the Roman Catholic Church in the last years of her brief life. Weil's religious turn mystifies those who, following the secularization thesis, associate religion with irrationality and toxic disciplining power. This distaste or discomfort regarding religion also helps explain Weil's divided reception, whereby some of her readers embrace her ethical and political writings and bracket the religious, whereas other readers bracket the political and focus on the religious, evidently delighted to have a twentieth-century genius pitching for the Christian team. A similar reception history follows several literary writers influenced by Weil, including Annie Dillard, Fannie Howe, and Denise Levertov, whose own religious propensities mystified many of their readers and energized others.

To be clear, the writers I discuss in this book are by no means representative of a broader North American or European public: in addition to being markedly privileged in education and mostly white, they are also well-published literary writers who share an attraction to Simone Weil. Yet it's telling to trace their biographical trajectories and note a plurality of religious commitments, and in particular a tendency among some toward what we might call resacralization or a return to religion. Some, like Annie Dillard, were raised by non- or marginally religious parents in nominal Protestantism that they later rejected before turning in adulthood to religion with a difference. In Dillard's case, that was a stint with Roman Catholicism. Kate Daniels similarly grew up Southern Baptist but converted to the Catholic Church. Mary Gordon, by contrast, was a cradle Catholic (also daughter of a Jewish convert) who has openly grappled with the Church even as she stays within it. Anne Carson, for her part, was raised in Roman Catholicism but chose not to stay. And Rich, raised in nominal southern American Protestantism, turned after decades of rejecting religion to a reassessment of her own Jewish heritage, although she did so in a nonreligious frame.

These biographical sketches contradict the secularization thesis writ small, a teleology that would have those who reject religious belief and observance—or those raised by parents who have rejected religion—continue on a thoroughly secularizing trajectory in the implicit name of progress. Instead, the stories highlight both the plurality of twentieth- and twenty-first-century religious experience among European and especially North American individuals and also the possibility of a return to religion even after its rejection, though in many cases religion with a difference. But the writers' reception histories, no less than Weil's, remind us that even if the secularization thesis is dead, that is not to say that it does not still shape our imaginations. Antireligious bias leads to a certain squeamishness among some readers about religiously inflected texts, and it can lead to a defensiveness among those who do choose to write about religion, as Branch documents.

In one sense, one might call Weil and these other writers who turn to faith after their parents' (or their own) earlier rejection of it "postsecular": their individual or genealogical stories show a movement from religious to secular commitment, followed by a return to religion. This is one sense in which scholars have used the term "postsecular," to signal a return to religion after an evident decline, whether sociologically or in disciplinary spaces. John McClure's influential *Partial Faiths: Postsecular Fiction in the Age of Pynchon and Morrison* (2007) figures the postsecular as a return to religion with a difference, a "partial" reenchantment coupled with progressive social values.[35] For McClure, postsecular fiction questions both religious and secular dogma, coming instead to a vision of communal caring, mystery and wonder, and "weakened" religion rather than moral or institutional authority. Amy Hungerford's *Postmodern Belief: American Literature and Religion Since 1960* (2010) similarly describes a transfer of religious value from dogma and doctrine to literature and language itself, a sort of contentless belief.[36]

These figurations of the postsecular suggest a provocative negotiation between the religious and the secular, but their frameworks do not fully illuminate Simone Weil. While Weil's turn to Christianity admittedly took her only so far as the "threshold" of the Catholic Church, her religious turn was not contentless belief but specifically Christian, her grappling with the Roman Catholic institution in particular, even as she maintained an interest in world religions and insisted on a universal presence of the divine. In this way, Weil's story undermines an oft-remarked implicit Protestantism in the literary conversations about the (post)secular. Fessenden notes that in many imaginations of the postsecular, a homogeneous and domineering religiosity gives way to secularism, which is followed by a (post-Protestant) "spirituality" as code for "good religion." By contrast, Fessenden invites a more careful and nuanced "religious and historical literacy," a call that I think echoes Lori Branch's invitation to her students to consider the "particular religiousness" of a text rather than generalizing.[37] Simone Weil calls for just such a particular reading, not of her abstracted "religiosity" but for her specific attraction to—and refusal of—a particularly understood Roman Catholicism, a dynamic at work most perhaps explicitly in the Catholic literary imagination of Mary Gordon.

Weil's religious turn also undermines a frequent postsecular recuperation of religion as a moral force cleansed of its mystical content, a risk Michael Tomko notes.[38] By contrast, Weil's religious turn was indisputably motivated by a series of mystical encounters with Christ—encounters in which she felt herself overtaken. These encounters led to an ever-deepening ethical vision, but the mystical and prayerful—even in Weil's recitations of George Herbert's poem

"Love" (III) and the Lord's Prayer in Greek, admittedly literary practices—persisted as a spiritual practice. Again, the provocative ethical paradigm of attention for which Weil is famous is inseparable from her cruciform theology. For all these reasons, I don't take frameworks like McClure's and Hungerford's as a starting point in my approach to Weil and her later literary interlocutors, although at points their insights do resonate.

Scholars like Fessenden and Furani who are troubled by the prevailing figurations of the postsecular frequently raise the concern that this scholarly paradigm reinscribes the assumptions of the secularization thesis, even as it seeks to overturn them: assumptions of progress, teleology, accruing knowledge. Furani admits, "My disquiet comes from a sense that postsecular formulations maintain an allegiance to secularism's dualities rather than contest them, and fail to adequately recognize the genealogy and elasticity of the secular."[39] These scholars suggest various solutions to the problem. Fessenden, for her part, invites a carefulness about the spiritual authority we grant literature as an alternative to religion, about our schema of "good" and "bad" religion (and its implicit Protestant bias), and about historical and cultural particularity.[40] Furani goes so far as to echo Coviello and Hickman in suggesting that perhaps "the secular" is not the paradigmatic sign under which we should discuss modernity, and that instead looking back to 1492 and the instigation of modern imperialism and globality may be a better project—one that resonates with Weil's own deep concern about the uprootings wrought by colonization and industrialization.[41] To conceptualize religion in the modern age, however, Furani advocates for a more careful look at the secular itself: "Questioning the secular requires looking into it, not beyond it." He thus offers a history of the secular that roots it in the theological to begin with, showing how over time the word and concept—beginning two thousand years ago with the pre-Christian Latin *saeculum* and its meaning of finitude and transience—developed within Christian discourse for centuries before moving "outside" religion with the Enlightenment. Historicizing in this way allows for a more "elastic" sense of the secular not as religion's other but as a signal of becoming worldly in any given time, worldly in the sense of recognizing "the frailty within finite existence as the condition of possibility for the religious."[42]

I don't intend to resolve the debates over figurations of the secular and postsecular in the pages that follow. Instead, I hope to follow Furani, Branch, and Fessenden into a more careful and attentive reading of the ebbs and flows of particular religious belief and practice and particular iterations of the secular in Simone Weil's work and in her critical reception and literary afterlives. I am interested in how the secularization thesis and its assumptions about religion have shaped readings of Weil, how her engagements with Christianity and specifically Roman Catholicism appealed to and repelled various readers since her death. I'm interested in how to make sense, alongside Weil's literary interlocutors, of her deeply discomfiting critiques of Judaism and the Hebrew Bible, variously interpreted as internalized racism or outwardly focused anti-Semitism, paradoxically consistent with her outrage at Hitler or the result of profoundly poor reading. And I'm interested in how Weil's particular critiques of Christian tradition—the Crusades, the Inquisition, the Catholic Church's imperial power and anti-intellectualism—continue to challenge us, how her universalism undermines a narrow celebration of her legacy, and how her later readers critique other aspects of Weil's religiosity, including a cruciformity that threatens to tip over into masochism.

Beholding writers' own sympathy and struggles with Weil's outlooks on Jewish and Christian traditions, we are left to ask: How do both the religious and the secular, variously understood, engender both critique and affirmation, questioning and goodness, none of which are mutually exclusive? How do literary writers grappling with and memorializing Weil negotiate what Lissa McCullough calls "her beyond-the-edge radicality," which "is not mere accident or appearance but is the direct expression of a stark, unsentimental, disenchanted, and nevertheless profoundly joyful late modern religiosity, bringing light to bear on the darkest of times?"[43]

FEMINISM AND EMBODIMENT

Within the framework of a secular age understood as a time in which options for belief, disbelief, and critique of religion abound, Weil's religious turn presents obvious challenges. It leads, for example, to an occasional bracketing of her mysticism or an erasure of her work altogether, as in Claude Gendron's article in 2016 on moral attention and feminist care ethics, which acknowledges Weil as "'pioneer' of the contemporary reintroduction of this concept of ethics" but chooses to focus on her "direct 'descendent'" Iris Murdoch rather than discussing Weil herself, evidently because Weil treats attention "from a religious standpoint" and Murdoch does not.[44] Gendron's essay highlights both the discomfort some readers share at Weil's later religiosity and her perhaps surprising influence on a wide range of feminist philosophers, including Nel Noddings, Sara Ruddick, and Joan Tronto. Chris Cuomo traces Weil's influence on feminists in part to the very relationship Gendron notes, namely, her strong appeal to Iris Murdoch, whose writing went on to shape generations of feminists, although Cuomo is quick to note the surprise and challenge of this discursive lineage: "Simone Weil certainly does not make a very good feminist hero, but the echoes of her work are resounding. In fact, it can be argued that she is an invisible mother of feminist thought."[45]

Weil's appeal arises from both her person and her writing: as a woman who rejected feminine norms in early twentieth-century France, studying philosophy and participating in labor activism and war efforts, Weil models resistance to bourgeois patriarchal rule.[46] Further, while Weil never frames her ethics of attention or her political philosophy of responsibility over rights as deriving from women's experience the way later feminist philosophers like Carol Gilligan did in the 1980s, her suggested ethical and political ideals in some sense formalize the good of practices otherwise known as "women's work."[47] Even the vocabulary Weil uses in her widely known essay "Reflections on the Right Use of School Studies with a View to the Love of God" borrows from implicitly gendered language her schoolmate Simone de Beauvoir would later go on to highlight as part of an implicit binary opposition within patriarchal systems, although, again, Weil never acknowledges the unspoken socialized femininity of these ideals. She writes, "Attention consists of suspending our thought, leaving it detached, empty, and ready to be penetrated by the object. . . . Above all our thought should be empty, waiting, not seeking anything, but ready to receive in its naked truth the object that is to penetrate it." Weil's insistence on passive, empty, receptivity—not to mention her repeated vocabulary of being penetrated—aligns with the feminine side of the Western construct of gender norms, even as the same paragraph offers the metaphor of "a man on a mountain."[48] Similarly, her elevation of the activities of truly looking at other people and noticing details, asking others what they're going through and listening to their stories, and feeding and otherwise taking care of people, privileges as an ethical model activities typically associated with mothering and women's broader social roles. Later feminist ethicists of care follow Weil's writing on attention in commending a more general ethics and politics of relationality and care-giving, as Sophie Bourgault notes in her essay "Beyond the Saint and the Red Virgin: Simone Weil as Feminist Theorist of Care."[49] Ruddick, for example, in her influential book *Maternal Thinking: Toward a Politics of Peace* (1989), draws on both Weil and Murdoch to sketch a picture of "attentive love," which is both risky and beneficial:

"Attentive love is prey to the self-loss that can afflict maternal think-ing; indifference, passivity, and self-denial are among its degenera-tive forms. Attentive love is also a corrective to many defects of maternal thinking, including an anxious or inquisitorial scrutiny, domination, intrusiveness, caprice, and self-protective cheeriness."[50]

Ruddick's characterization of Weil's ethic of attention as paradox-ically both a core feature of desirable caregiving and a possible threat to women's well-being highlights a key tension in Weil's reception among feminist thinkers. The modern Western women's movement is predicated on a rejection of self-sacrifice and an exposé of the degree to which Christianity was implicated in women's subjection. In this, it is consistent with a wider trajectory, for as Johannes Zachhuber and Julia Meszaros explain in their introduction to *Sacrifice and Modern Thought*, "one major narrative of European modernity involves the notion of its systematic and increasing repudiation of sacrifice."[51] In 1895 Elizabeth Cady Stanton commented, "Men think that self-sacrifice is the most charming of all the cardinal virtues for women, and in order to keep it in healthy working order, they make oppor-tunities for its illustration as often as possible." Stanton further connected this lesson in feminine self-sacrifice to the church, writing in her introduction to *The Woman's Bible*, "From the inauguration of the movement for women's emancipation, the Bible has been used to hold her in the 'divinely ordained sphere' prescribed in the Old and New Testaments."[52] Second-wave feminists like Adrienne Rich con-tinued Stanton and her co-laborers' earlier project of exposing the degree to which Jewish and Christian religions were responsible for a general expectation of women's self-sacrificing service of men and children in projects like Rich's book *Of Woman Born*, and the mid-century women's movement further reclaimed women's embodi-ment, sexuality, and self-determination in consciousness-raising circles and Take Back the Night marches. Concurrently, a rising group of feminist and womanist theologians like Rosemary Radford

Reuther, Elizabeth Shüssler Fiorenza, and Delores Williams continued to apply a hermeneutic of suspicion and liberation to the biblical texts and religious traditions, exposing what was death-dealing to women while elevating what was life-giving in the faith, while others like Mary Daly abandoned theology altogether. And these trajectories of examining women's socialization continued in later projects like philosopher Iris Marion Young's work on a phenomenology of women's embodiment and Susan Bordo's work on hysteria, agoraphobia, and eating disorders—two projects that highlight the way women have been socialized to make themselves small and take up less room in private and public life.[53]

It is no wonder, then, that many feminists have been troubled by Weil's ethic of decreation and her not unrelated religious turn, encapsulated in assertions like her claim in the essay "Human Personality" that "the only way into truth is through one's own annihilation."[54] Despite her appeal to Weil in work like *Maternal Thinking*, Ruddick admits, "I was repelled by Weil's self-hatred and anti-Semitism that was one expression of it. Her strenuous, unremitting moral seriousness depressed me."[55] Ann Loades names Weil's fascination with Christian "sacrifice and eucharist" as the very source of her "destruction."[56] Francine du Plessix Gray, one of Weil's more recent biographers, admits in an essay that she's among the ranks of Weil's readers characterized by a "mercurial pattern of alternately loving and hating her." The features that "make [Gray] want to throw a book at her" include Weil's view of the body "as the source of all evil (a belief she practiced in real life by gradually destroying her own body)."[57] This comment reminds us that for many feminists, Weil's difficulty isn't just in her theories but in her life story, her legacy of ultimate self-erasure. Weil scholars debate over whether anorexia is an appropriate descriptor of Weil's relationship to food, but even those, like Gray, who believe Weil to have been anorexic still see in her later years not just an illness but a willful drive toward self-sacrificing risk.

Commenting on this drive, Cuomo writes, "Her ethics and spirituality are ultimately disturbingly embodied." Cuomo traces this challenge both to socialized gender and to religion: she compares Weil to "many earnest young women predisposed to hating their bodies" and wonders over her ultimate demise, asking whether it was due to "Physical illness? / Anorexia Philosophia? / Suicide-by-Catholicism?"[58] And as Cuomo and others point out, Weil's enfleshed decreation is all the more troubling when one considers the degree to which it seems to have added to the (implicitly gendered) hagiographical approach of many of her admiring commentators. A similar logic is at work in those who dismiss Weil as crazy, as Charles de Gaulle famously did: it relegates her to the realm of female hysteria. In other words, for as much as Weil seems to have distanced herself from feminine social norms and rooted her rigorous theories of self-diminishment in Christ along with a male-dominated philosophical tradition and classical literary metaphors of militarism, Weil's *reception* regenders her life, returning her legacy to the realm of womanly self-sacrifice or (and) emotional excess.

These challenges are central to many of the literary writers at the center of this book, who find in Weil a provocative interlocutor and exemplar of an ethics and politics that is honest about power and pain but who also find in her life and work a risky hyperbole entangled with gender and God-talk. To varying degrees, these writers grapple with Weil's enmeshment in histories of female self-diminishment and Christic kenosis, or self-emptying, joining philosophers and other scholars in their attempt to think alongside Weil without replicating her mistakes. In so doing, they implicitly weigh in on long-standing debates among Weil scholars, who variously interpret Weil's embodiment, Christianity, gender, and yearning toward action, even when it meant putting her life on the line. Springsted, for his part, writes in his introduction to the *First and Last Notebooks* that while Weil "has so often been accused of masochism and dolorism," she nevertheless "believed that suffering should be avoided, when legitimately possible, but she knew it is often unavoidable, and she knew its potential value."[59] Bourgault similarly comments that while "Weil thought there was a type of suffering" "that called for a thoughtful and stoic consent," there was another type of suffering "that ought to be addressed (and that justified revolt)."[60] This is quite a different perspective from Cuomo's assessment of both "body-hating and self-sacrifice" as "central" to Weil's philosophy."[61] Women's literary engagements with Weil's legacy bring nuance to these competing views of the philosopher-mystic, the possibilities of figurative and imaginative language offering a way into the apparent paradoxes that discursive prose often seems to disallow. In so doing, these literary writers untangle—or at least loosen—knotted questions of secularization and feminism, questions about the contemporary wisdom of ancient faith traditions and postures that threaten to reify old limitations even as they carry the potential to disrupt reigns of injustice. In poetry and prose, these texts wonder with and about Weil and the possibilities of attention, radical integrity, sacrificial responsibility, belief, and a world in which everyone who hungers has plenty of food.

SELECTION AND ORGANIZATION

In this book, I focus on the most sustained and impassioned literary engagements with Weil I have found in English, examples from poetry, fiction, and literary nonfiction that exemplify Weil's perpetual and at points surprising presence in anglophone literature. I could have written about others—Fanny Howe, for example, or perhaps Christian Wiman—whose work manifests long conversations with Weil, or focused on a wider collection of writers who show occasional interest in Weil in single poems or essays. I try to mention such writers throughout the book to highlight the breadth of Weil's literary appeal, even as my choice to focus on a smaller group allows me to focus on the depth of their engagements.

As a result of this rubric of selection, the writers at the center of this project are overwhelmingly women, and they are overwhelmingly white. To be clear, I did not set out to write a book about white women. In a decade of research, I looked far and wide for all the anglophone literary engagements with Weil I could find, eventually narrowing my focus to those whose writing to, about, and in the tradition of Weil struck me as the most intensive and whose engagements with Weil had received the least scholarly attention. These writers represent various diversities of sexuality, disability, region, and relationship to religion, but they are all women, and they understand themselves as white within the racialized framework of contemporary North American life. When this racial dynamic became apparent, I searched harder to find writers of color engaging with Weil, curious and concerned at the project's developing shape.

Writers of color do cite Weil. Cornel West, as I noted, admiringly quotes Weil in interviews. The womanist theologian M. Shawn Copeland briefly cites Weil's work on suffering and affliction to discuss enslaved women's experiences, echoing Weil's recognition of Christianity as "the religion of slaves."[62] One of Michelle Cliff's early essays was a piece on Weil as a sister of sorts and, as I discuss in conversation with Mary Gordon's fiction in chapter 3, offers one of the most astute readings of Weil's relationship to her own Jewishness, in comparison with Cliff's own observations of internalized anti-Black racism. Cliff cites Weil briefly, as well, in her last published books, both fiction and nonfiction, showing an interest in Weil across the decades.[63]

Yet for Cliff, as for M. NourbeSe Philip, who cites Weil as an influence in an essay and several interviews as I discuss in this book's conclusion, Weil's writing and life seem to offer a footnote rather than a primary source. These writers nod at her in passing, recognizing her sympathetic perspectives, but they focus the main emphasis of their literary texts—their poetry, fiction, and nonfiction—on other historical figures and phenomena, often from within their own cultures' traditions of anticolonial and antiracist resistance. So, for example, rather than a biographical fictionalization of Weil, Cliff writes a novel of Mary Ellen Pleasant, the nineteenth-century Black abolitionist and entrepreneur, and multiple novels about resistance movements in Jamaica, including the semiautobiographical *Abeng* and the widely read *No Telephone to Heaven*.[64] Philip writes a coming-of-age novel about a girl inspired by Harriet Tubman and an experimental poetry sequence subverting both language and colonialist missionary Dr. Livingstone.[65] Both writers excavate the horrifying history of the ship the *Zong*, bearing witness to their ancestors—or, in a term Weil shares with many other decolonial thinkers, to their roots.[66] Weil appears here and there in their work as a tangential source, but she is not their primary exemplar of moral seriousness, the struggle with Christian religion, or questions of suffering and attention: both Cliff and Philip seek to establish other genealogies of resistance. In this way, perhaps ironically, Weil is relegated to the margins to amplify the stories and voices of uprooted peoples, fully in keeping with her own philosophy of antioppressive attention and a self-erasure that makes room for an other to exist.

Sigrid Nunez's work focuses somewhat more sustained attention on Weil. Nunez, the American daughter of a postwar German immigrant mother and a Chinese-Panamanian father, has written of Weil several times over the course of her career as a novelist. Weil's work appears in passing in Nunez's National Book Award–winning novel *The Friend* (2018)—in fact, in conversation with both Adrienne Rich and Flannery O'Connor—and offers the title and epigraph to her novel *What Are You Going Through* (2020), although Weil doesn't feature in most of her other books.[67] However, Weil appears most fully at the center of Nunez's novel *The Last of Her Kind* (2006), in which the narrator, Georgette George, reflects on her relationship with her college roommate, Ann Drayton, a white woman born to economic privilege she unendingly seeks to abdicate. As students at Barnard College in the late 1960s, George and Ann are caught up in political movements, but whereas Ann idealizes those without privilege, George, who grew up poor, doesn't see why oppression would lead to moral superiority. The novel's central conflict finally arrives years later, when Ann fatally shoots a police officer who was threatening Ann's Black fiancé, leading to a high-profile murder trial that surfaces the conflicted discourses of gender, race, and class in 1970s New York. In an interview after the trial, Ann's attorney comments that she reminds him of Simone Weil, leading George to research Weil, whom she had known only in passing as one of Ann's favorite writers, and to meditate on the two figures' similarities. Both women were from childhood "unusually sensitive to the suffering of others"; both long to rescind their privilege; both believe that those who are oppressed are closer to the truth; both struggle with eating when they knew others didn't have enough food; both admire (and possibly romanticize?) Blackness; both take their care for others to an uncommon extreme; both are woefully misunderstood; both have their lives cut short.[68]

What's fascinating about Nunez's appeal to Weil in *The Last of Her Kind* is that while it explicitly addresses race, it does so with Weil as the model of a certain specifically *white* woman's struggle with her racial and class privilege. In other words, Nunez could be said to expose through her character Ann Drayton an implicitly racialized dynamic in so much of the anglophone literary work on Weil, the quest for a historically proximate white foremother in political and moral seriousness, an exemplar less far-off than Joan of Arc or the medieval saints—figures also noted by Nunez and by many other writers as parallels to Weil—who suggests what it might mean to go against the grain, to come to terms with a social role one is born into at the cost of others' flourishing within an unjust society. This is just one trend in the literary writing on Weil, perhaps most explicit in Adrienne Rich and Mary Gordon, but it is a current that flows throughout the poetry and prose, one to which I repeatedly return in this book. Of course, it is risky to surmise about authorial motivations, and I try not to fall into armchair psychology but instead rely on interviews, archives, and the literary texts themselves to clarify what draws so many white women writers to Weil. It is also risky to write about absences: Why don't more men write these sustained engagements with Simone Weil? Why don't more writers of color? But perhaps a more fitting question is: Why *would* they? Or why *should* they?[69] Again, rather than assumptions or arguments from absence, I focus on how Weil functions in the literary texts where she *is* so insistently present: What is she doing in them? How do they make her somehow alive, and why, by the texts' own logic?

The book's chapters follow a roughly chronological trajectory based on their main subjects' initial published engagements with Weil, although all four chapters include texts published in the twenty-first century. In chapter 1, I consider how Adrienne Rich's reading of Weil contributed to Rich's ethical commitments, particularly an ever-expanding vision of relational attentiveness scholars increasingly locate at the heart of Rich's poetic legacy. Reading Weil's presence in Rich's ethico-poetic project—in published work, interviews, and archives—shines light on one of Rich's central philosophical sources that has so far been wholly overlooked. Yet Rich doesn't just draw on Weil's ethics of attention: she also grapples with Weil's decreative impulses and their embeddedness in gendered and religious frames. This areligious feminist engagement with Weil's work complicates a conversation in Weil scholarship about the division of her reception among those interested in her religious-mystical interests and those interested solely in her politics. Rich's poetic explication of Weil's writing—and life—shows a path that doesn't ignore Weil's Christian turn but instead struggles with it—and rejects it—in a way that is in fact entirely consistent with Weil's own contestation of the Christian tradition.

Chapter 2 turns to Annie Dillard, whose initial interest in Weil is not ethico-political but metaphysical. Unlike the other writers I focus on in this book, Dillard does not struggle with Weil on feminist terms: instead, rather like Weil, she generally brackets gender and more than any other writer here embraces Weil's theory of decreation. Because Dillard follows Weil so fully into metaphysics and theology, she is also uniquely situated to question the more extreme points of Weil's religious theorizing. Yet Dillard is also changed by Weil over the decades, I argue, resulting in a shift in Dillard's work scholars have not yet noticed. Tracing Weil's influence through Dillard's non-fiction trilogy *Pilgrim at Tinker Creek*, *Holy the Firm*, and *For the Time Being*, as well as her widely read *The Writing Life*, I show how Dillard's initial Weil-inspired but apolitical decreative *poetics* develops, over the years, into a decreative ethics. Such a movement supports a reading of Weil that refuses to separate the mystical or metaphysical from the ethical and political. It also shows how Weil's challenging ideas, translated without frequent reference into Dillard's work, have faced much less resistance in this setting, both highlighting how Weil's influence is present in one of the twentieth century's most lauded prose stylists and raising questions about the differences between the two women's reception histories.

In chapter 3 I turn to fiction, and in particular to the work of Mary Gordon, who, like Dillard, began reading Weil in the 1970s and whose interest in her has not waned. I read three twenty-first-century texts by Gordon—the novels *Pearl* and *There Your Heart Lies* and the novella *Simone Weil in New York*—that struggle with Weil's legacy by fictionalizing aspects of her life and work. Gordon's long-form fiction allows for a unique degree of nuance, exploring both the gifts and the challenges of Weil's writing and biography through fictional characters who share her propensities. Gordon's approach combines Rich's feminism with Dillard's openness to Christianity, and specifically Roman Catholicism, as well as strategies of triangulation and comparison that allow for a tempered criticism of Weil's riskier extremes. The result is a series of narratives that refuse to reject Weil's ethical and political challenge, or even her religious turn, while also exposing the troubling inconsistencies within her life and work as well as the troubled context of her reception, both during her life and after her death. Gordon is particularly sensitive to the gendered risks of a decreative ethics, Weil's notorious critique of Judaism, and the contestations of Catholicism. As such, Gordon's narratives open a frank discussion of what can possibly be compelling in Weil—and the Church—in a secular (or postsecular) age, when so many wrongs have been exposed.

Chapter 4 finally offers a comparative reading of six anglophone poets who take up Weil's work and biography in extended form, either in poetic sequences or in book-length collections starting in the 1980s. Seeking points of resonance and dissonance among them, I consider both their poetic strategies and their content, interrogating Weil's appeal. What about Weil invites such repeated versification? What does it mean to do poetic justice to the philosopher-mystic-activist's life? And what can Weil scholars in other disciplines learn from the poets' approach that may help with the tangle of contradictions complicating Weil's textual and biographical legacy? Ultimately, I find in these various lyrical approaches a nonhagiographical championing of Weil's extraordinary integrity embedded in critical—and often mournful—attention to her drive toward self-decreation. These tender creations of Weil often self-consciously represent the act of attending to her—and thereby creating her in her tangle of paradoxes—in a way that is uniquely possible in poetry.

In the conclusion I summarize Weil's importance as a figure who welcomes her literary creators to grapple with the risks and gifts of both Christianity and a decreative ethic in an age that demands accounting for historical and contemporary violence and oppressions, including religious, colonial, racial, gendered, economic, and ecological challenges. The writers struggle with these challenges in conversation with Weil's philosophy but also in creative attention to her life, both her wisdom and her pain: in rendering imagined Weils through poetry and prose, many of the writers find a unique opportunity to explore the limits of their own responsibilities and longings. The fact that the majority of Weil's literary interlocutors are white women arises again here not as an accidental or invisible feature but as a manifestation of the search for inspiring if imperfect models in the pursuit of ethico-politically responsible ways of attending to raced, classed, and global modes of privilege. In these literary treatments, Weil emerges not as a saint but as a locus for struggle, her word-enfleshed body brought to life as an imperfect yet inspiring forebear. Such engagements continue even in very recent years, as writers struggling with the not unrelated contemporary crises of attention, decolonization, and climate emergency, including Casey Schwartz, M. NourbeSe Philip, and Terry Tempest Williams, continue to find in Weil a provocative inspiration for both literary writing and action that brings beauty, truth, and goodness into the world.

1

FORCE

Weil as a Source for Adrienne Rich's Expanding Solidarities

One of the most exquisite pleasures of human love—to serve the loved one without his knowing it—is only possible, as regards the love of God, through atheism.

—Simone Weil, *First and Last Notebooks*

The 1973 paperback edition of Simone Weil's *Waiting for God* bears four endorsements. The first is a famous quote by André Gide naming Weil "the most truly spiritual writer of this century." The next is from Robert Coles, psychologist and later Weil biographer, lauding her "example" for modern pilgrims. The third is from the *New York Times* celebrating the "brilliant, paradoxical figure, this left-wing mystic." The last names Weil "one of the most neglected resources of our century." This claim is attributed to Adrienne Rich.

Anyone with a passing familiarity with both Rich and Weil will recognize the surprise of this affirmation. Simone Weil, notorious for her fraught relationship to embodiment and Judaism as well as her attraction to a markedly cruciform Christianity, seems a strange "resource" for Adrienne Rich, radical feminist and poetic leader in a movement committed to women's bodies who famously reappraised and embraced her own Judaism from a staunchly nonreligious perspective. Yet the two writers do share some notable commonalities: born into families with Jewish roots, both women were recognized as gifted by their doctor fathers; they were raised on the classics; they were treated as "exceptional" women in early adulthood—Weil in 1930s France; Rich in the 1950s United States. Both Weil and Rich lived with chronic pain from a young age—Weil with headaches; Rich with rheumatoid arthritis—and both wrote the pain into their work while also resisting its tyranny. Both writers theorized about and practiced the power of language and shared a commitment to increasingly global understandings of economic and decolonial justice. Both wrote prolifically in their pursuit of that justice, although Rich lived into her eighties and Weil only her early thirties.

While scholars have generally overlooked their textual relationship, Rich draws on, names, and at points struggles with Weil from at least the late 1960s through the last years of her life. Rich's engagement with Weil's vocabulary, ideas, and biography appears in both her poetry and her prose repeatedly over this four-decade span in a way that suggests careful study and sustained thought. Still, their differences are too sharp to ignore, raising the question of how and why Rich found in Weil such a persistent source and interlocutor. What was the source of Weil's fraught and long appeal to Rich? How might we trace their textual conversation?

I argue in this chapter that Rich's forty-five-year-long writerly engagement with Weil rests on a shared ethics of attention to the other—and to an increasingly expansive sense of others—that is inescapably relational, sensitive to suffering and violence, rooted in the power of language, and oriented toward justice. Reading their long textual conversation clarifies both writers' legacies. In recent years, scholars have begun to reappraise a critical tendency to emphasize only the midpoint of Rich's career—the height of her radical feminist writing—as though the three decades that followed were denouement.

In contrast, Albert Gelpi, Miriam Marty Clark, and Jeanette Riley, among others, argue that the second half of Rich's career manifests an urgent and perpetually developing aesthetic and ethical sensibility. Meanwhile, Weil's reception similarly faces a challenge, what Deborah Nelson calls a "bifurcation," as many readers focus exclusively on her legacy as a political thinker or a mystical thinker, ignoring the other aspect of her work.[1] Reading Rich and Weil together, however, offers mutual illumination: recognizing Weil as one of Rich's primary influences highlights Rich's long commitment to a poetics of ethical and political responsibility and illuminates one of her as-yet underacknowledged sources for this commitment. At the same time, Rich's embrace of Weil as source of political and ethical insight—and her concomitant critique of Weil's turn toward religiously inflected self-sacrifice—complicates a treatment of Weil that ignores either her political or her mystical approaches. Despite Rich's outright poetic wrestling with Weil's self-diminishing impulses and turn to faith, I argue that the poet, in working with *all* Weil's writings, including the religiously motivated ones, actually echoes Weil's own treatment of the Christian tradition, sharing a hermeneutic that embraces the life-giving while critiquing the embedded harm. In this way, Rich's literary attention to Weil models a feminist approach to reading religion in a secular age.

RICH READING WEIL

Adrienne Rich likely began reading Simone Weil's work in the early 1960s. In a column for the *American Poetry Review* in 1973, Rich recalls reading Weil along with social critic Paul Goodman when she was "living in a university community that prided itself on its intellectual razor-sharpness"—almost certainly Harvard, where her husband Alfred Conrad was a professor, and away from which they moved in

1966. Rich claims in the column that Weil helped her find "the courage to trust my—then almost purely intuitive—sense that the Vietnam War was an abominable enterprise."[2] These recollections imply that for Rich, Weil's concern with suffering, force, and colonization was part of her early appeal.

Rich may have first encountered Weil through Susan Sontag's piece on her challenge and admirable "seriousness" in the inaugural issue of the *New York Review of Books* in February 1963, to which Rich herself contributed a review of Paul Goodman's collected poems.[3] Weil was in the American intellectual air in the 1960s, which saw the publication of volumes including *Selected Essays, 1934–43* (1962), *Seventy Letters* (1965), *On Science, Necessity, and the Love of God* (1968), and *First and Last Notebooks* (1970). These publications followed on the initial translation of Weil's work into English in the mid-1940s and early 1950s, including Mary McCarthy's translation of "The *Iliad*, or the Poem of Force" for *politics* and the books *Waiting for God, Gravity and Grace*, and *The Need for Roots*.

Like Sontag in her attraction to Weil's seriousness, Rich initially seems to have appreciated her moral courage in opposition to postwar conservatism. Above all else, Simone Weil was a "philosopher of oppression," as Rich calls her in the poem "For a Friend in Travail."[4] This plumb line runs through her philosophical writings, and while over time Weil developed and even thoroughly revised her concepts and key words, as A. Rebecca Rozelle-Stone and Benjamin P. Davis argue, "she was consistent in her acute attention to and theorizing from the situation of the oppressed and marginalized in society."[5] This moral edge may help explain why, despite the challenges of her philosophical and embodied self-emptying and her related turn to a kenotic Christianity, Weil's work was notably popular in the women's movement of the 1970s, in which Rich became a key figure. Michelle Cliff recalls that a colleague at Norton gave her a copy of the *Selected Essays* in 1970, and Cliff was immediately attracted to

Weil's contradictory mind.[6] Cliff and Rich met a few years later as Cliff was copyediting Rich's *Of Woman Born*, which includes several references to Weil, and Rich wrote in a letter to Tillie Olsen that she and Cliff hit it off talking about the philosopher—sparking a partnership that would last the rest of Rich's life.[7] Sigrid Nunez similarly recalls first encountering Weil in the 1970s through Susan Sontag, who continued to admire Weil for her "seriousness."[8] Weil seems to have been in the New York intellectual conversation in the 1970s as much as she was in the 1950s and 1960s, so much that Elizabeth Hardwick wrote a reflection on Weil in the inaugural issue of the feminist journal *Signs* in 1975.

Hardwick's piece may offer further clues as to why Weil held such fascination for midcentury writers, including feminists like Rich. Hardwick begins by quoting an introduction to Weil from 1954 that notes she "has been variously described as a victim of spiritual delusion, a social prophet, a modern Antigone or Judith, and a new kind of saint." In her own sketch of Weil, Hardwick emphasizes Weil's "passionate style" of writing with "its stirring, affecting intensity." Weil's appeal seems to lie, for Hardwick, in both her poetics and her ethics: her care for "the lives of the humble," her commitment to "immediate justice, present compassion, and attention to the pains of the moment." Hardwick doesn't shy away from the "fiercely knotted complications" of Weil's biography, including her "suicide by starvation," her "aura of a willed immolation" approaching "neurosis," and her "religious longings." Nevertheless, Hardwick insists on Weil's "pure ethical vision," agreeing with Leslie Fiedler's 1951 introduction to *Waiting for God* that Weil's "was a mind that connected with the radical, alienated, secular intellectuals of the time."[9]

Rich, of course, did not begin as a "radical, alienated" intellectual. Her first book, *A Will to Change*, published like Weil's *Waiting for God* in 1951, was a collection of mostly conventional poems. However, Rich's trajectory through postwar motherhood and then teaching racially and economically marginalized university students in New York City, surrounded by civil rights and antiwar activist colleagues, resulted in a perpetually developing and passionately engaged ethico-political commitment until her death in 2012. Yet Rich is often anthologized (and was eulogized) primarily for her work in the 1970s, the peak of her radical feminism. As Albert Gelpi argues, "Many of Rich's readers have focused so narrowly on the sixties and seventies that they overlook the full reach of her purpose and vision in the second half of her career."[10]

In contrast, with a growing collection of contemporary scholars, I understand Rich's work in the 1970s as important but not the pinnacle of her achievement. Although Rich maintained her radical commitment to women's flourishing, her political and poetic commitments continued to complexify through intersectional analyses of race, economics, and global politics through the end of her life. In emphasizing the whole scope of Rich's poetic career, I follow critics like Miriam Marty Clark, Jeanette E. Riley, and Ed Pavlić, who read in the second half of Rich's career a challenging and ongoing pursuit of "global responsiveness and responsibility" that continually revitalizes her poetics.[11] As Riley argues, in the second half of her career, Rich's voice "transformed from a feminist voice to a national voice."[12] Maggie Rehm calls her a "citizen poet," "an artist with a strong sense of being engaged in and accountable to her world."[13]

What scholars in this developing conversation have not yet traced is the degree to which Simone Weil is a key source for this "responsive and responsible" poetics. Rich's work from the 1980s through 2012 manifests an impassioned attention to human suffering, a clear-sighted analysis of power in its many forms, a refusal of dehumanization and domination, a defense of the inseparable nature of theory and practice, an anticapitalist and anticolonial critique of modern global politics, and an inescapable responsibility as citizen-philosopher and citizen-poet—all of which ring out in concert with Weil's written and lived commitments.[14] In his book *Outward: Adrienne Rich's Expanding Solitudes* (2021), Pavlić doesn't name Weil, but his astute readings of Rich's poetry and complexifying commitments ring out, again and again, with Weil's vocabularies, either in his own words or in quoted sections from the poems: Pavlić writes, for example, of "attention," "affliction," "gravity," "force," "the realm of pure necessity," being "rooted," and "uprooted rootedness."[15] These vocabularies support Pavlić's important argument that "the music of Rich's most powerful work tunes itself into subversive, relational solidarities and sounds its way toward engaged mutual presences in contest with (not detachment from) history's dangers and trials"—a fact that suggests, again, a much stronger affiliation between Rich and Weil than scholars have yet traced.[16]

Beginning to properly trace these points of influence turns us to both the printed work and the archives. Rich's first published reference to Weil by name is in the poem "Pieces" (1969), included in *The Will to Change*: "This morning: read Simone Weil / on the loss of grace."[17] Two poems from 1968, "Leaflets" and "The Blue Ghazals," show an indisputable reference in quoting Weil's famous line from her essay "Reflections on the Right Use of School Studies with a View to the Love of God," "tell me what you are going through," and variations of this line also occur in "Shooting Script" (1969–1970) and "From the Prison House" (1971).[18] The frequency with which Rich quotes this phrase of Weil's in the years 1968–1971, in conjunction with a similarly high frequency of Weil's keywords "attention," "force," and "affliction" in this period, suggests that it was an intense time of engagement with Weil's thought for Rich, further supported by the frequency with which Rich cites Weil in the essays collected in *On Lies, Secrets, and Silence: Selected Prose 1966–1978*. These essays include "Teaching Language in Open Admissions" (1972), "Jane Eyre: The

Temptations of a Motherless Woman" (1973), "Toward a Woman-Centered University" (1973–1974), and "Conditions for Work: The Common World of Women" (1976).[19] Rich here references not just Weil's writing on suffering and her troubling turn to a masculine God but also her theorizing about education and history, suggesting the breadth of Rich's interest in Weil's work, both the ethical and the explicitly political.

In an interview with Rich and Mary Daly in 1977, Valerie Miner prompted a turn in the conversation by commenting, "Talking about feminism and philosophy, Simone Weil seems the next likely subject for discussion." Rich's response is worth quoting at length:

> I found her work fascinating because she seemed to be trying—without succeeding, to make some of the very connections we've been trying to make. Especially in her notebooks, she had flashes of illumination that never got worked through. There was tremendous self-hatred, self-denigration, a lot of attributes we're used to seeing in brilliant women who simply feel unable to follow through with the power of their vision. But I agree with you that she's being made a cult figure and people are not really reading her. They see the suicide, the victim-woman, the woman who failed, who did not come through, that whole suffering, ascetized aspect of her. That's not what interests me about her.[20]

The conversation offers further evidence of the 1970s feminist interest in Weil and demonstrates Rich's familiarity with her work, including her notebooks. Rich's response highlights her sensitivity to the feminist challenges with Weil—"self-hatred, self-denigration"—but also roots them not so much in Weil's particular personality as in the structural challenges for "brilliant women" within patriarchy, a dynamic she writes about in poems like "Power," which describes Marie Curie "denying/ her wounds   came   from the same source as her power."[21] Rich also rejects the fetishization or hagiographic reading of Weil's asceticism. Instead, she goes on to describe what does appeal to her in Weil's work: "Something like the essay *On Human Personality* was very valuable to me in a pre-feminist stage because it gave enormous insight into questions about survival which I was trying to work through."[22] "On Human Personality," which Weil wrote in her life's final year, expresses perhaps the fullness of her thinking, addressing the negotiations of individual and collective, attention and affliction, beauty and justice, encapsulating many of the concepts in Rich's written engagement with Weil.

The scope of that engagement is substantial: drawing just on the explicit citations Rich included at the ends of poetry collections and in prose footnotes, we know that in addition to "On Human Personality," Rich read *Waiting for God*; *Selected Essays, 1934–43*; *Oppression and Liberty*; the *First and Last Notebooks*; and "The *Iliad*, or the Poem of Force." This list, which includes volumes first published in English in the 1950s, 1960s, and 1970s, suggests a sustained study rather than a passing fancy, as does the fact that Rich continued to publish poems referring to Weil in the 1980s, 1990s, and 2000s. Rich also endorsed the 1976 paperback version of Simone Pétrement's hefty biography of Weil, calling it "an essential document" and Weil a "visionary woman."[23]

The archives are also illuminating. In addition to clips of interviews and columns referencing Weil, Rich's papers in the Schlesinger Library at the Radcliffe Institute also include two unpublished manifestations of her thinking about Weil. The first of these is a list, written in felt-tip pen on a page from an undated, debound small spiral notebook in a folder marked "after 1974." The list, headed simply by the word "Weil," includes references to six books by Simone Weil, with dates and publishers. Only seven pages of the notebook were saved, and it's striking that this is one of them (the back of the leaf includes a shopping list for vitamins).[24]

Even more illuminating are notes for lectures Rich gave as a visiting professor at Brandeis University in 1972–1973. The folder includes, first, a handwritten series of apparent brainstorming notes comparing Simone Weil and Sylvia Plath as "2 extremes of female genius."[25] Rich's notes link Weil's "inwardness" to "a transcendence she called God" and her "outwardness" to concern for "the oppressed." Weil is "critical of society. A radical."—"painfully ascetic yet passionate." (This is in contrast with Plath's "female" inwardness and lack of outwardness.) The handwritten notes go on to list Mary Wollstonecraft and Joan of Arc. Later in the folder appears a partial typewritten manuscript, much marked up with editorial changes, that moves from a reading of Marianne Moore to an explication of Weil's fragment from 1942 published as "Prologue" in the *First and Last Notebooks*, which poetically imagines an archetypal masculine presence and a quasi-erotic mystical encounter. Rich then transitions to a reading of Emily Dickinson, but the manuscript page at this point is literally cut off.[26]

It appears Rich revised Simone Weil out of the talks she finally gave, as the folder holds three typed lectures without the drafted Weil material.[27] Two of the lectures were later published—as "Jane Eyre: The Temptations of a Motherless Woman" and "Vesuvius at Home: The Power of Emily Dickinson"—and collected in *On Lies, Secrets, and Silence*. Weil appears in passing in the Jane Eyre essay, in a list of "gifted imaginative women in the Christian era" who choose "a masculine God" instead of "the love of earthly men (or women)."[28] The archival record thus manifests a fascinating thought process whereby Rich closely read Weil's writing and then revised her out of the final draft. But references to Weil remain in dozens of published poems and essays, and the pressing question, once one begins to recognize their persistence and scope, is what they all mean for Rich's perpetual development and Weil's perpetual presence in contemporary American poetry.

"WHAT ARE YOU GOING THROUGH?" WEIL'S ETHICS OF ATTENTION

Rich's prose writing and interviews suggest that her primary interest in Weil was as an ethicist and political thinker, with particular focus on her ethics of attention, a deeply relational response to suffering and injustice. This focus aligns Rich with other second-wave feminists, including the feminist care ethicists Sophie Bourgault argues were drawn to Weil mainly for her "concept of attention."[29] Such an alignment resonates throughout Rich's poetry, which Miriam Marty Clark, without reference to Weil, sees emphasizing "attentiveness" as well as "global responsiveness and responsibility," "obligation," and a "widening" scope of care.[30] We can trace an ethics of attention in Rich back to the poem "Like This Together" (1963), with its reference to the creative power of "fierce attention" that recalls Weil's discussion in the essay "Forms of the Implicit Love of God," published in *Waiting for God*, of "creative attention," an act of attending to "what does not exist" in order to bring it into being.[31] Rich writes that "through mere indifference/we could prevent" winter from ending. The poem spends most of its five sections meditating melancholically on relational understandings and misunderstandings as well as changes that imply endings and losses, like developers "tearing down the houses/we met and lived in." But the poem ends with this image of attention bringing about another sort of change in an erotic figuring of new life:

Only our fierce attention
gets hyacinths out of those
hard cerebral lumps,
unwraps the wet buds down
the whole length of a stem.[32]

It's not certain that Rich's "fierce attention" here borrows from Weil, but it does echo the philosopher's sense of the creative, life-bringing potential of attention with the image's implied interpersonal commentary.

"Leaflets," written in 1968, does clearly borrow from Weil, whom Rich cites in an endnote.[33] Here we see Rich's first use of Weil's famous question, "What are you going through?"—again, a question around which Weil builds her ethics in her widely cited "School Studies" essay, also published in *Waiting for God*. In this essay, Weil argues that attention—understood not as "muscular effort" but as a sort of open expectant passivity, "empty, waiting, not seeking anything, but ready to receive"—is at the heart of both prayer and care for others.[34] This mode of attention, Weil the schoolteacher insists, can be exercised in students' studies, suggesting a significance for geometry homework that exceeds even Weil's famous devotion to truth for its own sake.

At the end of the essay, Weil turns her argument about school studies as a discipline with spiritual outcomes into an interpersonal and ethical application: "Not only does the love of God have attention for its substance; the love of our neighbor, which we know to be the same love, is made of the same substance." This is because "those who are unhappy have no need for anything in the world but people capable of giving them their attention," although Weil insists that attending to another in their suffering is "a very rare and difficult thing." She explicates this claim by retelling the legend in which the Grail, which in Weil's telling "satisfies all hunger," "belongs to the first comer who asks the guardian of the vessel, a king three-quarters paralyzed by the most painful wound, 'What are you going through?'" Weil insists that the capacity to ask this question is itself "the love of our neighbor in all its fullness."[35]

Asking this question, she further argues, involves "a recognition that the sufferer exists" in all their particularity, not as an abstraction or example, but as a fellow human; in order to see this particularity and shared humanity, one must be able to look at another with the open mode of attention Weil has been describing, one that can receive the other. Weil concludes by bringing this attention full circle back to "a Latin prose or a geometry problem," insisting that such efforts in school may prepare us to attend to another and thereby "save" them. And while Weil has been tying this practice specifically to prayer, she notes that this capacity can be exercised "quite apart from any particular religious belief."[36]

Rich writes variations of Weil's central ethical question into at least half a dozen of her poems. In "Leaflets," the title poem in a collection Wendy Martin argues "reflects her growing awareness of the profound connection between private and public life," Rich experiments with a new form, rejecting stanzas and conventional punctuation.[37] Claire Keyes claims that this shift signals a new form of power as Rich rejects formal expectations of ordering and explanation.[38] The poem is certainly more allusive and associative than her earlier work, a tendency Rich will follow in the decades to come; the poem moves from picturing a night sky and its speaker's postprotest musings as "the head clears of sweet smoke / and poison gas" into allusions to Chekhov and Russian penal colonies, Ché Guevara killed in Bolivia, a "Dahomeyan devil" and a self-immolating girl in a "dyed butterfly turban," and Crusaders and "Jewish terrorists, aged 15," all within the context of addressing some "you."[39] This dizzying array of geographical and historical allusions is situated in the interpersonal, activist-to-activist conversation that drives the poem's first and last numbered sections, an apostrophe-mediated meditation on "life without caution," love, beauty, and the power of poetry imagined as political leaflets.

Weil's question comes in section 2, in a collection of lines that begins with the "coal-black, ash-white" image of an unspecified building explosion, perhaps a newspaper story about some thwarted activist effort. *"Who'd choose this life?"* a voice asks, and the speaker seems to reply:

> We're fighting for a slash of recognition,
> a piercing to the pierced heart.
> *Tell me what you're going through—*
> but the attention flickers
> and will flicker[40]

Weil's ethical question is offered here as a corollary to the activist work toward recognition for the unrecognized. Rich doesn't offer it as a solution but an engagement that could be powerful if it were truly practiced. The poem continues, implying not just the ongoing work toward justice and peace but also the interpersonal tensions within the political movement, between the speaker and this "you," given that they "almost miss each other/in the ill cloud of mistrust, who might have touched/hands quickly, shared food or given blood/for each other."[41] Rich's vision here is of a solidarity rooted in shared understanding, shared attention, that seems possible but not quite achieved.

Weil's line also appears in the poem "9/21/68" in the sequence "The Blue Ghazals." The poem addresses yet another "you," this time one with whom the speaker has been "sleepwalking" for "fifteen years," in the context of a nighttime bedroom with its ticking clock, "muttering" walls, and trees "turning, turning their bruised leaves." In the middle of the poem, the speaker urges, "Talk to me with your body through my dreams./Tell me what we are going through."[42] Again, the wish seems to be for an intersubjectivity that is not granted, despite the fifteen years of sleepwalking together. As Pavlić notes, this intersubjectivity is characteristic of Rich's ghazal sequence more generally: "Everywhere in the ghazals appear images of the interactive urge to relational speaking, thinking, dreaming, and being."[43]

The quest for intersubjectivity continues in "Shooting Script" (1969–1970) with lines like "Your clarities may not reach me; but your attention will," spoken to a "You" who "are beside me like a wall." A variation on Weil's Grail question appears in the following section to describe "Someone who never said, 'What do you feel?'"[44] This is yet another instance of Weil's question illustrating its own power in a *failure* of curious and compassionate attention. But the failure also implies the question's value, for, again, as Pavlić writes, "the most salient legacy (of many legacies) of Adrienne Rich's work establishes 'relationship' as a political category."[45] Here he builds on Craig Werner's claim from 1988 that Rich's "radical poetic voice" turns "silence into conversation," James McCorkle's emphasis in 1989 on Rich's use of dialogue and interconnection, and Nick Halpern's focus in 2003 on the centrality of conversation for Rich.[46] Underlying all these insightful readings is Weil's ethics of attention as a formative latent influence embedded in Rich's characteristic ethics and poetics of intersubjectivity from its earliest development.

Another variation of Weil's line appears in "From the Prison House" (1971), but this time the poem's speaker is not describing a relational dynamic so much as an assessment of the world's suffering— the ethical weight turns from the intersubjective to the collective and political, an expansion that tracks with Rich's trajectory toward ever-wider affiliations and concerns. Indeed, this is an early poem that exemplifies Rich's ethics of witnessing injustice. Opening the sparse twenty-eight-line poem, the speaker describes "another eye" that "has opened" beneath her closed lids as she sleeps, one that "looks nakedly / at the light / that soaks in from the world of pain." This eye "regards" not just "everything I am going through" but also more, including "clubs and rifle-butts," a "policewoman / searching" a sex worker's body, "roaches dropping into the pan / where they cook the pork / in the House of D." These vivid images describe the poem's titular prison house in a way that invites readers to likewise see the "violence embedded in silence."[47] Here Weil's line refers to both the speaker's own pain and struggles—which notably go entirely undescribed—and the act of attending to others' experience of injustice. The "House of D" refers to the New York Women's House of Detention, a women's prison in Manhattan notorious for its racial discrimination and abuse.[48] Echoing Weil's concern for a steely commitment to the truth, whatever it may be, along with attention to others' suffering, Rich's speaker concludes that "This eye" must aim for "clarity" in witnessing such injustice. The point is not "weeping" ("though tears are on my face") but an unstinting attention to others' pain even as it also engages in self-witnessing. Within the broader scope of Rich's work, this witnessing is one component of a dogged commitment to clarity of vision, clarity of thought, and active work for gender, racial, and economic justice.

The phrase "what are you going through" returns nearly two decades later in the poem "For a Friend in Travail" (1990), a more thorough meditation on Weil herself I discuss later in this chapter, as well as the poem "This Evening Let's" (2001), another apostrophe-driven poem evidently addressed to a friend from another country.[49] The latter poem takes us full circle back to Rich's work of the late 1960s that invokes Weil's question as an invitation to interpersonal connection, although this poem is more playful, evidently more hopeful about the possibility of such a relational connection, asking the friend with whom she wishes to order Greek "retsina / cracked olives and bread" to linger with a "smile" in the "mercy" of friendship.[50]

This ethics and politics of asking another what they're going through is evident not just when Rich borrows Weil's Grail question but also in the language of attention itself, which extends from "Like This Together" and "Leaflets" through poem XIX of the sequence *Twenty-One Love Poems* (1974–1976), which again speaks of "the fierc-est attention" as a relational goal between the "two women together" at the sequence's center, engaged in the "work / heroic in its ordinariness" of seeking to be together.[51] Attention appears again in "Toward the Solstice" (1977) as another habitual practice of care, this time toward not another person but a house: "A decade of perform-ing/the loving humdrum acts/of attention to this house/transplant-ing lilac suckers, washing panes, scrubbing" and so on, engaging in "woman's work."[52] While this iteration of attention is not interper-sonal, it still embodies Weil's sense that attention to another in need of care is a creative act that can bring that other into being—and it implicitly links Weil's ethic to labor Western cultures have tradition-ally associated with women.

The interpersonal attention appears decades later in the poem "Scenes of Negotiation" (2009), where Rich describes "a resistance cell?" in which "men and women" squat together in an "uncaulked" "shed," where they laugh together around food in "a kind of close mutual attention."[53] The scene implies that this way of being together undergirds and empowers ongoing courage and resistance. The poem "The School Among the Ruins," written six years earlier, similarly imagines attention to an other as a courage-bolstering practice. In this case, Rich's poem devastatingly pictures a school reduced to rubble in a bombing, the teachers' and children's lives suddenly taken from the simple "love of the fresh impeccable/sharp-pencilled yes" and "fresh bread" to hiding in the school without food and water. The poem's imagined teacher gently cajoles the students, as "all night the pitiless pilotless things go shrieking/above us," to "pay attention to our cat   she needs us." This triangulated invitation for the chil-dren to attend to the cat—to perceive the cat's hunger and need—is an invitation that seeks to preserve the children's humanity in their desperate circumstances. It models for the poem's *readers* a similar tri-angulation, inviting readers to witness the bombing victims' suffer-ing so that our own "faces" don't "turn to stone."[54]

The poem powerfully exemplifies Rich's commitment to an eth-ics of attention, one that doesn't just thematize attention in the ways

I have been discussing here but also insistently invites readers into an attentive practice, one that clear-sightedly looks at the reality of others' vulnerabilities and pains in order to forge the kinds of intersubjectivities that might lead toward shared work for shared flourishing. In this way, Rich follows other midcentury feminists in borrowing from Weil's relational focus, locating in Weil's work a protofeminist resource for an ethics of intersubjectivity and care. As Rich's ethical and political focus expanded in the 1980s, broadening to consider the implications of race, colonialism, class, globalizing economies, and other injustices in conjunction with gender-based oppression, Weil's ethics of attention continued to provide a framework for the relations across difference—the personal-and/as-political dynamics—necessary for resistance and justice. But her ethics of attention is by no means the full extent of Weil's influence on Rich.

SUFFERING, AFFLICTION, AND THE THREAT OF FORCE

Rich's engagement with Weil is wide-ranging, far exceeding the somewhat limited focus on an ethics of attention Bourgault locates in many feminist care ethicists' appeals to the philosopher.[55] Rich further turns to Weil as a resource for discussing suffering and violence, again, as concepts that help develop a feminist critique of patriarchal power in the 1970s but then extend still further in the second half of Rich's career.

Weil writes in *Waiting for God* not only of an ethics of attention but also of an important distinction between what she calls "suffering" and "affliction" (in French, *malheur*). Rich draws on this distinction in *Of Woman Born: Motherhood as Experience and Institution* (1976) in a chapter called "Alienated Labor," in which she writes about the current and historical obstetrical practices that reduce women to passivity, whether painfully undrugged or drugged and disempowered. Rich asks, "Can we distinguish physical pain from alienation and fear? Is there creative pain and destructive pain?" To help answer her questions, she discusses how "the remarkable philosopher-mystic Simone Weil" "makes the distinction between suffering—characterized by pain yet leading to growth and enlightenment—and affliction—the condition of the oppressed, the slave, the concentration-camp victim forced to haul heavy stones back and forth across a yard, endlessly and to no purpose." She continues:

> [Weil] reiterates that pain is not to be sought, and she objects to putting oneself in the way of unnecessary affliction. But where it is unavoidable, pain can be transformed into something usable, something which takes us beyond the limits of the experience itself into a further grasp of the essentials of life and the possibilities within us. However, over and over she equates pure affliction with powerlessness, with waiting, disconnectedness, inertia, the "fragmented time" of one who is at others' disposal. This insight illuminates much of the female condition, but in particular the experience of giving birth.

Rich reads Weil's distinction in the centuries during which women were told they must suffer in childbirth to pay for Eve's sin and also in the passivity of mid-twentieth-century anesthetic practices: both, she claims, involve "forced labor" and a lack of agency. Rich wonders whether avoiding the pain of childbirth is closer to Weil's "affliction" in its passivity and disconnection than the purposeful, active suffering involved in an unmedicated birth. In other words, Rich asks with Weil whether some modes of pain might bring us closer to a clearsighted sense of reality, one that refuses to "lose touch" with the "painful sensations" or "with ourselves." In this reassessment of affliction versus suffering, Rich supports her book's memorable central thesis that "to destroy the institution is not to abolish motherhood. It is to

release the creation and sustenance of life into the same realm of decision, struggle, surprise, imagination, and conscious intelligence, as
any other difficult, but freely chosen work."[56]

Rich also appeals to Weil's specific vocabulary of "affliction" in
numerous poems across the years, including "When We Dead
Awaken" (1971), "Contradictions: Tracking Poems, #27" (1983–1985),
and "From Sickbed Shores" (2008).[57] In all these instances, Rich's use
of the term follows Weil's description of multimodal alienation and
destruction, an "uprooting of life" that involves "social, psychological, and physical" pain and degradation.[58] In poem 27 of "Contradictions: Tracking Poems," for instance, Rich's speaker imagines
"Tolstoyans" and "Afro-American slaves" who knew the power and
danger of literacy, the risk of death for spreading it against the law,
and admits, "I used to think the worst affliction/was to be forbidden
pencil and paper." But the speaker goes on to admit that this view
has shifted, another feature of Rich's later poetry and prose, which
often narrates change and admits past wrongs: having learned both of
poets staying alive by reciting poems in prison cells *and* what she calls
elsewhere the "politics of location," whereby "where you stand" and
how literacy functions in a given place alters its power. The speaker
goes on, "I think now the worst affliction/is not to know who you
are or have been," an insight resonant with Weil's assertion in *The
Need for Roots* that "to be rooted is perhaps the most important and
least recognized need of the human soul" that involves having connections to community, history, culture, and shared identity.[59]

Uprooting results from violence: military conquest and colonization in its most large-scale form, but also the social, psychological,
and physical pain that results in individual affliction, most of which,
Weil writes, is caused by "human crime." Social uprooting parallels
personal affliction, which Weil writes "is anonymous before all things;
it deprives its victims of their personality and makes them into
things."[60] In her essay "The *Iliad*, or the Poem of Force," Weil further

expounds on this idea: "To define force—it is that x that turns any-body who is subjected to it into a *thing*." Force turns people into things most literally by bringing about their deaths and rendering them corpses, but "the force that does *not* kill" sounds very much like what she elsewhere calls affliction. For Weil, force—ultimate power over another—is almost impossible to wield justly: it is "as pitiless to the man who possesses it, or thinks he does, as it is to its victims; the second it crushes the first it intoxicates."[61] (Here, I think, we can hear resonance with Rich's description of drones in "The School Among the Ruins" as "pitiless pilotless things.") In Weil's reading of the *Iliad*, force itself is "the true subject," as she claims in the essay's arresting first line; it blithely subjects any character who possesses it to its own inclinations.

Rich borrows Weil's vocabulary of "force" in the late 1960s and early 1970s in poems like "The Blue Ghazals" (1968), "Diving into the Wreck" (1972), and poem XVI of "Twenty-One Love Poems" (1974–1976).[62] Always keenly attentive to power—working against patriar-chal "domination, depersonalization, and dehumanization," to quote Rachel Blau DuPlessis's assessment in 1975—Rich engages with Weil's concept of force as a sort of gravity, the way things work, the inexorable pull of violence and power-over.[63] She returns to this con-versation in the 2009 poem "Reading the *Iliad* (as if) for the First Time." Although this poem doesn't include the word "force," it's an implicit conversation with Weil's essay (which Rich quotes in the end-notes) and its take on the anonymizing power of force, the concrete-ness of violence and suffering, and the role of beauty within Homer's narrative. Rich's explicit, verbally fragmented depictions of war's violence—"Lurid, garish gash / rended creature struggles to rise"—wonders at the aestheticized rendering of agony. Describing the war scene on "a grecian urn / Beauty as truth," the speaker exclaims, "Beauty!   flesh before gangrene" and in the white-space-riven line disrupts the aestheticization. Following further descriptions of gore, the poem ends with horses weeping and beauty now not as an exclamation but a question:

> Beauty?
> a wall with names of the fallen
> from both sides   passionate objectivity[64]

Rich here echoes Weil's interest in the *Iliad*'s treatment of violence. Weil writes, "Whatever is not war, whatever war destroys and threatens, the *Iliad* wraps in poetry; the realities of war, never. No reticence veils the steps from life to death."[65] Against Keats's "Ode on a Grecian Urn," Rich extends Weil's claim that the *Iliad* refuses to aestheticize war, highlighting the devastating role of force for both sides and the beauty of love, friendship, and hospitality shown only in brief glimpses of contrast to the horrors of violence. Ultimately, Rich's poem from 2009 reminds us that even forty years after Weil's first appearance in her work, the philosopher remained as a persistent interlocutor in Rich's interrogations of poetics, ethics, and politics.

"SELF-HATRED BATTENING ON HER BODY": RICH'S CRITIQUE

Weil's influence threads through Rich's work, but the poet resists her source at important points. Rich's most obvious grappling with Weil's influence occurs in later poems like "A Vision" (1981) and "For a Friend in Travail" (1990), but we can trace it back to the poem "Hunger" (1974–1975).[66] Rich dedicated this poem to her friend Audre Lorde, and the poem is an early example of Rich's examination of the interplay of universal and particular sufferings and solidarities. In four sections, Rich directs her speaker's gaze from a "Chinese painter's" inked scene of "two human figures recklessly exposed" to famine in West and Central Africa, to the German painter Käthe Kollwitz's paintings of working-class grief, and finally a newspaper photo of a generic "woman" who "shields a dead child from the camera." Rich recognizes patriarchal rule and its inadequate response to hunger as a unifying force across these contexts, insisting:

> The decision to feed the world
> is the real decision. No revolution
> has chosen it. For that choice requires
> that women shall be free.

The poem's speaker does not presume to fully understand women's experience in other places, but she also refuses to imagine that they are unconnected:

> I know I'm partly somewhere else—
> huts strung across a drought-stretched land
> not mine, dried breasts, mine and not mine, a mother
> watching my children shrink with hunger.
> I live in my Western skin,
> my Western vision, torn
> and flung to what I can't control or even fathom.[67]

This paradox of connection—recognizing sufferings "mine and not mine," acknowledging the particularity of Western "skin" and "vision" while also naming its connection to otherness—previews Rich's work on the politics of location that would emerge in the 1980s in essays and poems like "North American Time" (1983) with its insistence that if "you want to write / of a woman braiding / another woman's hair," you need to know about the type of braid, the hair, the motivation, her overall experience, even politics in her country.[68] This insistence

on responsibility and rejection of easy appropriation is a counterbal-
ance to the risks of Rich's impulse to trace global affiliations among
women under patriarchy, a tendency that was prominent in 1970s
white feminism, perhaps most famously exemplified by Mary Daly's
Gyn/Ecology, which Lorde would go on to criticize for appropriation
and generalization in "An Open Letter to Mary Daly" (1979).[69]

Rich runs the risk of feminist universalizing in "Hunger" but also
resists it through her references to particular modes of hunger and
her rejection of a hierarchy of suffering. She asks:

> Is death by famine worse than death by suicide,
> than a life of famine and suicide, if a black lesbian dies,
> if a white prostitute dies, if a woman genius
> starves herself to feed others,
> self-hatred battening on her body?[70]

Rich goes on to name famine (act of a "male god") in "Chad, in
Niger, in the Upper Volta," as well as the "male State" ostensibly in
North America with its "terrorists of the mind" seeking to control
women and children. These various modes of suffering—and iterations of patriarchal control—reduce women and children to survival
rather than creative resistance, as does the patriarchal insistence that
the pain "belongs in some order," creating an atmosphere of competition rather than allowing for networks of solidarity. Rich imagines
in section 3 that these rules have resulted in a fear that keeps women
from "touching / our power," leading women instead to "starve ourselves / and each other": internalizing patriarchal rule rather than
embracing what it "could be to take and use our love."[71]

It is hard not to read Rich's "woman genius" as Simone Weil,
although she never names Weil in this poem. Not only is Weil the
most widely recognized twentieth-century "woman genius" whose
death arose in part from "self-starvation," but Weil's work is rife with

vocabularies and metaphors of hunger. For Weil, hunger was a double-voiced discourse that undergirded both an ethics of attention and responsibility and an ethics of what she called decreation, or self-diminishment, where love, friendship, and care for others looks very much like hungering but not eating. She writes in *The Need for Roots*, "It is an eternal obligation toward the human being not to let him suffer from hunger when one has the chance of coming to his assistance"—she means this literally and uses it as a paradigmatic example of a universal human obligation to meet everyone's physical and moral needs.[72] As Bourgault explains, "In *L'enracinement* [*The Need for Roots*] Weil suggests that the human need for food is so self-evident and compelling that we should anchor our entire vision of politics in this most fundamental need."[73] At the same time, Weil repeatedly returned to metaphors of unfulfilled hunger, and choosing not to eat, to describe the desire for beauty, goodness, friendship, and the divine.[74]

In the space of the poem, the Weilian character exemplifies internalized patriarchy of both the "male god" and "male State" mind control, the "self-hatred" and self-starvation modes of self-sacrifice the poem cannot applaud. Weil the "genius" is listed here as neither more nor less a victim than those dead of famine, than a "black lesbian" or "white prostitute": the implication is that all these women are afflicted by similar forces even in their particularity. Rich's conclusion is ultimately one of connection and care for others, those deep in what Weil described as affliction, with its social, physical, and psychological isolation and its robbery of language. Rich writes, "I'm alive to want more than life, / want it for others starving and unborn": her speaker's own life and voice implies a responsibility to desire more than simple survival for other women and children, wherever they are, however they suffer under the patriarchal "terrorists of the mind." The poem concludes, "Until we find each other, we are alone."[75] The implication is that only communal efforts will shift the structural violence that leaves women literally or figuratively hungry around the globe.

"Hunger" resonates powerfully with Weil's vision of the obligation to attend to and care for suffering others: Rich turns her gaze outward to women suffering in other parts of the world and in bearing witness to their suffering in the poem in some sense creates them. She explicitly names hunger as a unifying suffering, echoing Weil's point in *The Need for Roots* that the obligation to feed the hungry is the paradigmatic human—and literal—responsibility to pursue justice. Indeed, Rich writes a few years later in a 1983 essay of "the bedrock significance of hunger as a feminist issue."[76] Yet even as Rich shares Weil's ethical impulses, Weil herself appears as one of the suffering women to whom Rich attends, a victim of the internalized patriarchal force that has turned so many women toward self-starvation, self-hatred, and self-sacrifice.

Rich wrestles even more explicitly with Weil in "A Vision," written in 1981, which is Rich's first poem wholly given over to engagement with Simone Weil. With the epigraph "(thinking of Simone Weil)," the poem addresses either Weil or some other who reminds Rich's speaker of Weil. She characterizes this "You" as powerfully and willfully committed to the project of staring at the sun as a "test," one that is related to maintaining "focus" and "loss of self/in a greater thing"—a decreative practice. The poem emphasizes that this staring at the sun is painful—it describes the "stubborn lids that have stayed open/at the moment of pouring liquid steel." The staring is also risky, and the poem twice repeats the phrase "your fear of blinding."[77] In a way, the poem seems a reiteration or renegotiation of the eye that "looks nakedly/at the light//that soaks in from the world of pain" in the earlier poem "From the Prison House."[78]

Rich alludes here to Weil's repeated metaphors of blindness and sight. In *The Need for Roots*, for example, Weil writes of how through colonization and industrialization, "men of the white race have

everywhere destroyed the past, stupidly, blindly," resulting in the horrifying injustice of uprooting people from their traditional cultures.[79]
Throughout her work, blindness is a problem, but, as in Rich's poem,
vision is often painful. Weil repeatedly references Plato's allegory of
the cave, celebrating the way the sun's light helps humans see "naked
reality," including pain.[80] For Weil, the sun's light allows humans to
take in all that is and to somehow accept and even love it, even the
most painful parts of it.[81] This dynamic extends to God—important
to Rich's questioning later in the poem—as Weil writes, "We know
we cannot see [God] without dying and we do not want to die." Drawing again on the allegory of the cave, she emphasizes the pain of
coming to the entrance and "the light," which "not only blinds but
wounds us. Our eyes turn away from it." Nevertheless, Weil writes,
it is a "horrible idea" to turn away from the light, from seeing both
God and reality "face to face."[82]

Rich's allusion is even clearer in the poem's second stanza, which
plays with Weil's vocabulary of "force" and "attention":

this
unfair struggle with the forces of perception
this enforced
(but at that word your attention changes)
This enforced   loss of self[83]

Weil insists that one must not look away from reality, including
the reality of suffering, even when every impulse pulls one's attention
back. This is what Hardwick describes as her "obsessive concentration upon affliction."[84] Rich's wordplay here, though, suggests that
the struggle not to look away from suffering, even when it hurts, is
itself a manifestation of force, which for Weil carries the negative
connotations of violence. Force is not really bent by human agency;
no matter who wields it, force reduces its object to a thing—either a

corpse or a slave robbed of humanity. In this, "A Vision" parallels "Hunger" in its suggestion that Weil's self-diminishment is not a free ethical action but an internalized violence against her own self.

In the fourth stanza, Rich narrates the relational process of writing, the "problem" of "writing to you," a return to Rich's common theme of ethical intersubjectivity—but despite these imperfections, "I am writing this almost / involuntarily," the paragraph begins; "the words create themselves," it ends.[85] This involuntary creation recalls Weil's sense that attention, truly practiced, is an open and passive waiting, and that such an open and receptive stance is at the heart of creative work. It echoes Weil commendation in her "School Studies" essay of "a way of waiting, when we are writing, for the right word to come or itself at the end of our pen, while we merely reject all inadequate words."[86] Again, even as Rich questions Weil, she seems to embrace another aspect of Weil's thought.

The final stanza asks the "you" why she is "forced to take this test / over and over and call it God." Rich wonders, "why not call it you and get it over?"[87] Here is Rich's most explicit rejection of Weil's cruciform Christianity, which insists on a full embrace of suffering for the sake of divine union. The poem reads Weil's suffering-servant faith in a fully desacralized space: for Rich, this impulse in Weil is motivated by a blind misperception about the divine, an internalized play of self-harming force. Yet even then, the poem ends with a question rather than a definitive statement, expressing both an openness to further understanding Weil or the Weil-like figure and a commitment to ongoing conversation.

Rich questions Weil's sense of personal versus divine motivation again in the poem "For a Friend in Travail" (1990). The poem sets up a scene of postsurgical pain and nighttime musing, addressing another unnamed "you." Yet the first phrase—"Waking from violence:"—suggests a broader significance than the surgical mistake that follows in the line; in its more general possible meaning, the phrase suggests any number of other modes of violence, including dream violence, which characteristically links embodied, particular suffering with a broader pain.[88] The speaker describes wandering awake at night, and in referencing the "Drinking-Gourd" weaves still broader lines of affiliation by referencing African American resistance history.

The second stanza quotes Weil's famous Grail question for the first of the poem's two times and refers to Weil, implicitly, in the third person:

> *What are you going through?* she said, is the great question.
> Philosopher of oppression, theorist
> of the victories of force.[89]

This is the only time in Rich's poetry that she explicitly links Weil's question to her person. In calling Weil "philosopher of oppression" and "theorist/of the victories of force," Rich gives insight into her own reading of Weil's importance: Rich herself is widely known as a poet (and theorist) concerned with oppression and power, a word that appears again and again in her work and commentaries thereon.

The next line, "We write from the marrow of our bones," asserts that writing—including philosophizing and theorizing no less than poetry—comes from deep within us and our embodiment. Rich links the theoretical here to the personal, and the realm of ideas to the realm of embodiment, and thus, implicitly, to pain. This claim resonates with a tension over Weil's passion for objective and general truth and decreation—even in her self-absenting prose style, as Joan Dargan notes—and the inescapably personal origins of many of her insights. Rich goes on to note another tension or absence in Weil: "how victims save their own lives."[90] Rich here seems to be diagnosing a deficit in Weil's thought, with its insistence that salvation is possible only through divine or at least divinely driven interpersonal intervention. Rich seems to embrace an alternative vision, one that recognizes inner strength and agency rather than complete powerlessness in affliction.

Yet in the next stanza, with its description of a dream of crawling over a ledge and the waking and dreaming in suffering, she goes on to describe dawn and "Love for the world" of which "we are part": Weil's dogged *amor mundi* must, logically, encompass "us." A stoic love for all creation, if it is logically consistent, implies self-love and self-acceptance since the self is part of creation, however much self-love seems to have eluded Weil herself. Echoing Rich's earlier line and paralleling imagined victims' self-saving, the stanza ends, "How poppies break from their sealed envelopes/she did not tell."[91] This natural image suggests the mystery and beauty of flowers' unfolding and an implied parallel natural blooming rather than diminishment for humans.

But despite Rich's questioning of Weil throughout the poem, she still ends it with Weil's own question, posed to the friend the poem addresses: "What are you going through?"[92] In other words, Rich embeds a critique of Weil's decreative self-diminishment in a poem that still relies on her ethics of relational attention, particularly in the context of suffering. This, I'm saying, is characteristic of Rich's whole forty-five-year engagement with Weil. For all her questions and critiques—specifically of Weil's self-sacrificing and religious impulses bound by a fascination with the Christian cross—Rich turns and returns to Weil's basic premises about attention, suffering, and force. And paradoxically, Weil's insights—about love for the world, the obligation to ease others' hunger, and attentive care for the oppressed—are precisely the lens through which Rich interprets Weil's unsatiated body in the poems that address the philosopher of oppression.

SEEKING ROOTS, READING RELIGION

Rich's resistance to Weil's Christian turn, to the "transcendence she called God," bound up with the impulse to "starv[e] herself to feed others," never caused Rich to turn away entirely from her source. Nor did it lead her to fall into common patterns among Weil's readers who bracket either the mystical or the political writings. Rich was among Weil's most astute and expansive literary readers, turning to her less widely known works—*The Selected Essays, Oppression and Liberty*—to discuss political power and labor practices in essays like "Conditions for Work: The Common Work of Women" (1976) or the separation of science from the bigger picture in the essay "Toward a Woman-Centered University" (1973–1974), collected in *On Lies, Secrets, and Silence.* Weil also hovers over some of Rich's important later reconsiderations. For example, Rich's 1980s reappraisal of Marxism—only recently beginning to receive thorough attention from scholars—rings out with Weil's own refusal of a division between thought and action, imagination and economic justice, as Rich writes about these dynamics in essays like "Raya Dunayevksaya's Marx" (1991), collected in *Arts of the Possible.*

More personally—although also, inevitably, politically—Weil's influence is present in Rich's reappraisal of her own Jewish roots. This reappraisal occurred in the 1980s, when Rich was in her fifties, and is represented in poems like "Sources" (1981–1982) and "Yom Kippur, 1984" (1984–1985) and essays like "Split at the Root: An Essay on Jewish Identity" (1982) and "If Not with Others, How?" (1985), collected in *Blood, Bread, and Poetry.* In these pieces Rich recalls being raised as a "white southern woman" and "social Christian," her assimilated Jewish father "building/his rootless ideology."[93] Weil's theory of the importance of roots is implicitly present throughout these searching poems and essays, as Rich links her retrieval of her own Jewishness with her emerging politics of location and accountability to settler colonialism and anti-Black racism, tracing the lines of her experiences of oppression as a woman and a lesbian, her plain luck at not being born a Jew in Europe in 1939 or experiencing other manifestations of anti-Semitism, and her embeddedness in the privileges of whiteness. In "Sources," Rich characteristically layers the personal and the political, addressing both her father and her late husband to admit that in reconsidering their—and her own—Jewishness, she was able to read them in a new light: "It is only now, under a powerful, womanly lens," she writes, addressing her domineering father, "that I can decipher your suffering and deny no part of my own."[94] Writing to her erstwhile husband, who took his own life shortly after their separation, she writes tenderly of his thwarted need for roots, to have a place and people "among whom we can sit down and weep," echoing Psalm 137: "No person, trying to take responsibility for her or his identity, should have to be so alone."[95] Rich's poignant assessment of the need for roots extends not just to the Jewish men in her younger life but also to herself: she may not embrace the spirituality of Judaism, but she retrieves the identity, seeking community and expanding layers of solidarity. And the need for roots extends to the political, as she writes in "If Not with Others, How?": in order to undo racisms global and American, she insists, "The depth of the work we do depends on its rootedness—in our knowledge of who we are and also where we are—a country which has used skin color as the prime motive for persecution and genocide, as Europe historically used religion."[96]

Weil echoes throughout these texts, not just in her concept of rootedness but in her keenly antioppressive and explicitly anticolonial outlook. Of course, it's hard to miss the irony of Weil's role as a motivator for Rich's rediscovery of her own Jewish heritage, given Weil's refusal of her own Jewishness. Rich doesn't write about Weil's own anti-Jewish biases at any length, although she was certainly aware of them: it's possible she shared her partner Michelle Cliff's assessment that Weil's anti-Jewishness was a sort of internalized racism, paralleling the gendered "self-hatred battening on her body."[97] It's also possible that if Weil had lived into her own sixth decade, she might have engaged in a similar project of rerooting, one that joined Rich both in finding fuller community—"no person . . . should have to be so alone"—and also in "enlarging the range of accountability" as she assessed the complexity of her own social location.[98]

Rich's study of her Jewish heritage included a reengagement with the Bible and a broader reassessment of the ways religious feminists and Black Christians, in particular, drew on their religious roots to resist oppression. It did not, however, lead Rich into religious faith. And it does not resolve the tension that persists in her treatment of Weil, a tension present in many twentieth- and twenty-first-century engagements with religion in a secular frame that leaves room for belief, unbelief, and critique of religion. That tension includes the question of whether one does an injustice to a philosophical source when one embraces an aspect of its wisdom while snipping and tugging that wisdom away from its religious origins. Can one, in other words, embrace Weil's ethics of attention, her assessments of suffering, force, and the need for roots, apart from their profoundly theological underpinnings?

I have argued elsewhere about these deracinations as a problematic feature of later twentieth-century engagement with religiously committed philosophers.[99] One major example of this trend in literary studies is in appeals to the philosopher and Talmud scholar Emmanuel Levinas (himself one of Weil's later readers who famously accused her of misreading the Hebrew Bible—more on this in chapter 3). As Adam Zachary Newton convincingly argues, something significant is lost when literary scholars and other writers borrow the ethical insights of a philosopher like Levinas while suppressing their inextricably woven religious—and in Levinas's case, specifically Jewish—reflections.[100] Eric O. Springsted expresses similar concern that to approach Weil only in terms of her philosophy misses—"often

deliberately—a genuine and central theological commitment in Simone Weil the thinker." Springsted argues for an approach to Weil
that takes her Christianity seriously, not as "an addendum," but also
recognizes her as a rigorous philosophical thinker, "not just an anthology of mystical insights."[101] Rich could be said to participate in a
similar pitfall as she snips and pulls Weil's provocative writings about
suffering, affliction, and attention out of a text woven through with
references to prayer, divine love and self-limitation in creation, Jesus's
story about the good Samaritan, and the cross.

There's also a strong argument to be made, however, that Rich's
treatment of Weil's Christian turn—bracketing it in some texts, critiquing it in others—is in full alignment with Weil's own sensibility.
The philosopher was passionately drawn to cruciform Christianity in
her later writings; this is incontrovertible, and it developed not out of
an intellectual conviction but from a series of mystical experiences.
The third of these led her to feel Christ's "sudden possession": "I only
felt in the midst of my suffering the presence of a love, like that which
one can read in the smile on a beloved face." But readers who find
this religious turn discomfiting often overlook the degree to which
Weil critiqued oppression within the Christian tradition. Her sense
of the divine took on specific features after her mystical experiences
in Christian spaces, but Weil continued to insist on the truth present
in world religions: this insistent universalism contributed to her refusal
to be baptized. In a letter that came to be known as her "Spiritual
Autobiography," Weil writes,

> So many things are outside [the Church], so many things that I love
> and do not want to give up, so many things that God loves, otherwise
> they would not be in existence. All the immense stretches of past cen-
> turies, except the past twenty are among them; all the countries inhab-
> ited by colored races; all secular life in white peoples' countries; in the
> history of these countries, all the traditions banned as heretical, those

of the Manicheans and Albigenses, for instance, all these things resulting from the Renaissance, too often degraded but not quite without
value.

Weil refused baptism—and thereby was disallowed communion in
the Catholic Church, though she dearly longed for it—in solidarity
with these past and present communities excluded by the Church, and
in protest of the Church's power to exclude and excommunicate,
which she linked to the evil of totalitarianism, tracing current totali-
tarian regimes back to the Church's model. Wishing for the Church
as an institution to admit to such past crimes as the Inquisition, she
also wrote that the institution's current dogmas prevented its mem-
bers from exercising "intellectual honesty," another reason for her to
remain outside it.[102]

For all her desire to join Christ on his cross, Weil's critique of the
Church is sharp. And for those, like Rich, whose integrity requires a
critique of Christianity that distances them still further from its
tenets, Weil argues that ethics and aesthetics, properly pursued, are
enough. In the essay "Forms of the Implicit Love of God," she writes,

> In affliction some men, in spite of themselves, develop a hatred and
> contempt for religion because the cruelty, pride or corruption of cer-
> tain of its ministers have made them suffer. There are others who have
> been reared from their earliest youth in surroundings impregnated with
> a spirit of this sort. We must conclude that in such cases, by God's
> mercy, the love of our neighbor and the love of the beauty of the world,
> if they are sufficiently strong and pure, will be enough to raise the soul
> to any height.

In other words, while Weil maintains her own sense of the divine as
an ultimate reality she meets in Christ, she finds its truth both in all
the world religions ("Each religion is an original combination of

explicit and implicit truths; what is explicit in one is implicit in another") and in pure-of-heart atheism.[103]

The fact that Rich openly wrestles with Weil's religiosity in relation to the harms Rich critiques in the Christian tradition, especially in relation to Christian patriarchy, in some sense does more justice to Weil's oeuvre than those who simply ignore her religious commitments. For one, it shows Rich's fuller engagement with Weil's writings. For another, it enters into the conversation Weil invites around not just the benefits but also the harms of organized religion: the imperialism, violence, and exclusion Weil herself openly decried in the same texts that express her attraction to the Church.[104] In this way, Rich's engagement with Weil offers a model of secular—or perhaps postsecular—engagement with belief and unbelief, one predicated not on an embarrassed erasure of ideas or interlocutors but on a frank critique of the lamentable that nevertheless embraces the life-giving—a practice I'm arguing we find modeled both in Weil's own writing and in Rich's long dialogue with Weil as a key source for her ethical, political, and poetic commitments.

It should come as no surprise that Adrienne Rich and Simone Weil are characterized in similar ways: not just for their "intensity" (a frequent refrain) but for their unflagging commitments to the common good of their countries, indeed, of the world. Commenting on Rich as "citizen poet," Maggie Rehm writes, "This is one of the great strengths of Adrienne Rich's writing—that she situated herself politically to acknowledge and interrogate the ways a citizen is implicated in and inextricable from her own moment of her own country, while also exploring both the limits and the necessity of human relationships."[105] In 2006 Craig Werner wrote of Rich's "belief in the value of embodied political passion."[106] Weil's role as a "citizen philosopher" and her commitment to "embodied political passion" likewise characterize every facet of her work. As E. Jane Doering writes, "For Weil, theory was never separate from action."[107] Rich follows Weil, her source and provocateur for more than forty-five years, in this passionate seriousness. In a late essay called "Jacob and the Angel"—one that, incidentally, showcased Rich's later return to Jewish sources— she writes, "Poetry can't give us laws and institutions and representatives, the antidotes we need: only public activism by massive numbers of citizens can do that. To read, to listen, to write, to wrestle with contradictions, to engage with others—this is, indeed, the verb without tenses, the conversation without an end."[108] Rich wrestled with Weil, but she did not cease to find wisdom in her; she questioned Weil, but she did not cease to address her. Theirs was a conversation rooted in the search for justice no less than beauty, a conversation we continue to find documented in Rich's impassioned poetry and prose: a conversation without an end.

2

ATTENTION

Annie Dillard Waits for God with Weil

In art and science of the 1st. order, creation is self-renunciation.
—Simone Weil, *First and Last Notebooks*

In a profile of Annie Dillard in 1995, Philip Yancey recalls the first time he met Dillard, nearly two decades earlier: "Acquainted with her only through her writing, I expected to find either a fey, neurotic poet like Emily Dickinson or a gaunt mystic like Simone Weil." Instead, Dillard "wore blue jeans and an embroidered shirt. She loved Ping-Pong and softball and dancing. She reveled in a good joke. Neither Dickinsonian nor professorial, she was rather the kind of person you'd put first on your guest list to liven up a dinner party."[1] Yet while Yancey tellingly represents Dillard as decidedly *not* "like Simone Weil" in her exuberant embrace of pleasure—an exuberance that features in most interviews with Dillard, which inevitably mention her love of softball and a good joke—the rest of his piece points to striking similarities between Dillard and Weil, although Yancey does not acknowledge them as such. These include not just the writers' shared focus on religion and metaphysics—questions of reality, existence, time, and space that transcend sensory observations—but also their reception bordering on hagiography. He writes, "Most involuntarily,

Annie Dillard became a modern saint, an icon," echoing Leslie Fiedler's famous opening claim in his introduction to *Waiting for God* that Weil is "a special exemplar of sanctity for our time."[2]

Dillard's ascension to fame followed the publication of *Pilgrim at Tinker Creek* (1974), which won the Pulitzer Prize, became a best-seller, and set Dillard on a path to becoming one of the most admired American nonfiction writers of the twentieth century. *Pilgrim* famously joins the tradition of American nature writing—in 1968 Dillard had completed a master's thesis on Thoreau's *Walden*—to combine her poetic observations of the Roanoke Valley where she lived with meditations on the relationships of beauty and brutality, matter and meaning, and the role of the artist. Yancey links the book's remarkable success in part to the "secular culture" into which it was released: "Spirituality in those days had no place on the New York literary landscape, and in that desert, *Pilgrim* shimmered like an oasis for the soul."[3] Dillard's combination of sharp prose, keen attention to the world, and frank spiritual exploration met with enormous success, appealing to many of the same interests that drew so many readers to Simone Weil's spiritual writings at this same moment in the 1970s, a time George A. Panichas characterizes in his preface to the *Simone Weil Reader* (1977) as parched for spiritual insight.[4]

The comparisons with Weil are by no means unfounded. Given the philosopher-mystic's presence in *Pilgrim at Tinker Creek*, Dillard has been reading Weil since at least the early 1970s.[5] In their 1995 meeting, Dillard told Yancey that in terms of sources, "theologically, she feels closest to Simone Weil's *Waiting for God*, and she calls Rabbi Abraham Joshua Heschel the greatest religious thinker of the century."[6] In an interview with Mary Cantwell in 1992, Dillard likewise named Heschel and Weil the two writers who "have everything [she] needs."[7] Yet while Dillard has been open about Weil's influence and occasionally cited Weil in her work, scholars have mostly overlooked Weil's insistent presence across Dillard's expansive oeuvre. Her twelve original books, excerpts of which are remixed in editions of collected work, include volumes of poetry, fiction, essays, memoir, and long-form nonfiction narrative. Weil's presence is an undercurrent throughout, particularly in the long-form nonfiction triology, where Dillard cites her not just in *Pilgrim at Tinker Creek*, the first book, but also in the last, *For the Time Being* (1999), and intensively engages with her thought in the middle book, *Holy the Firm* (1977), and, to a lesser degree, in *The Writing Life* (1989). Dillard never names Weil in *Holy the Firm*, but she reports in an essay that she was reading Weil's notebooks during the time of the book's composition, after she had moved in an implicitly Weilian act of ego-containment across the country to escape the temptations of fame that accompanied her Pulitzer Prize.[8]

In fact, one might go so far as to say that Dillard constructs her published first-person author-persona in the nonfiction as a kind of Weilian alter-ego: a polymath inquiring into science, philosophy, and literature as well as the supernatural world, intensely interested in what *is*—nearly obsessively attentive, quasi-monastic, and hyperbolic, even self-sacrificial. Like Weil, Dillard writes in a curiously self-absenting prose. She finds herself drawn in adulthood to the Roman Catholic Church, into which she was received around the year 1990, although she struggles with the nonsensical within it, studiously embraces a wide range of world religions, and writes for spiritual outsiders rather than insiders. (For at least two decades, her website has listed her religion as "None.") She breaks boldly into masculine-coded fields—philosophy, theology, and nature writing, like Weil broke into philosophy, theology, and politics—but like Weil she does not take up the work of writing *about* gender. (We might say Annie Dillard is to Adrienne Rich as Simone Weil is to Simone de Beauvoir.) More than anything else, she seeks to give herself over to the writing, to a practice of attention and a purity of commitment that does justice to the material.

But as with Rich and Weil, key differences persist. Against Weil's virulent critiques of pre-exilic Judaism, in her work, Dillard increasingly embraces the Jewish tradition, especially Hasidism. Against Weil's insistent ethico-political edge, Dillard's early work is unconcerned with what *ought* to be, instead focusing nearly exclusively on what *is*. Shared penchant for chain-smoking notwithstanding, against Weil's otherwise embodied asceticism, as Yancey points out, Dillard's way of being in the world is exuberantly convivial. In a piece that evokes Weil in passing, Geoff Dyer writes in 2016, "Dillard is content to throw a lot overboard to make room for the metaphysics. But there is nothing desperate, anorexic or body-denying about her preoccupation with questions of the spirit."[9] Perhaps most important, Dillard's life didn't end in her early thirties, shortly after the publication of both *Pilgrim at Tinker Creek* and *Holy the Firm*: she lived. This meant both that she lived to continue to develop her own mind, like Rich did, and also that she lived to manage, to some degree, her own reputation. Dillard is one of the most well-known American writers of the twentieth century, her work widely anthologized, her essays and her book *The Writing Life* taught in workshops, her nature writing lauded among the masters of the genre. She was granted the National Humanities Medal in 2014 by President Barak Obama "for her profound reflections on human life and nature."[10] Yet she has lived a private life, careful to avoid the spotlight, giving only very limited public readings and lectures, refusing to commodify herself. In the words of Michael Joseph Gross, "By refusing to build a public image that adds to or explains the voice of her essays, Dillard has crafted a writing life of uncommon integrity."[11] Her website is humorously self-effacing, turning away those who would seek her spiritual, moral, or professional advice: on the contact ("or not") page, a black-and-white image of young Dillard boasts what appear to be crisscrossing bandages over her mouth, with the heading "The Secrets of the Universe as Decoded by the Unhinged."[12] Dillard insists, time and again, that her writing and her life are not the same, that no one in daily life can live up to the purity of the writing. In this way, she resists the hagiographical pressures in a way that Simone Weil may have sought to do but could not from beyond the grave.[13]

Dillard's early brush with the pressures of sanctity may not be unrelated to her uniquely *non*biographical approach to Weil. Unlike most writers who render Weil's life through their literature, Dillard writes almost nothing about the difficulties posed by Weil's person. She engages with Weil's written work, leaving Weil's life story out of the conversation. To be sure, Dillard is not unaware of Weil's biography: in "How I Wrote the Moth Essay—and Why," she calls Weil "brilliant, but a little nuts," pointing to her "fanaticism" in "deliberately starv[ing] herself to death to call attention to the plight of French workers" (a slightly exaggerated claim).[14] But in the long-form nonfiction, Weil's life—and especially her death—do not feature at all, and unlike Adrienne Rich, Mary Gordon, or the various poets who devote long sequences to Weil's life, Dillard never draws Weil's "fanaticism" into conversation with gendered critiques of religious self-sacrifice. In this way, Dillard could be said to prefigure Yoon Sook Cha's approach in her book *Decreation and the Ethical Bind: Simone Weil and the Claim of the Other* (2017). Cha asserts, "This book departs from scholarship on Weil that pathologizes the difficulties to which such an ethics gives rise, particularly that which transposes these difficulties onto Weil's person. Indeed, it is common to find studies that psychologize Weil's thinking by redacting details from her life, effectively reducing Weil's thinking to her biography."[15] Such an effort to focus on Weil's ideas rather than her person is consistent not just with Weil's stated desire but also with Dillard's advice to another writer struggling with success: "Separate yourself from your work. A book you made isn't you any more than is a chair you made, or a soup. It's just something you made once."[16]

In her books, Dillard consistently separates Weil from her work, and attending to the presence of Weil's *ideas* in Dillard's own famous work illuminates elements of both. First, it highlights the degree to which, in a so-called secular age, plenty of readers have remained keenly interested in questions of ultimate meaning, framed in both metaphysical and religious terms—questions at the heart not just of Weil's philosophical writings but of Dillard's best-selling and award-winning nonfiction. Second, recognizing Weil as a major influence on Dillard's heady discussions of self-sacrifice—discussions that have not tended to provoke the same critique as Weil's own legacy—clarifies the source of readers' objections to Weil. Commentators may tend to call Dillard "a little nuts," echoing her own assessment of Weil, but her hyperbolic figurations of sacrifice haven't caused critics much worry about Dillard's well-being or her example for women more generally.[17] This less contentious reception of Weil's decreative ideal in Dillard's work—figured repeatedly as attentiveness, emptiness, even literal self-sacrifice, but seldom linked directly to Weil's name—highlights the degree to which concerns with Weil's self-suspending ethics respond to her life rather than her writing and exposes the double-sided tension of gendered expectations of Weil, with which Dillard has also contended.

Third and finally, reading Dillard's long-form nonfiction with Weil's influence in mind illuminates a heretofore unacknowledged trajectory of development in Dillard's work from an exclusively aesthetic practice of attention in *Pilgrim at Tinker Creek* to a more integrated, and I would argue Weilian, ethics of attention in *For the Time Being*. In other words, Dillard's decades-long engagement with Weil's writings leads to her own work's fullest flourishing and to some of the most lauded nonfiction in twentieth-century American literature.

A BEATEN BELL:
PILGRIM AT TINKER CREEK

Annie Dillard is perhaps best known known for the way her writing embodies, invites, and thematizes the practice of attention. As Pamela Smith notes, "Her attentiveness is remarked on by virtually all the Dillard reviewers and scholars."[18] Dillard doesn't name Weil until near the end of *Pilgrim at Tinker Creek*, but her focus on attention is signaled early, in the second chapter, titled "Seeing," which theorizes Dillard's practice of purposeful looking: "Unless I call my attention to what passes before my eyes, I simply won't see it."[19] Such seeing doesn't come easy; it "is a discipline requiring a lifetime of dedicated struggle" that Dillard associates with global monastic and mystical movements (32). The rest of *Pilgrim* unfolds as evidence of this dedication, as Dillard turns her keen eye to frogs and spiders, coots and butterflies, praying mantises, sycamores, goldfish, and rotifers, gazing into the creek, the sky, and the lens of a microscope, not to mention any number of contemporary and ancient books. Indeed, as thick as the text is with descriptions of the ecosystem, it is also full of references to Dillard's reading: the Bible as well as the Quran, Thoreau and Emerson, Van Gogh and Einstein, Pliny and Martin Buber, Thomas Merton and Pascal, as well as any number of anthropologists, physicists, and entomologists—Dillard describes *The Strange Lives of Familiar Insects* as "a book I couldn't live without" (168).

The result of this blending of ecological observation and wide-ranging citation is something broader than a nature journal: Dillard's fundamental interest is metaphysics, how matter and spirit, immanence and transcendence intersect. In this interest she also closely follows Weil, whose metaphysical interests Lissa McCullough summarizes with a similar list of linked dualisms: world and God, necessary and good, immanent and transcendent, created and uncreated, temporal and eternal.[20] With Weil, Dillard is curious about

beauty and brutality, the problem of pain and its collisions with wonder. Dillard is intellectually omnivorous, but she is also inescapably
theological and primarily rooted in the Jewish and Christian traditions. In these specifically confessional theological interests, Dillard
departs from her Transcendentalist influences, whose metaphysics led
to pantheism rather than Christian or Jewish discourse, as James
McClintock has noted.[21] Reading Weil's overlooked metaphysical
influence here, rather than just Thoreau and Emerson, illuminates
Dillard's approach, which follows Weil's insistence on attending to
the real—to things as they are—and to the problem of suffering,
which, especially in the later work, draws together Weil's appeals to
Greek philosophy, tragic Christian sensibility, and traditions both
Western and Eastern.[22]

This resonance becomes explicit near the end of *Pilgrim*, in the
third to last chapter, when Dillard at last quotes Weil outright to
describe this commitment to a shared *amor mundi*: "Simone Weil says
simply, 'Let us love the country of here below. It is real; it offers resistance to love'" (242). The quotation comes from the long essay
"Forms of the Implicit Love of God," published in *Waiting for God*,
in a section that discusses the Stoic commitment to loving the world
as it truly is, not as we imagine it, but in its actual beauty and difficulty.[23] Dillard's chapter is about eating and being eaten, the hard-
to-watch realities of parasitic insects and the threat of a copperhead
Dillard sat next to and watched a mosquito feast on. Parasitism leads
Dillard into metaphysical musings: "Chomp. It is the thorn in the
flesh of the world, another sign, if any be needed, that the world is
actual and fringed, pierced here and there, and through and through,
with the toothed conditions of time and the mysterious, coiled springs
of death" (234). Pages later, she concludes, "I have to love these tat-
ters" (241). In appealing to this particular quotation from Weil, Dillard exposes a deep affinity in their work, for as E. Jane Doering and

Eric O. Springsted note, Weil's "most basic and driving mechanism" is "the desire to know and love things as they are."[24]

Like Weil, Dillard associates her discipline of attentive seeing with a stance of remarkably passive waiting. "The secret of seeing," she writes, is "the pearl of great price": "although the pearl may be found, it may not be sought" (33). Weil ends her "School Studies" essay with a similar image of the pearl of great price, insisting on the ultimate value of "academic work," which she theorizes exercises students' capacities for attention to others and to God. Throughout the essay Weil famously associates attention not with "muscular effort" but with "negative effort," a form of open, patient receptivity: "We do not obtain the most precious gifts by going in search of them but by waiting for them."[25] This mode of waiting tracks throughout *Pilgrim*. In the chapter on "The Present," Dillard describes the experience of the present in precisely these terms: "pure devotion to any object"—or "innocence"—"is at once a receptiveness and total concentration" (82). Indeed, attentive waiting is the book's central practice: sitting for hours looking into the creek, watching the sky, trying to observe a skittish muskrat. Without waiting, none of it would be. "I find it hard to see anything about a bird that it does not want seen," Dillard writes. "It demands my full attention" (188). As the book rises toward its passionate conclusion, she insists, "The waiting itself is the thing" (258).

The practice of watchful waiting, or patient attention, extends still further in *Pilgrim* to a persistent motif of emptiness that sounds very much like Weil's. Again and again, Dillard describes herself as emptied-out: "Experiencing the present purely is being emptied and hollow; you catch grace as a man fills his cup under a waterfall" (80–81). In the chapter on stalking a muskrat, she writes, "When I stalk this way I take my stand on a bridge and wait, emptied" (184). Describing the difficulty of such a practice, she explains, "I could not, or would not, hold still for thirty minutes inside, but at the creek I slow down, center down, empty": "I retreat—not inside myself, but out-side myself, so that I am a tissue of senses" (200–201).

Weil's conception of attention in "School Studies" likewise insists on emptiness: "Above all our thought should be empty, waiting, not seeking anything, but ready to receive in its naked truth the object that is to penetrate it." This emptiness is essential to Weil's combined scholarly, artistic, ethical, and spiritual sense of attention. She fur-ther explains, "The soul empties itself of all its own contents in order to receive into itself the being it is looking at, just as he is, in all his truth."[26] This emphasis on *truth* aligns with Weil's (and Dillard's) commitment to the real, and it helps explain Dillard's practice of looking at pond water through a microscope: "I don't really look for-ward to these microscopic forays": "I do it as a moral exercise; the microscope at my forehead is a kind of phylactery, a constant reminder of the facts of creation that I would just as soon forget" (121). This emptied commitment to attending to the truth also helps explain why Dillard spends so many pages describing observations of insects—and professes to have "favorite entomologists"—even though she also admits repeatedly to not really *liking* insects. Her commitment is to see what really is in and around Tinker Creek, and thereby to receive the truth of the "shreds of creation that flourish in this valley," "to keep myself open to their meanings, which is to try to impress myself at all times with the fullest possible force of their very reality" (137).

This empty, receptive, and attentive waiting opens Dillard—and Weil—to both brutality and beauty, to both gravity and grace. Dil-lard recognizes the ever-present death, waste, and violence, the ines-capable pull of how things are throughout creation (177), which Weil calls gravity, laws of the universe that involve the perpetuation of suf-fering.[27] Dillard theorizes a similarly universal structure: "The terms are clear: if you want to live, you have to die; you cannot have moun-tains and creeks without space, and space is a beauty married to a blind man. The blind man is Freedom, or Time, and he does not go anywhere without his great dog Death" (181). Translating her meta-physical metaphor into science, Dillard connects it to "the Second Law of Thermodynamics" (181), the natural law of entropy, which explains that over time energy diminishes and order devolves into dis-order. The world lives toward death.

Yet Dillard's practice also leads her to see the beauty that is there whether she watches it or not (8); her forays to the creek lead to an "unmerited" grace, a coincidence of the stretch of Tinker Creek her backyard backs: "You wait for it, empty-handed, and you are filled" (102). Time and again, Dillard's attentive waiting (manifested in both her patient observations of Tinker Creek and her devotion to read-ing) delivers beauty and even wonder. "The texture of the world," she writes, "its filigree and scrollwork, means that there is the possibility for beauty here, which answers in me a call I do not remember call-ing, and which trains me to the wild and extravagant nature of the spirit I seek" (139). She insists near the book's end, "I've gone through this a million times, beauty is not a hoax"; "Beauty is real. I would never deny it; the appalling thing is that I forget it" (266). This is true alongside the reality of death that punctuates *Pilgrim*; the book is just as insistently concerned with the glory of a mockingbird's elegant "free fall," the "awesome wonders" of sharks seen in Florida waves' translucent rising (8), budding tulip-trees whose "two thin slips of green tissue shaped like two tears" enclose, "like cupped palms shel-tering a flame, a tiny tulip leaf," "lambent, minutely, with a kind of pale and sufficient light" (111). Weil likewise insists on the world's beauty as well as the role of desire and joy in the practice of atten-tion.[28] Indeed, for Weil, the beauty of the world is one of the three sites of God's presence "here below," along with religious ceremonies and our neighbor, as she argues at length in "Forms of the Implicit Love of God." Such beauty is as essential a component of the best art as is honesty about death: "Every true artist has had real, direct, and immediate contact with the beauty of the world."[29]

For Weil, the world's beauty is inseparable from God's presence in it: "The longing to love the beauty of the world in a human being is essentially the longing for the Incarnation."[30] Dillard echoes this sense when she insists not just that waiting for the present, "empty handed," leads to fullness, but that this experience echoes the narrative of Christ: "You'll have fish left over. The creek is the one great giver. It is, by definition, Christmas, the incarnation" (102). Dillard poetically smashes together the Incarnation of Christ with the creek's gift of its never-ending flow and perpetual abundance: like Christ feeding the five thousand with leftovers to spare, like Christ's birth (and its associated holiday full of gifts), like the metaphysical mystery of the divine-in-flesh, being intersecting with time. Dillard connects these ideas, again, to subatomic physics but ends the chapter with a quotation from the Doxology: "world without end."

For both writers, the empty stance that opens one to receive the real, both its beauty and its pain, involves a diminishment of the self, figured in Dillard as both an unselfconsciousness (82, 198) and a willing self-giving or even self-sacrifice, which gains importance as *Pilgrim* unfolds. In the chapter "Nightwatch," Dillard makes light of the Christian doctrine of the fall, insisting on the world's beauty: "If this furling air is fallen, then the fall was happy indeed. If this creekside garden is sorrow, then I seek martyrdom. This crown of thorns sits light on my skull, like wings" (216). The world is riven, she is saying, but if inhabiting its riven beauty is what martyrdom looks like, then so be it. But the actuality of sacrifice becomes more pressing as the later chapters meditate more fully on death, and Dillard increasingly associates herself with a sacrificial offering: "I am a sacrifice bound with cords to the horns of the world's rock altar, waiting for worms" (242). In the vision, Dillard sees worms and moths, she feels wind, and then the sacrificial bonds are loosed so that she can walk away, having confronted and found freedom in "the real" (242). In the next chapter, anticipating yet another winter, she describes "the death of the self of which the great writers speak" not as a "violent act" but as "the slow cessation of the will's springs and the intellect's chatter" (258): like Weil's passive, self-quieting waiting, the empty self is able to receive. "Not only does something come if you wait, but it pours over you like a waterfall, like a tidal wave. You wait in all naturalness without expectation or hope, emptied, translucent, and that which comes rocks and topples you; it will shear, loose, launch, winnow, grind" (259). These are not innocuous actions: the waiting self Dillard describes undergoes pressure that verges on violence: cutting, purification, even diminishment.

Weil explores the diminishment accompanying attention in the essay "Forms of the Implicit Love of God," in which she writes that attention involves "renunciation." The one who attends "accepts to be diminished by concentrating on an expenditure of energy, which will not extend his own power but will only give existence to a being other than himself." In this, attention is a creative act, even redemptive, because one exchanges oneself for the other's existence: "Creative attention means really giving our attention to that which does not exist." For Weil, this creative attention has an ethical and social dimension, whereby one attends to a suffering or afflicted other and thereby literally brings them back into being, as well as an aesthetic and scholarly dimension, whereby attending to an academic or creative work brings it into being. Both these dimensions—the ethical and the aesthetic—involve self-diminishment: "work of the very highest order, true creation, means self-loss."[31]

For Weil, the inescapable model of this creative self-loss is God, who in the triad of the creation, the incarnation, and the Passion of Christ models this "generosity and compassion." In Weil's theological imagination, creation involves God's own self-diminishment: "On God's part creation is not an act of self-expansion but of restraint and renunciation. God and all his creatures are less than God alone. God accepted this diminution. He emptied a part of his being from himself." According to Weil, this model is reenacted in the kenosis of the incarnation, whereby Christ "emptied himself" to become a human, as recorded in the ancient hymn recorded in Philippians 2:5–11. It is further pictured on the cross as Christ suffers. This creation-incarnation-cross triad offers Weil her model of human attention and creativity: "By this creative act he denied himself, as Christ has told us to deny ourselves."[32] Dillard shares Weil's vision of a self-diminishing Creator in *Pilgrim*, although it becomes much more explicit in later books.

This self-emptying has, for Dillard, a specific aim: it renders her an artistic medium, or renders *through* her very existence art, beauty, and proclamation that tends toward praise. Again, this is not the *ethics* of attention Weil forwards, whereby the emptied-out self in some sense gives life to a suffering other; it is an *aesthetics* whereby the attentive self creates art. In both cases, however, the attentive waiting extends into spiritual effects. Dillard figures her writerly praise-lifting in repeated images of herself as a bell waiting to be rung, a photograph plate waiting to be inscribed (198), an instrument to be played on (218), and a sacrificial animal waiting to be lifted in the choreographed liturgy of Hebrew praise. The image of the bell bookends *Pilgrim*, as Dillard describes how "some enormous power brushes me with its clean wing, and I resound like a beaten bell" at the end of the first chapter (12), then in the penultimate chapter describes, again in relation to the "death of the self," "waiting like a hollow bell with a stilled tongue" (258). In the final chapter, she speaks again of the "bell under [her] ribs," not perhaps "flung" but "blown" by a breath that "burgeon[s] into flame" (268)—suggesting an image of fire that will become central to her next book, *Holy the Firm*. These are lovely images of song, but they are by no means innocuous, nor is the insistence, "I would pare myself or be pared that I too might pass through the merest crack, a gap I know is there in the sky" (269), a vivid image of self-diminishment in pursuit of the real, the beautiful, and the true.

This self-emptied artist, echoing the pattern of the self-renouncing Creator, receptive to the not-yet-created Other, results in a curious stylistic tendency for both Weil and Dillard whereby these notoriously distinctive writers, hyperbolically given to contemplations of the real, write much less about their own personal experiences and bodies than one might at first assume. Of course, everything they write is in a sense self-revelation, but Dillard and Weil both include remarkably few personal details in their nonfiction prose. Deborah Nelson notes that Weil's style is characteristically self-erasing, bare, impersonal: Weil "voids" her writing of "location, history, and cultural specificity" so that it may be universal. At the same time, she writes with concrete though general nouns, in "horror of abstraction."[33] Joan Dargan reads Weil's "tending to eliminate personal reference in favor of an impersonal form of expression" as "a significant characteristic of Weil's style," one that performs her ideals of self-renunciation.[34]

This is no accident, for Weil is explicit about her preferred prose style. "A work of art has an author," she writes in *Gravity and Grace*, "and yet, when it is perfect, it has something which is essentially anonymous about it." Later she writes, "Attention alone—that attention which is so full that the 'I' disappears—is required of me."[35] Rozelle-Stone and Stone summarize, "Any *good* artist, therefore, imitates divine creation via decreation: 'In creating a work of art of the highest class the artist's attention is oriented towards silence and the void; from this silence and void there descends an inspiration which develops into words and forms'"; "our attentiveness, being creative in its renunciation, makes it more likely that others will see reality as well."[36]

Dillard, that paragon of American personal nonfiction, may not at first seem to align with Weil's ideals of a nearly anonymous artist, but commentators have in fact noticed her reticence. *Pilgrim* describes any number of things she *sees* and *reads*, but it is notably silent on other aspects of her life, including her marriage, her friendships, and her daily activities apart from reading and the Tinker Creek excursions. The books that follow are slightly more personal, but not much. In the words of Suzanne Clark, "When we read Annie Dillard, we don't know who is writing. There is a silence in the place where the might be an image of the social self—of personality, character, ego."[37] Michael Joseph Gross goes so far as to insist that "the achievement of her career has been to reinvent the personal essay in a way that minimizes egoism as thoroughly as an American can."[38] Even in her memoir *An American Childhood*, Dillard herself admits, she was at pains to focus on the subjects that interested her more than her own person. She offers commentary on the memoir: "I want to direct the reader's attention in equal parts to the text—as a formal object—and to the world, as an interesting place in which we find ourselves. So another thing I left out, as far as I could, was myself."[39] Dillard maintains this stance across the decades: commenting on her much-anthologized moth essay, Dillard writes, "I don't recommend, or even approve, writing personally. It can lead to dreadful writing."[40] Her own commentary joins her readers' assessment in sounding very much like Weil's ideal and practice of writing that is emptied of "that which says I."[41]

But this recognition of Dillard's approach to personal nonfiction is generally untroubled by concern about gender politics, whereas many of Weil's commentators hear troubling feminine echoes in her call to self-emptying. These commentators almost invariably point to the way this sacrificial ideal played out in her *life*, as in Adrienne Rich's poem "Hunger," composed in the same years Dillard published *Pilgrim*. Again, Rich situates women's unmet hungers within global patriarchal political and religious systems, alluding to Weil as a "woman genius" who "starves herself to feed others," beset by "self-hatred," in a characteristic alarm.[42] For all Dillard's hyperbolic appeal to Weil's ideals of attention and self-emptying, scholars and reviewers have not tended to express anything like the same degree of concern for Dillard.

That's not to say there's been none altogether. In a scholarly essay in 2008, Richard Hardack bewilderingly characterizes Dillard's tendency to use male pronouns in *Pilgrim* as "a violent form of (male) parasitism, nature dispossessing (female) identities." He likewise calls her self-erasures "the trickster fiction, or tinkering, of a postmodern confidence woman." Hardack seems to be arguing that Dillard's decreative aesthetic, which he links not to Weil but to transcendentalism, requires that her "potentially reproductive female body" "disappear."[43] I think Hardack is attempting an argument aligned with feminist concerns over Weil: a woman shouldn't need to sacrifice herself in order to matter. Yet in contrast with Weil's concerned commentators, Hardack's worry isn't that Dillard overdoes self-emptying in her life but in her writing: calling her "simulation of male personae" "problematic," he ultimately argues that "one of the central questions Dillard's work poses is whether having a female or reproductive body is desirable."[44]

I do not see this as one of the central questions of Dillard's work, and neither have most of the other readers who write about her work. Indeed, Hardack's approach to Dillard's so-called con is interesting primarily as a notable outlier in the scholarly reception of her oeuvre, and it strikes me as illuminating not of Dillard's writing but of the double bind in which twentieth-century women writers like Dillard and Weil find themselves, judged from all sides for being both too feminine and not feminine enough. The archival record indicates that Dillard was well aware of the gendered pressures on a woman aiming to join the literary tradition to which she sought entrance. As Diana Saverin reports in her piece "The Thoreau of the Suburbs" (2015), Dillard shaped *Pilgrim* to occlude her midcentury housewife existence in order to gain it entry into the highly masculinized realm of American nature writing. Dillard wrote in her journal as she composed the book, "It's impossible to imagine another situation where you can't write a book 'cause you weren't born with a penis. Except maybe *Life With My Penis*."[45] She similarly acknowledged the gendering of philosophy in a 2016 interview: "It's metaphysics. And it turns out that not a lot of people are comfortable with that, but I was. I guess that's why they told me I had a masculine mind. At the same time, I also had a boy's arm."[46]

Dillard's characteristic humor here both plays into and subverts gendered binaries, not to mention the mind/body divide. It also reminds us again of the fact that she has had the opportunity to manage her public persona—which she consistently performs as buoyantly hale, against expectations like Yancey's—in a way that Weil's early death precluded. But again, Dillard's approach to the issues of gender, like Weil's, was not to thematize them in her published writing but to persist in her focus on other topics heretofore barred to women. It may well be that a context of less patriarchal pressure would have produced a different sort of authorial presence in both women's writing, but it is also the case that judging either of them for not performing a certain feminine-coded self in their writing or lives can be its own kind of patriarchal pressure.

Hardack's approach does highlight one useful reminder, which is that Weil is not Dillard's only source for the ideal of ego-undoing, which she also learned from the transcendentalists, especially Emerson. Sharon Cameron's book *Impersonality: Seven Essays* is instructive here, as Cameron examines writers interested in "the making and *un*making of personality," including not just Weil and Emerson but also T. S. Eliot (who wrote the introduction to the English edition of Weil's *The Need for Roots*) and D. T. Suzuki, from whose essays Weil learned about Buddhism, and who also wrote on Emerson.[47] Cameron's comparative reading reminds us that Weil's decreative theory is by no means unique, but rather part of a global conversation about the risks of egocentrism and the benefits of self-gift. Reading Weil in this broader discursive context—as many of the poets I discuss in my fourth chapter do—depathologizes her approach to self-emptying by highlighting that it is neither an exclusively feminine nor entirely quixotic project. The fact that most of Dillard's commentators have situated her in such richly philosophical, theological, and literary contexts helps explain her capacity to popularize some of Weil's more challenging ideas, not just in *Pilgrim at Tinker Creek* but in her next book, *Holy the Firm*, which is both more explicitly gendered and more emphatically given to the ideal of Christ-like authorial sacrifice.

LIKE CHRIST ON THE CROSS, IN TOUCH WITH: *HOLY THE FIRM*

In *Pilgrim at Tinker Creek*, Dillard figures herself as an anchorite, her house an "anchor-hold" along Tinker Creek (2). She cites and then questions Julian of Norwich, "the great English anchorite and theologian," to trouble the concept of God's presence in all things and active work ordering the world (177). Dillard's early association of the discipline of seeing with monastic habits (32) bears implicit resonance with her claims to be a beaten bell, resounding (12, 268), kindled by a "generous, unending breath" (268), a "wave breast" and "heave offering" of thanksgiving (271). These themes carry through *Holy the Firm*, published just three years after *Pilgrim*, in which the themes are elevated in the text's poetic pages to an even more insistent image of a self-sacrificing, nun-like artist figure whose self-immolation lights the world in explicit imitation of Christ on the cross, one that more than any other of her books figures Weil's heady ideal of self-emptying.[48]

Dillard does not name Weil in *Holy the Firm*, but the philosopher's influence is intensely present throughout the book. This influence would be hard to miss even if Dillard hadn't later admitted to reading Weil while writing *Holy the Firm* in her short piece "How I Wrote the Moth Essay—and Why." Describing the stretch of time in 1975 when she moved to an island in Puget Sound and drafted her third book, she admits, "My reading and teaching fed my thoughts. I was reading Simone Weil, *First and Last Notebooks*. Simone Weil was a twentieth-century French intellectual, born Jewish, who wrote some of the most interesting theology I've ever read. . . . I was taking extensive notes on Weil." Dillard explains that she had moved to the island in part to escape the "temptations" of fame after the success of *Pilgrim at Tinker Creek* and to "rededicate [herself] to art and to God." In this context of personal experience and textual influence—Weil is the only reading she cites in the essay, apart from recollections about Arthur Rimbaud—her central concerns were "dedication, purity, sacrifice."[49]

Sacrifice is at the heart of the book that resulted. Dillard herself claims in *The Writing Life* that the themes of *Holy the Firm* are "the relation of eternity to time and the problem of suffering innocents": these questions are metaphysical and theological.[50] Much of the scholarly work on the book focuses on the theological—the problem of pain—with less attention to the related central question of time and eternity, or matter and spirit.[51] Tracing out Simone Weil's influence on the slim text helps clarify the book's metaphysics as well as the relationship of metaphysics to theodicy, the question of God's possible goodness in light of human suffering.

Dillard's appeal to "eternity and time" is theological shorthand for the divine realm and human realm, or spirit and matter.[52] These varieties of language pervade the book from the opening page, which, following Emerson, depicts the "days" as "gods," divine presence inseparable from daily life "wrapped in time like a husk" (11). The day, she insists repeatedly, is "real" (12)—a word that, as in *Pilgrim*, accrues importance as the narrative proceeds. For those living on Puget

Sound, the mountains are the rim of the real (20); the god riding on her shoulder "call[s] things real" (28). In this first section, the created world is itself real, ripe with "time" and "matter" abundant (29). The first section describes a world of immanence: the spiritual/metaphysical/infinite/eternal pervades earthly life, the days themselves gods who "socke[t] into everything that is, and that right holy" (30). Dillard's speaker lives "at the fringey edge where elements meet and realms mingle, where time and eternity spatter each other with foam" (21), a description that starts a paragraph thick with resonances and overlaps between time and land, matter and space. In this first, exuberant narrated day, there is no separation.

The problem introduced in part two, on day two, on which "into this world falls a plane" (35), is multiple: the not-so-subtle fall from grace and innocence, signaled in insistently repeated vocabularies and images of falling through the chapter, the mystery of how a good and powerful God could allow innocents to suffer, and the question of whether there is any connection between eternity and time—or God and humanity—in the first place. Here Dillard moves from a vision of immanence, where god is (and is in) everything, to one of emanation, whereby god or God creates the world but in doing so leaves it to itself. Julie Norwich—the seven-year-old girl whom Dillard self-consciously writes as her own double and names after the medieval mystic—is the instigating figure for the section's metaphysical and theological investigations, as her face is horrifically burned in the plane crash. Abandoning the first section's description of a richly abundant created world, Dillard now insists, "we are sown into time like so much corn," "souls sprinkled at random like salt into time and dissolved here, spread into matter" (41). The picture is one of orderless and therefore meaningless abandonment to time and matter, a god who plants and leaves. "Has he no power?" she asks (43). "No," she answers. "The gods have no power to save. There are only days. The one great god abandoned us to days, to time's tumult of occasions, abandoned us to the gods of days each brute and amok in his hugeness and idiocy" (43). Dillard insists now that "only the good is real": time and space are illusions, the "flimsiest dreams" of God, who is "spirit" (44). Alas, "the pain is also, and undeniably, real," because love is also real, and the world's workings lead again and again to loss and grief (44).

She goes on to describe God as "abandon[ing] us, slashing creation loose at its base from any roots in the real; and if we in turn abandon everything—all these illusions of time and space and lives—in order to love only the real: then what are we?" (46). Her answer is that thought and knowledge become "impossible," our existence an illusion, and that trying to love such a God is nonsensical because he is "less lovable than a grasshead," a "brute and traitor, abandoning us to time, to necessity and the engines of matter unhinged" (46).

Dillard seems here to be grappling with Weil's ideals of loving the world as it is, even its "necessity," as she borrows Weil's terminology.[53] Contra Weil's stoicism, Dillard refuses to fully submit to *amor fati* and *amor mundi*; instead, she rails against God in the mode of a desperate Psalmist. Julie Norwich's suffering, she writes, is "evidence of things seen" that leads her to "look at the world stuff appalled" (46). Continuing her apparent explication of Weil's ideas, Dillard explains, "Faith would be that God is self-limited utterly by his creation—a contraction of the scope of his will; that he bound himself to time and its hazards and haps as a man would lash himself to a tree for love" (47). Again, here she seems to gloss Weil's idea of God's creation as self-limiting, parallel to the Passion, which explains God's evident lack of control over human pain: Weil writes, "Either God is not almighty or he is not absolutely good, or else he does not command everywhere where he has the power to do so."[54] Weil sets up the tension starkly: one cannot maintain that God is both all-powerful and all good.

Dillard insists, "I know it as given that God is all good" (47), echoing Weil's insistence that "the essential knowledge concerning God is that God is good. All the rest is secondary."[55] Weil's answer to the riddle is that God, in creation, limits his power, leaving the world to the workings of "blind necessity"—the order of things. Dillard rephrases the question as one of whether God "touches anything," given the world's plainly evident evils (47). This is a matter of both creation and incarnation: Are we to understand Christ's "descent" as "kenotic suicide" or his "ascent" as abandonment (47–48)? Or even if Christ makes some connection between "eternity" and the "souls of men," is matter itself not somehow connected to time (48)? If God creates and then abandons creation, separate from it, the universe lacks meaning, fails to "participate" in "the holy," in "being itself," in "the real"—all terms Dillard's sentences continue to parallel as interchangeable (48). This association of God with the real follows Weil closely, for, as McCullough explains, "only God is maximally real for Weil," although he exists "beyond space and time."[56] But Dillard struggles here with a way to understand how solving the problem of evil by naming the creator's choice to absent himself doesn't introduce a bigger metaphysical problem of the material world's ongoing relationship to that creator, who is the very source of reality.

To be clear, these thought experiments demand a great deal from Dillard's readers: she herself admits that writing *Holy the Firm* was uniquely exhausting, "work I myself could barely understand."[57] They also demand a degree of willingness to follow Dillard into explicitly Christian vocabularies, a challenge within a secular age's cacophonous relation to religious traditions. And after the impassioned railing of the second section of *Holy the Firm*, the opening of the third confronts readers with a bit of a shock: "I know only enough of God to want to worship him, by any means ready to hand" (55). The shift from shaking her fist to declaring praise is abrupt. In fact, the transition is there, but it is subtle. The very last image of section two is of new land appearing at the water's horizon revealed by lifting haze (50–51). The implication is that the section has not yet plumbed the mystery: there's still more, perhaps even more active creation on the part of the Creator, suggesting not abandonment but ongoing relation. Here Dillard follows Weil's claim that creation is both "an act of love" and "perpetual."[58] On day three Dillard thus moves from her celebration of immanence and her excoriation of emanation to a mystical reconciliation of the two that relies on an ongoing practice of creative attention. She ultimately rejects an antimaterialist dualism that sees no union between matter and spirit—a Platonic or Gnostic vision some commentators associate with Weil, although others, including McCullough, insist that Weil's perspective never abandons her materialism.[59] As David Tracy writes, "Weil is more materialist than any other Platonist even as she shares Plato's love for the purely intelligent forms"; indeed, she turns Plato materialist.[60] This union of matter and spirit is the stance *Holy the Firm* doggedly seeks.

The pages that follow approach the linked questions of the problem of pain and the relation of matter to spirit with a stacked series of images and encounters that suggest parallel resolutions mediating between the two. Dillard addresses the "scandal of particularity"— the specificity of Christ's human incarnation and the broader fact that God reveals ultimate truths through concrete points of space and time—which is also manifested in church practice, in all its scandalous and sometimes nonsensical particularity (55–59). In a description of one such particular, Dillard narrates the process of walking to buy communion wine for her church, then walking back with the image of "Christ with a cork," "holiness splintered into a vessel" (64)—offering yet another picture of spirit in matter in a distinctly sacramental vision. The wine in her backpack seems to give rise to what follows, namely, a mystical vision of folks holding a beachside baptism transfigured into Christ being baptized, a "reality" (65) that leads Dillard to see, in a single drop of water falling from his body, "all that time contains" (67). In the mystical union of all things that follows—"this everything"—there is "no time" (68). Dillard's vision echoes Weil's own unexpected mystical encounter with Christ, which answered some of Weil's own "arguments about the insolubility of the problem of God" through a completely unexpected experience: "I had vaguely heard tell of things of this kind, she writes, "but I had never believed in them."[61]

The mystical experience seems to open the possibility of Dillard's next discovery. Arriving finally at the book's titular concept, she reports on reading about a "substance" posited by "Esoteric Christianity," deep within the planets, that is "in touch with the Absolute, at base" and called "Holy the Firm" (69). Holy the Firm solves the tension between emanation—God's radical absence from the material world—and immanence—God's undifferentiated presence within the world—for Dillard, by allowing for the "Absolute" to be "in touch with" matter, allowing "time and space" to have "eternity" socket into it in the base of creation and its apogee, the Incarnation, so that "matter and spirit are of a piece but distinguishable; God has a stake guaranteed in all the world," and by extension, "the universe is real" (71).[62] Ultimately, Dillard seems to need a concrete solution to Weil's perpetually paradoxical sense that God and the world are both "one" and "infinitely distant" from each other, which the concept of Holy the Firm provides in a poetic conceit.[63] In fact, although Dillard never uses the term, Holy the Firm is an example of *metaxu*, the Greek word Weil borrowed from Plato to describe "intermediaries" that mediate between the physical and the metaphysical, the human and the divine. In an excerpt collected in *Gravity and Grace*, Weil explains this mediation: "Two prisoners whose cells adjoin communicate with each other by knocking on the wall. The wall is the thing which separates them but it is also their means of communication. It is the same with us and God. Every separation is a link."[64]

Almost immediately, though, Dillard acknowledges that Holy the Firm, this link between holiness and matter, is a conceptual frame rather than an ontological claim: "These are only ideas" (71). And as the narrative proceeds, it becomes clear that Holy the Firm isn't just an image of divine matter deep in the planets: it's a metaphor for the artist herself, who is also in a very important sense an example of *metaxu*, an intermediary. Drawing on the first section's imagery of the moth-turned-candle wick, the self-giving nun, and her own communion-wine-bearing body turned to light-filled buttressed space, Dillard paints the artist as a self-sacrificing servant to the work and the world:

> His face is flame like a seraph's, lighting the kingdom of God for the people to see; his life goes up in the works; his feet are waxen and salt. He is holy and he is firm, spanning all the long gap with the length of his love, in flawed imitation of Christ on the cross stretched both ways unbroken and thorned. So must the work be also, in touch with, in touch with, in touch with; spanning the gap, from here to eternity, home. (72)

The images form a palimpsest here: the artist—and the artist's work—are figured as the gap-spanning activity and object, joining time to eternity, like both Christ on the cross and Holy the Firm at the center of the planets. The work is sacrificial; it draws on "materials," like both Christ and Holy the Firm "in touch with" matter and spirit, the created world and the Absolute. In this cruciform space of spanning the gap in mediation, the artist lights "the kingdom of God for people to see": he (or she?) helps others really see the real. And he does it for love.[65]

It's hard not to hear echoes of Weil here. Writing evocatively in the essay "The Love of God and Affliction," Weil describes the love of God coming "over the infinity of space and time" and planting a seed in those who consent to it, which grows into a tree. This tree is like the so-called Tree of Calvary that helps the love arc back to God across "infinite distance." Paralleling Dillard's artist's tree, Weil's tree is made in the "likeness" of the cross, and love is "a direction." Even in the space of extraordinary suffering, "though the nail pierces" the soul, if one directs one's love toward God, Weil writes, one finds oneself "nailed to the very center of the universe. It is the true center; it is not in the middle; it is beyond space and time; it is God." Weil's picture here is of a sufferer—one truly afflicted—who in this way finds that "the soul, without leaving the place and the instant where the body to which it is united is situated, can cross the totality of space and time and come into the very presence of God. // It is at the intersection of creation and its Creator. This point of intersection is the point of intersection of the arms of the Cross."[66] Spanning the gap from here to eternity, Dillard echoes, the self-sacrificing artist, in "flawed imitation of Christ," crosses the totality of space and time to bear witness to the point where creation and Creator intersect. Borrowing from Weil, Dillard's picture of the artist here elevates the motif of a self-renouncing creator—in imperfect imitation of the self-renouncing Creator—to an almost exultantly metaphysical aesthetic mysticism.

But the next paragraph in the section ambiguously begins "Hoopla!" (72), making space for readers who cannot follow Dillard into her exuberant kenosis. The paragraph that follows describes the world's beauty, its evocation of praise—"A hundred times through the fields and along the deep roads I've cried Holy" (72–73)—which once again supports the previous paragraph by describing the artist's vocation to connect the created world and the divine. And the final three pages then return from metaphysics to the problem of suffering in the experience of Julie Norwich, painting her a victim of suffering whose unasked-for pain gives her unique access to the Absolute, "baptized at birth into time and now into eternity, into the bladelike arms of God" (73). This imagery is direct from Weil, whose descriptions of the cross-shaped link between eternity and time Dillard has been borrowing are more immediately rooted, for Weil, in abject unasked-for suffering than in an artist's choice to serve. According to Weil, those who experience affliction have the most direct possible experience of the real, the Absolute. As McCullough explains, "The only joy possible for one in such a condition [of affliction] is transcendent joy—a joy not of this world but from beyond the world, outside it—an incommensurate joy that passes understanding."[67] Dillard, addressing Julie Norwich directly, remarks that no one on earth will love her without a face, but now she has wisdom, "you got there early, the easy way" (74). "You might as well be a nun," she writes, advising Julie to give her life over to prayer and to the "power" of mystical encounter (75). The language is elevated, advocating to Julie a future of "the smash of the holy" (75). It is also gruesome: "Wait till they hand you a mirror, if you can hold one, and know what it means. That skinlessness, that black shroud of flesh in strips on your skull, is your veil" (74).

This is not how one speaks to a suffering seven-year-old. Is this Dillard's hyperbolic exposé of the evident heartlessness of Weil's commitment to the real? Is Dillard pushing Weil's rhetoric of *amor fati*, her celebration of the divine revelation made most possible in affliction, that "marvel of divine technique," to its furthest reaches in an implicit critique?[68] For Dillard then introduces questions to her own horrific rhetoric, addressing either the imagined Julie or reader: "Do you think I don't believe this? You have no idea, none" (75–76). (Indeed, we do not.) She extends the meditation on Julie's future by imagining her star-lit nights, like "moths," eyes "bright as candles and as sightless, exhausted," with mystical visions like Elisha seeing

Elijah carried away in the flesh to eternity, "Held, held fast by love in the world like the moth in wax, your life a wick, your head on fire with prayer, held utterly, outside and in, you sleep alone, if you call that alone, you cry God" (76). The addressed figure of Julie has shaded into Dillard's own self-description of the artist-moth-nun, sacrificed utterly, loving the world, given over to praise, mediating between time and eternity. Read with an awareness of Weil as Dillard's insistent interlocutor during the composition of this text, one can see how the Dillard–Julie Norwich dyad shades into a triad—or we might say a trinity—of immolated women, for Dillard's description of Julie Norwich could just as well characterize not just her own artist-persona but also her inspiration, Weil's "life a wick" if any could be called such.

In yet another turn, however, after several pages of this heightened advice that the physically ruined Julie give herself over to God, in the book's very last paragraph Dillard changes her approach entirely by suddenly insisting, "Surgeons will fix your face" (76). She imagines for Julie a husband, children, common daily pleasure in life. "So live," she admonishes in the book's final lines. "I'll be the nun for you. I am now" (76). It is a heady ending, ebullient, exultant, but shockingly abrupt in its trade of Dillard (or her narrator) for Julie Norwich in the position of flame-faced mystic nun. Read apart from Dillard's implicit conversation with Weil, it can seem manic and cruel, and so it's perhaps not surprising that most commentators on the text elect not to discuss it or do so only in passing. Read *with* and *against* Weil, by contrast, the ending questions its own advocacy for a redemptive stance toward Julie Norwich's suffering, which is not to be celebrated for the little girl's early and "easy" encounter with the Absolute but shown as heartless and horrific. Dillard translates Weil's idealization of affliction as a unique opportunity to be "in touch with" God into a particular child's suffering and shows its cold comfort.

At the same time, Dillard substitutes, instead, the self-sacrificing figure of the artist who patterns herself after Christ to bear witness to the divine, to the real. The artist is both a creator figure and a redeemer figure whose self-emptying work stretches across the gap between time and eternity and makes room for praise. This continues Dillard's vision of a decreative writer in *Pilgrim at Tinker Creek*, still paralleling Weil, who writes in *Gravity and Grace*, "Even in art and science, though second-class work, brilliant or mediocre, is an extension of the self; work of the very highest order, true creation, means self-loss."[69]

Holy the Firm's questions and negotiations make a lot more sense when one reads it with the awareness that its author was "taking extensive notes" on Weil's *First and Last Notebooks*. Yet for all its heady hyperbole, Dillard's Weilian sacrifice in this book is not self-starvation, not to speak of death: it's artistic discipline. It's the hard work of writing, of reading, of devoting a life to metaphysical musings and attention to life's difficulties, albeit with a penchant for metaphors of fire. For reasons she never articulates, Dillard never names Weil in this book where her thought is so insistently present, in some sense decreating Weil according to her stated wishes, or perhaps saving Dillard's work from critique-by-association. Just as she implicitly exposes the cruelty of Weil's celebration of affliction's spiritual efficiency, Dillard softens Weil's cruciform vision, rendering it more accessible. It's about *writing*, in the end, for Dillard: the most concrete example of sacrifice in the book is Dillard's instructions to her students that to be a writer, "you can't be anything else. You must go at your life with a broadax" (18). She textures this vision of writerly sacrifice still further in *The Writing Life*, at the same time extending her engagement with Weil, not just in the pragmatics of self-gift but also in an ongoing encounter between the imaginary and the real.

IMAGINATION OR THE REAL:
THE WRITING LIFE

In *Holy the Firm*, Annie Dillard holds an extended, albeit implicit, poetic conversation with Simone Weil about how the material world intersects with the spiritual, how the presence of suffering intersects with divine goodness, and how the writer can do anything like justice to these dynamics. The book's resolution relies on a Weilian substitution, whereby the self-giving artist figure embraces life as a self-immolating nun to give Julie Norwich her happy future. The question *Holy the Firm* implies on further reflection, however, is whether this aesthetic salvation is enough. If Julie Norwich is a fictional name for an actual child, the book raises questions of ethics. Does Dillard *use* a suffering human's experience to make her art? And are those final pages of address meant to comfort an *actual* child? Dillard's insistence, in the end, that Julie will be "fixed" by doctors seems like false assurance: How can Dillard know, a mere day after the accident, what the little girl's future will be? How can she be so sure?

On the other hand, if Julie Norwich is fully fictional, Dillard's own creative power suggests something quite different from the power of the Creator with whom she, as artist, seeks to be in touch. If the creator God cannot—or does not—prevent abject suffering, how can Dillard insist herself, as creator of literature, on preserving the character from protracted pain, given the reality in which children *do* in fact suffer from horrific accidents without being "fixed," in which suffering *does* wholly alter the trajectories of their lives? Does Dillard do more here to rescue her character than the God she claims to seek to illuminate, within the reality she claims to wish to see in all its truth? Does she here fall prey to the temptation of the imagination, a temptation Weil insistently warns against, choosing to tidy up an ending that reality would leave to open-ended pain?

There's a way of reading Dillard's subsequent long-form nonfiction as correctives to these unresolved questions about the ending of *Holy the Firm*, correctives that continue Dillard's long implicit conversation with Weil. Such a reading answers to a weakness in some of the recent scholarship that interprets all of Dillard's writing—a more than thirty-year project—as fully coherent and consistent, participating in one stable argument. By contrast, I argue that Dillard's concerns persist, but the focus shifts, as does the approach. Reading Weil in Dillard helps clarify this narrative of change and developing thought, one that offers, first, a corrective on the matter of attending to the real, and second, of representing ethical attention. We can recognize a growth that Dillard herself has noted she wishes she could have seen in Weil over the course of a longer life—the benefit of a human mind maturing and changing in light of lived experience—indeed, in light of further encounters with the real.[70]

For all the insistence on attending to the real in *Pilgrim at Tinker Creek* and *Holy the Firm*, both its beauties and its brutality, Dillard is an imaginative writer, and she does not pretend otherwise. As she describes her process in essays and in interviews, it becomes clear that Dillard's nonfiction is an unabashedly *crafted* artifact. The cat that opens *Pilgrim* with its bloody paw prints is borrowed, according to Dillard in an interview with Diana Saverin; the elevated layered imagery of gold hair, gold fur, and golden light in *Holy* is likewise a carefully constructed set of parallels.[71] Dillard's insistent twinning of her speaker and Julie Norwich likewise raises questions about the small girl's actual reality.

On the one hand, Dillard's creative attention to her subject follows Weil's pattern in that it makes something out of nothing. On the other hand, Dillard's imaginative approach to the real she conveys in her ostensible nonfiction stands in possible tension with Weil's troubled approach to the imagination, for while Weil is a devoted reader of literary writing, she is also notoriously suspicious, following

Plato, of imaginative writing's access to truth. As Nelson notes, Weil worries that imagination blocks reality.[72] She writes in *Waiting for God*, "We live in a world of unreality and dreams. To give up our imaginary position as the center, to renounce it, not only intellectually but in the imaginative part of our soul, that means to awaken to what is real and eternal, to see the true light and hear the true silence."[73] In *Gravity and Grace*, she writes, "The imagination, filler up of the void, is essentially a liar."[74] As Rozelle-Stone and Davis explicate, "The imagination—problematized on epistemological grounds in her early thought—is criticized once again in her religious philosophy for its insidious tendency to pose false consolations that at once invite idolatry of self-satisfaction, both of which obviate real contemplation."[75]

Read in this light, Dillard's ending to *Holy the Firm* may be guilty of such false consolation, abruptly turning away from Julie Norwich's wounds in the book's final paragraph to imagine for her a future of full and total healing. This imagined resolution contemplates neither real beauty in the world nor the tragic lack of resolution suffering so often takes. It solves the problem through a poetic figuration of substitution—"I'll be the nun for you. I am now"—that may not fully answer the actual pain the book conveys. In so doing, it also raises further questions as to whether Julie Norwich, or the girl after whom she is modeled, ever really existed in the first place.

Of course Julie Norwich's name is poetic license, borrowed from the medieval mystic to whom Dillard at other points alludes in the text. In interviews, Dillard refers to a plane that crashed "nearby," but even in recent essays scholars wonder over whether an actual little girl was hurt or whether this aspect of the narrative is an imagined stretch. However, in the last section of her book *The Writing Life* (1989), which focuses in part on Dillard's process of writing *Holy the Firm*, she does recount an actual plane crash that occurred in 1976. In a sense, this last section of *The Writing Life* stands as an implicit correcting

supplement to the end of *Holy the Firm*, in that it attends to and com-
memorates the real: a real human's artistry and loss, in the person of
the pilot Dave Rahm, who may well have been the local friend whose
crash inspired Dillard's imagined scenario.

Dillard's sudden turn to a memorialization of Rahm in *The Writing Life* comes at the end of another book that bears the marks of her
long conversation with Weil. The vocabulary is there: "You attend,"
Dillard writes on the first page, describing the writing process (3).
You give "many years' attention"; you work with a "courage" that
"stands on bare reality" (4). Dillard quotes their shared friend Plato
in the epigraph to chapter 2, writing of "Beauty Itself" and becoming "the friend of God" (24). She makes repeated references to Weil's
beloved image of the Holy Grail (57) and to writing as "unmerited
grace" (75). She also quotes Weil, although curiously without attribution, again raising questions about Dillard's motivation for occluding her source: "In working-class France, when an apprentice got
hurt, or when he got tired, the experienced workers said, 'It is the
trade entering his body.' The art must enter the body, too" (69). In
this description of an artist letting her craft change her very shape,
her brain, Dillard borrows from Weil's discussion in the essay "The
Love of God and Affliction," which for Weil illustrates not just crafts-
manship but a radical openness to the real. Weil comments on the
anecdote: "Each time that we have some pain to go through, we can
say to ourselves quite truly that it is the universe, the order, and beauty
of the world and the obedience of creation to God that are entering
our body."[76] Dillard's application is somewhat less cosmic in scope but
effects a similar reframing of pain.

In a sense, *The Writing Life* translates *Holy the Firm*'s aesthetic mysticism into pragmatic visions of an artist's discipline (though without
abandoning poetic hyperbole altogether). She describes the difficulties of writing along with the joys, the frustratingly slow pace, the
isolations, the titrated caffeination, missed social gatherings, and

hyperfocus that lets the houseplants die. But when Dillard writes about the ultimate artistic sacrifice in this book, she doesn't just play up her own struggles. She turns to a true story of actual risk, actual death. The final chapter of *The Writing Life* begins with facts about the real world: "Dave Rahm lived in Bellingham, Washington, north of Seattle" (93). Dillard locates the place geographically and then Rahm in his craft: "Dave Rahm was a stunt pilot, the air's own genius" (93). Her repetition of his full name, and of the place, and then her inclusion of the date she first saw him fly, in 1975, further emphasizes the wholly nonfictional nature of this chapter's account. Dillard describes his extraordinary flight, his work as a geologist at Western Washington University, her "scant attention" (94), and then how she "reluctantly" began "paying attention" as "Rahm drew high above the world an inexhaustibly glorious line" (95). Dillard overtly compares Rahm's stunts with a writer's work: "the plane was a pen" drawing a "contracting and pillowing pen line" (95). She is in awe; she thinks about the performance for days (98). Later, thanks to a mutual friend, Dillard "flew with Dave Rahm" (note the full name again), in a terrifyingly close encounter with Mount Baker in the clouds, gaining new appreciation for the force a stunt pilot undergoes in his body. In conversation with a crop duster pilot, she also gains new appreciation for the risks such flights entail (106). Thus, when a visiting friend comes for coffee and asks in conversation, "Say, did we know that stunt pilot Dave Rahm had cracked up? In Jordan, during a performance: he never came out of a dive" (106–7), the news should not surprise, but Dillard recounts her own tears. She later locates a newspaper and offers the details: the crash occurred when he was flying for King Hussein of Jordan, where he was a visiting professor, with his wife and her daughter watching.

Dillard moves from the description of Rahm's death to another of his art, recalling a day she saw him flying: "He furled line in a thousand new ways, as if he were inventing a script and writing it in one infinitely recurring utterance until I thought the bounds of beauty must break" (109). Dillard knows, from the barrel rolls she asked (and received) from him on their flight, that Rahm bought such beauty at the price of his own physical misery, but that he didn't focus on "how he felt": instead, in an echo of Weil's ideal artist, he became anonymous within the craft. "Robed in his airplane," Dillard writes, "he was as featureless as a priest" (110). His "penetration of the universe" (a phrase Dillard borrows not from Weil but from Pierre Teilhard de Chardin) lay in "his inexpressible wordless selfless line's inscribing the air and dissolving" (111).

The lesson here, no less than in *Holy the Firm*, is of the artist's self-emptying, the prototypically Weilian erasure of "that which says I," in favor of the work, the art, the beauty, even to the point of death. What Dillard imaginatively figures in her earlier book, she reads in the literal sacrifice of Rahm, who could not have forged such beauty with his plane without risking what he risked. In one sense, Rahm's example simply extends the kenotic ideal Dillard forwards in *Pilgrim at Tinker Creek* and *Holy the Firm*, literalizing it beyond the metaphor of a writer's sacrificed hours, and literalizing it in a way that counterbalances fraught associations of self-sacrifice and femininity. On the other hand, if Dave Rahm's death in 1976, which aligns with the time when Dillard wrote *Holy the Firm*, was the real event that precipitated its imagined events, Dillard's account of him here—both her paean to his artistry and her closely hewed narration of the facts of his life and death—corrects an earlier straying from the real. In contrast to Julie Norwich, there is no happy ending for Rahm, no doctors who can fix his demise, not even the king who "dashes to the burning plane" (108): in Weil's words, no false consolations. There is no use imagining Dillard's substituted devotion to her art could redeem his life. Instead, the book concludes, his life itself was its own truth and lesson; the truth of his beauty as well as his death its own real story worth attention.

REPAIRING THE WORLD:
FOR THE TIME BEING

If *The Writing Life* corrects course from imagination to real, following Weil from the realm of the figurative to the literal, *For the Time Being* stretches Dillard from a primarily aesthetic to an ethical attention, ending the nonfiction trilogy within the holistic unity of Weil's vision of attention. This shift could not be more explicit. Dillard begins *For the Time Being* with an author's note that lays out the project's central questions: "Does God cause natural calamity? What might be the relationship of the Absolute to a lost schoolgirl in a plaid skirt? Given things as they are, how shall one individual live?"[77] The questions reiterate Dillard's persistent implicit conversation with Weil about the problem of evil and metaphysics, but with an added turn to ethics: How shall we live? The book's efforts to answer its questions extend through a patchwork series of explorations: of birth defects, Hasidic Judaism, the life and thought of French Jesuit paleontologist Pierre Teilhard de Chardin, sand, clouds, statistics about contemporary human populations, travels to Israel and China, and encounters with strangers. The resonances accrue as the text unfolds, supporting Dillard's conclusion that "given things as they are," we should live lives that try to repair the very world. Simone Weil is yet again an implicit presence throughout, although Dillard explicitly cites her influence—and again challenges her stoicism—only near the book's end.

Ethics is not a primary concern in Dillard's earlier work, as she herself notes. In *Pilgrim* she quotes the scholar of world religions Huston Smith: "In nature the emphasis is in what is rather than what ought to be" (238). In an interview for *Christianity Today* in 1978, she said: "No, I don't write at all about ethics. I try to do right and rarely do. The kind of art I write is shockingly uncommitted—appallingly isolated from political, social, and economic affairs. //There are lots of us here. Everybody is writing about politics and social concerns; I don't. I'm not doing any harm."[78] The gap between *is* and *ought* is a fraught one, as numerous commentators on Dillard note. Writing of Dillard's ecological commitments—or lack thereof—Pamela Smith admits, "What seems puzzling is her policy of nonintervention"; "Dillard is an active observer. She is not, however, an activist."[79] More recently, Jack Shindler has described Dillard as a "writer-activist" whose themes and characteristic syntax, rather than discursive moralizing, invite readers to *see* as a first step toward social engagement, but this argument relies a great deal on subtlety.[80]

If *For the Time Being* is more concerned with ethics than Dillard's earlier work, it is much less concerned with theorizing the writer's role; in fact, while Dillard recounts several encounters with strangers on her travels and visit to a hospital, in some ways this book is her most self-effacing yet: "This is a nonfiction first-person narrative," she begins the Author's Note, "but it is not intimate" (ix). It is also much less concerned with describing direct observations of the natural world than Dillard's earlier nonfiction, given over even more to reporting on Dillard's reading. One result of this shift is a much broader scope: Dillard moves from a meditation on the brutalities of the natural world as evident around Tinker Creek and the senseless accident of a falling plane contemplated off the coast of Washington to a view that traverses continents and millennia and encompasses not just accidental and natural disaster but also injustice, which she calls "moral evils" (116). This scope draws Dillard's attention to a book about birth defects (3) and histories of mass extinction (31) just as surely as it draws her to the recent genocides in Ireland, Cambodia, and Rwanda (58) as well as ancient Roman, Aztec, and Chinese human sacrifices (155).

This scale risks zooming out to the point that the stakes of human life blur, but in fact this tension is one of Dillard's questions throughout the text. How do we assess the sheer scope of human suffering without losing sight of its meaning? To survey evil, both natural and moral—in Weil's terms, again, to attend unflinchingly to the real—gives one a sense of its ubiquity across time and place. This era is not unique, Dillard concludes, neither better nor worse than any other: "Our time is a routine twist of an improbable yarn" (31). Nevertheless, she warns, returning to the theme, "each instance of human, moral evil, and each victim's personal death, possesses its unique history and form" (58). To lose sight of this particularity risks losing an essential moral sensibility, to follow the paired example of Ted Bundy and Mao Zedong, who, "awakened to the long view," defended serial killing and deadly public policy by insisting "there are 'so many people'" (160). By contrast, Dillard notes repeatedly, either no individual human life is precious or all of them are (58, 160). The number of humans affected by natural and moral evil—the 138,000 Bangladeshi people killed by tsunami in 1991 (107), the "more than two million children" per year who die from diarrhea and 800,000 from measles, the seven million Ukrainians Stalin starved in a year, the two million Cambodians Pol Pot killed (130)—they boggle the mind. They produce "compassion fatigue," "reality fatigue" (131), but Dillard does not cease her ethically demanding line of questioning. After the tsunami in Bangladesh, she asks, "Did your anguish last days or weeks?" (107). Repeating the story two pages later, she probes further, "What will move you to pity?" (109).

Dillard's searing questions extend to the divine, for her conclusion about the scope of suffering—that it is historically and geographically ubiquitous, but that each life is precious—raises still more urgent questions about God's involvement, returning us to Dillard's long-standing themes and their implicit conversation with Weil. In *For the Time Being*, Dillard focuses not on the Passion or incarnation as she did in the earlier books, but more fully on creation itself, drawing on Weil and to an even greater extent Isaac Luria to posit a creation theology that involves God's self-contraction. Dillard offers this theological vision within a context of frank and even impassioned questioning, however, once again deviating from Weil's stoicism and insisting that her own religious outlook is by no means facile, translating ancient theological questions into a register keyed to agnostics. Commenting on one rabbi's teaching about God's punishment through natural disasters, for instance, she observes, "It is, like every ingenious, God-fearing explanation of natural calamity, harsh all around" (30). She recounts her desire to "hammer the sky—crack it at one blow, split it at the next—and inquire, hollering at God the compassionate, the all-merciful" (53). She presents this questioning as a fervent long practice, her earlier books' answers notwithstanding: "Many times in Christian churches I have heard the pastor say to God, 'All your actions show your wisdom and love.' Each time, I reach in vain for the courage to rise and shout, 'That's a lie!'—just to put things on a solid footing" (85). The section continues with quotations from the Gospels and the epistle to the Romans about how God has "cast down the mighty" and "filled the hungry with good things," working all things together for good, and asks, "When was that? I missed it" (86). "*Deus otiosis*," she suggests calling him: "do-nothing God, who, if he has power, abuses it" (86). Later, describing how "some few wandering Hasids go into exile in order to 'suffer exile with the Shekinah,' the presence of God in the world," she comments dryly on that presence, "which is, as you have doubtless noticed, lost or strayed" (129).

Yet threaded through these unabashed criticisms are the pieces of a cumulatively built case for God's goodness, developed in narratives about Luria's Jewish tradition, Teilhard de Chardin's unique Roman Catholic perspective, and other forays into Jewish and Christian theologies and world religions. Dillard explains the growing importance of Hasidism on her thought since she published *Holy the Firm*: "For twenty-five years, with increasing admiration, I have studied these people: gloomy Luria because he influenced the exuberant Baal

Shem Tov, and the Baal Shem Tov because he and his followers knew God, and a thing or two besides" (22). Luria's importance to Dillard seems particularly to derive from his teaching about the creation of the world, in which "God contracted himself—*zimzum*. The divine essence withdrew into itself to make room for a finite world. Evil became possible: those genetic defects that dog cellular life, those clashing forces that erupt in natural catastrophes, and those sins human minds invent and human hands perform" (50). In complications that followed, "sparks of holiness fell to the depths," so that "God is hidden, exiled, in the sparks of divine light that the shells entrap" (50). Dillard brings this Kabbalistic creation account into conversation with Teilhard's insistence that it is "fatal" to believe "that we suffer at the hands of God omnipotent" (84) and causes many to turn away from faith. But it's an old idea that God is not omnipotent, Dillard insists (166), one that even Thomas Aquinas suggested (85).

Dillard names the resonance between Luria and Weil near the end of *For the Time Being*: "Simone Weil takes a notion from Rabbi Isaac Luria to acknowledge that God's hands are tied. To create, God did not extend himself but withdrew himself; he humbled and obliterated himself, and left outside himself the domain of necessity, in which he does not intervene. Even in the domain of souls, he intervenes only 'under certain conditions'" (168). Dillard is not alone in noting the uncanny resemblance of Weil's creation theology to Luria's, although it's unlikely Weil encountered his ideas. McCullough writes:

> Several scholars have commented on the striking parallels between Weil's conception of creation and that of the Jewish kabbalistic thinker Isaac Luria (d. 1572). As there is no clear evidence that Weil was aware of Luria's highly original theory of creation, we can only speculate that she may have absorbed the idea through indirect channels of exposure (perhaps via Böhme or Schelling). Although in the last years of her

life Weil began to read several major Christian mystics, her antipathy to Judaism seems to have kept her away from Jewish mystical traditions.[81]

Yet whether Weil was familiar with Luria or not, her work lays out this vision of a self-emptying God clearly in the essays collected in *Waiting for God* as well as the *First and Last Notebooks*, two of Dillard's primary sites of encounter with Weil's thought. "Already before the Passion," Weil writes in the *First and Last Notebooks*, "already by the Creation, God empties himself of his divinity, abases himself, takes the form of a slave."[82] This, she writes in *Waiting for God*, is the "creative renunciation of God" on which human self-renunciation is patterned, an influence present in Dillard's sense in *Pilgrim at Tinker Creek* that creation itself is a fall of sorts.[83] Glossing Weil's perspective on God's self-limiting in creation, McCullough uses language very close to Dillard's own: "Out of his omnipotence, God abdicates power with the result that his freedom is limited. God lets his hands be tied, so to speak, and he himself does the tying. 'God is more hidden in creation than in incarnation. . . . Everything is possible for him, but everything happens as if everything were not possible for him.' "[84]

Weil joins Luria and Teilhard in helping Dillard conceptualize a cosmic understanding in which God's goodness extends through God's self-limitation in the very act of creation. That is not to say, however, that these are easy ideas, and Dillard openly questions her interlocutors. In a passage from *For the Time Being* worth quoting at length here, she again both embraces and critiques Weil's thoughts:

> In *Gravity and Grace*, Simone Weil, that connoisseur of affliction, lists four "evidences of divine mercy here below": The experience of God is one; the radiance and compassion of some who know God are another; the beauty of the world makes a third. "The fourth evidence"—nice

and dry, this—"is the complete absence of mercy here below." This introduction of startling last-minute evidence requires two takes from the reader and one footnote from the writer: "NOTE: It is precisely in this antithesis, this rending of our souls, between the effects of grace within us and the beauty of the world around us, on the one hand, and the implacable necessity which rules the universe on the other, that we discern God as both present to man and as absolutely beyond all human measurement."

Life's cruelty joins the world's beauty and our sense of God's presence to demonstrate who we're dealing with, if dealing we are: God immanent and transcendent, God discernible but unknowable, God beside us and wholly alien. How this proves his mercy I don't understand. (164)

Calling Weil "that connoisseur of affliction" is the closest Dillard comes in her books to calling out the philosopher's lived example, though of course the phrase could still refer exclusively to her ideas. And Dillard's questioning here is also not reserved exclusively for Weil: Dillard levels a similar critique at Teilhard's claim that human souls form "the incandescent surface of matter plunged in God." In some sense Teilhard's concept of the incandescence of matter itself, rather than spirit, offers a solution to the problem of matter-spirit, but Dillard concludes the paragraph, "Still: what does this sentence mean?" (122). Elsewhere she refers to Teilhard's "nutty" admirers (102). She is similarly unsparing in her assessment of the Baal Shem Tov, who she notes approvingly followed two centuries after Isaac Luria but "dropped Luria's asceticism" and Kabbalistic "elitism" (137), but who also attributed both moral and natural evil to God's teaching and punishing aims (116). "Theodicy was not his bailiwick," Dillard drily summarizes, and likewise refuses to follow the Talmud's teaching that God "rewards us or afflicts as he judges": "No," she concludes. "It does not wash" (117).

The rhetorical effect of Dillard's open critique of her sources, including Weil, coupled with her railing against the divine, renders her a mouthpiece for doubt, so that the solution she suggests is all the more precious, a good-faith faith arrived at in a context of open struggle. As for Weil's claim that divine mercy is present in its absence, commentators generally understand this as consistent with the self-emptying creation narrative Dillard herself appropriates. Weil writes, "Because he is creator, God is not all-powerful. Creation is abdication. But he is all-powerful in this sense, that his abdication is voluntary. He knows its effects, and wills them."[85] The lack of mercy in creation evinces God's mercy *in creating in the first place*. McCullough writes, "In the dialectical terms of Weil's thinking, experience of the world negatively reveals the reality of the absent God."[86] But the robustness of Dillard's approach to Weil's dialectics is less important here than her rhetorical willingness to voice her readers' likely sense that these are difficult concepts to swallow in a secular age.

What this admittedly difficult creation theology of divine self-limitation allows, for Dillard, is nothing less than the redemption of God's goodness, for if God is "out of the physical loop" (168), then "God is no more blinding people with glaucoma, or testing them with diabetes, or purifying them with spinal pain, or choreographing the seeding of tumor cells through lymph, or fiddling with chromosomes, than he is jimmying floodwaters or pitching tornadoes at towns" (167). The result, for Dillard, is not full abandonment, though. Like Weil, she continues to recognize the mysteries of grace. "I cannot prove," she writes, "that with [the untied hand] he wipes and stirs our souls from time to time, or that he spins like a fireball through our skulls, and knocks open our eyes so we see flaming skies and fall to the ground and say, 'Abba! Father!'" (141). But of course the very heightened language of the unproven suggestion, and its parallel to other stories she tells of mystics throughout the book, suggests that Dillard holds this unproven grace to be. Later, after another insistence on what God does not do, Dillard admits, "Sometimes God moves loudly, as if spinning to another place like ball lightning. God is, oddly, personal; this God knows. Sometimes en route, dazzlingly or dimly, he shows an edge of himself to souls who seek him, and the people who bear those souls, marveling, know it, and see the skies carousing around them, and watch cells stream and multiply in green leaves" (167). Here Dillard subtly alludes back to her own mystical vision, related in *Pilgrim at Tinker Creek*, of an everyday tree: "I saw the backyard cedar where the mourning doves roost charged and transfigured, each cell buzzing with flame" (33). Here Dillard also follows Weil, for despite all her insistence on God's utter absence from the world "here below," Weil also famously recounted her own mystical experience when Christ would be "present" with her in a mysterious inner sense of grace.[87]

The metaphysical question of matter and spirit persists in *For the Time Being*, which Dillard seeks to resolve not through the esoteric substance of Holy the Firm or the self-sacrificing artist, but through the parallel senses of divine light, or sparks, or incandescence present throughout the created world in the thought of Luria, the Baal Shem Tov, and Teilhard, in particular, although Weil's language persists throughout in vocabularies of "attention," "blind chance" (87), and the real. The idea that matter emanated from spirit, as Weil and others suggest, "lacks all respectability" from a scientific perspective, but it offers meaning, a sense of "our role and raison d'être" (95). At the same time, Dillard ultimately concludes, miles away from her searching in *Holy the Firm*, these ideas are in the end not so important: "What to do? There is only matter, Teilhard said; there is only spirit, Kabbalists and Gnostics said. These are essentially identical views. Each impels an individual soul to undertake to divinize, transform, and complete the world" (172). Their answers about "what to do," Dillard notes, seem to in fact presume that both matter and spirit exist (173), as she herself seems to her in her final suggestion of pan-entheism, which holds that God is both "immanent in every-thing" and also that "everything is simultaneously in God, within God the transcendent" (176–77). "There is divine," she concludes, "not just bushes" (177). In this reading, Dillard echoes her gloss of Weil, "God immanent and transcendent, God discernible but unknowable, God beside us and wholly alien" (164).

But the emphasis here isn't so much on the nature of reality or even the relation of suffering to the divine but in the question of "what to do," which is a question of ethics. Dillard links "what to do" to both metaphysics and mysticism: "Having seen" God's surprising grace-filled action, she observes, "people of varying cultures turn—for reasons unknown, and by a mechanism unimaginable—to aiding and serving the afflicted and the poor" (168). Likewise, regardless of whether one sees all of earth as matter or spirit, or some union of the two, as she notes, the result is a call to repair. In Luria's Hebraic conception, this is the work of "*tikkun*"—redemption or restoration that "can restore God's exiled presence to his being" (51). God's presence on the earth, Dillard later suggests, following Teilhard and the "dear nutcase" Joel Goldsmith, is amplified by human holiness (140). Humans participate in the divine project, Dillard insists, citing Taoist and medieval Christian sources along with Teilhard and the Hasidic teachers (195), even "Christian fundamentalists": "God needs man; kenotically or not, he places himself in our hands" (200). She doesn't quote Weil here, but she could: "God is absent from the world," the philosopher-mystic comments in her notebooks, "except through the existence of those in the world in whom his love lives."[88]

Dillard illustrates this conclusion with a story woven through the book's final chapter, the tale of a fourteen-year-old girl named Suri Feldman who went missing in a Connecticut forest on a fieldtrip in May 1995 (189). In fragments throughout the chapter, Dillard tells of the search and of the stakes, as a twelve-year-old girl had disappeared and been murdered in the same forest only months before (196).

Reprising the initial question in her Author's Note, Dillard asks, "What is the possible relation between the 'oyster-like, gray, or quite black' Absolute and a Brooklyn schoolgirl in a plaid skirt? Well, that's just the question, isn't it?" She interrupts the story with a quote from Lawrence Kushner: "Without our eyes, the Holy One of Being would be blind," which reads as juxtaposed commentary on the next paragraph that reports that six hundred of the thousand volunteers who searched for Suri Feldman were Hasidic men who drove from cities across the eastern reaches of North America (196–97). Dillard heightens the tension, recounting the story's facts: a pillow for the bloodhounds to sniff, a sketch of a possible perpetrator, the threat of cold and rain (197). She interrupts the story with more theological musing, more cloud reports, more numbers about births and deaths against which to imagine Suri Feldman's existence (6,381 U.S. deaths per day, and 10,852 births) (199). At long last Dillard reveals the story's ending: "May 7, 1995: They found the Hasid girl." She's fine, unharmed. In the aftermath, "the Hasids in the woods danced," and back in Brooklyn, as volunteers tell the newspapers: "I've never seen so many people dance in a circle" (199). The story precedes Dillard's final insistence that "God needs man" (200).

How does the Absolute relate to a girl in a plaid skirt? Dillard asks. She answers: the Absolute relates through the people whose eyes, whose hands, whose feet searched a full day for her unspeakably precious presence in the Connecticut woods. The Absolute rejoices in the joy of the dancing searchers. God's mercy is evident, following Weil, in the "radiance and compassion of some who know God."

Within the context of the book's pressing questions, the story of Suri Feldman illustrates Dillard's point that suffering and joy, matter and spirit, human and divine, meet in the space of human work to redeem and repair the world. Within the context of Dillard's larger project, however, the story of Suri Feldman that ends *For the Time Being*, like the story of Dave Rahm that ends *The Writing Life*, offers an implicit corrective to the story of Julie Norwich that ends *Holy the Firm*. If Dillard's attention to Dave Rahm in his realness corrects course for the risks of imagination in Julie Norwich's story, her attention to Suri Feldman—and more precisely, to the embodied ethical attention others devoted to Suri Feldman—highlights the literally salvific power of an ethics of attention. The care to which Dillard bears witness in recounting this tale differs noticeably from the care she offers Julie Norwich, which is by no means embodied or literal. Dillard's attention to Julie, whether she is imagined or not, does not in fact heal Julie's face or life; an aesthetics of attention only goes so far. By contrast, the attentive care the thousand searchers offer Suri Feldman—the time, the cost, the miles driven, the energy expended— embody Weil's ideal of a Samaritan care, the literal life-saving power of the compassionate action to which Weil calls her readers as the fulfillment of her vision of God's own self-renunciation. Dillard, in effect, redeems or repairs her own vision by returning it, once again, to the material realm of real human needs and the human possibility of meeting them. In this, again, she echoes Weil's own holism, the ethical-aesthetic unity of her theological thought.

Throughout her writing life, Dillard has produced unflaggingly precise and beautiful prose, keenly attentive to the natural world and the human condition. Against any number of retrenching fundamentalisms, she has written a Christian faith marked by an openness to world traditions and agnostic questioning, one that is profoundly anti-triumphalist, even secular, in the postsecular sense not just of the end of faith but of a cacophony of belief, unbelief, and their mutual interrogation. As she writes in a 2020 piece for the *Christian Century*, "As a serious Christian—humor me—I'm at home with Orthodox Jewish dogma, Hasidic dogma, Islamic dogma, godless Buddhist wisdom, and probably many other views. Christianity is huge."[89] Dillard's later work also leads the way in a nature writing that is increasingly socially engaged, a tradition taken up by writers like Terry Tempest Williams, who has also found her way to Weil as I discuss in this book's conclusion. Weil is Dillard's persistent companion, interlocutor, and at points even implicit alter-ego in these artful negotiations, both persistently present in Dillard's work and also notably absent, in much the same way Dillard herself is absent from these texts, occluding the self in order talk about the work and the world and the divine from a place one can't quite locate. Weil's absent-presence in one of the twentieth century's most admired anglophone prose stylists suggests that Weil's legacy is even broader than many have realized—her concerns as urgent now, and as inescapably human, as they ever were, in their thirst for the Infinite and their dogged quest for beauty, truth, and justice. For as Lissa McCullough notes, according to Weil, "the point of 'waiting for God' is not to surrender oneself to God and to abandon the world, leaving the limitations of creatureliness behind. The objective is to redescend to live among creatures as a transparent mediator of creative-redemptive love."[90] Living among weasels and rotifers, falling planes and girls in plaid skirts, Dillard has attended to them with an "intense, pure, disinterested, gratuitous, generous attention" the name of which, Weil says, "is love."[91] And one need not look far to find objects of such love or the creator their very presence may imply—indeed, no farther than the creek in one's backyard or even the trapezoids that structure the skin on one's own hand: from where Weil and Dillard watch and wait, "anything whatsoever contains the infinite."[92]

3

HUNGER

Weil's Fraught Sacrifice in Mary Gordon's Fiction

Creation is a fiction of God's.
—Simone Weil, *First and Last Notebooks*

The December 1985 issue of *Ms.* magazine includes a two-page spread by Karen FitzGerald on "Eight Writers and Their Spiritual Reading." These writers include Elaine Pagels, Ntozake Shange, and Ursula Le Guin, among others, recommending books like *Their Eyes Were Watching God*, *Beyond God the Father*, and *Ceremony*. Only one book appears twice, recommended by both Annie Dillard and Mary Gordon: Simone Weil's *Waiting for God*.

Dillard advocates for Weil with an evident awareness of a feminist periodical's readers: "Simone Weil was a Jewish Frenchwoman who was interested in Christianity and Catholicism; she was also a fanatic. In *Waiting for God*, Weil wrote: 'Literally it is either total purity or death.' This fanaticism, this all or nothingness, both attracted and repelled me." Gordon echoes Dillard's focus on Weil's moral seriousness, though in a different register. Naming Weil along with George Herbert and John Donne, she focuses on the quest for love. "Simone Weil writes as a vision of God as love, and the relationship of the love of God to human life. It is rigorous, absolute, and passionate."[1]

Yet while Gordon is less self-consciously distancing in her brief contribution to *Ms.*, she admits to Weil's challenges elsewhere. In the introduction to her essay on Weil as a guiding figure in the book *Not Less than Everything: Catholic Writers on Heroes of Conscience, from Joan of Arc to Oscar Romero* (2013), she asks: "Who was Simone Weil? To what category should we link her name? Philosopher? Political activist and theoretician? Factory worker? Farmworker? Christian mystic? Self-hating neurotic? Self-hating Jew?"[2] This interpretive conundrum—which echoes many of Weil's commentators—is in fact at the heart of much of Gordon's writing, which shows Weil's persistent influence and challenge: in vocabularies of force, affliction, and attention; in dramatized ethical quandaries; and in questions about faith given Roman Catholicism's participation in injustice and domination.

Gordon's interest in Weil goes back to the mid-1970s moment important for Rich, Nunez, Dillard, and many others writing at the time. As she told Edmund White in an interview in 1978, Weil had become "an obsession," although "she also disturbs me because of her denial of pleasure."[3] She repeated the language in 2014 in an interview with Sean Salai, admitting, "I had also been obsessed with Simone Weil for years and years and years."[4] The interest—and tension—is not surprising, given Gordon's own background: like Adrienne Rich, Gordon shares Weil's Jewish heritage, and like Annie Dillard, she shares Weil's tenuous connection to Roman Catholicism, although Gordon is a cradle Catholic rather than adult convert. As with the poets discussed in the next chapter, Gordon transmutes Weil's life and work into quasi-biographical writing that blurs the line between fact and fiction, imagining afterlives of sorts while taking the liberties of literature to make sense of the philosopher-mystic's life. Gordon stands out in this project, however, not only as a writer of long-form fiction but also as a reader of Weil raised in the Catholic Church, one whose religious engagement is as explicit as her feminism. Like many of the poets in chapter 4, Gordon shares Rich's critical stance on Weil's commitment to self-sacrifice, but she's not willing to dismiss it altogether as some feminist commentators do.

Still, Gordon is by no means antifeminist, and in fact another point of resonance with Weil is her willingness to question the Church. For decades she has maintained the tenuous position of a practicing Catholic who openly criticizes the institution, including its stances on contraception and women's ordination but also its clericalism and anti-intellectualism, echoing Weil. In an interview with Judy Valentine in 2007, she admits, "I love being a Catholic in the same way that I love being an American, which is that most of the time I'm deeply ashamed to be both Catholic and American, and I have to believe that there is some tradition that is not immediately visible in current practice that I love very much." Pressed on the matter of the Church's inescapable patriarchy, she says, "You can't feel comfortable. You'd have to be, again, an idiot to feel comfortable in Catholicism. I'm not comfortable, and I'm angry all the time." Instead of comfort, she says, to be a feminist in the Church is to be in an "embattled position," to be "historically patient while screaming."[5]

Many of Gordon's characters turn away from the Church because of precisely these issues, leading to a repeated trope of the generational shift from religious to areligious. She traces the movement, often in family lines, from strict religious observance to rejection of religion to later generations raised without religion, illuminating the tensions that arise in the lack of shared vocabularies, practices, and understandings. Many of her novels imagine both what is gained and what is lost, not abstractly but concretely, in a movement away from Catholicism. In this way Gordon renders discussions of the secular within the frame of narrative, especially family and relationship. These particular family stories track with the broader sociohistorical phenomenon of secularization understood postsecularly, that is, again, not as the end of religion but as the proliferation of possibilities for belief and unbelief, a fracturing of previously assumed shared religious understanding—another point of resonance with Weil, whom E. Jane Doering and Eric Springsted insistently connect to the question of "just what it might mean to recover a usable spiritual tradition."[6]

In this chapter I turn to three works of fiction Gordon has published in the twenty-first century: *Pearl* (2005), *Simone Weil in New York* (2014), and *There Your Heart Lies* (2017). These narratives, to three very different degrees, render Weil in literary imaginings and alter-egos in ways that allow Gordon to suss out the philosopher-mystic's importance and difficulty. *Pearl* never names Weil, but her presence haunts the text, from allusions to Weil's vocabulary and themes in *Waiting for God* to its late twentieth-century reimagined family drama of a young woman committed to starving herself to death for the sake of a political cause. The novel, I argue, interrogates the value of sacrifice in a secular age, particularly given the constraints of gender. *Simone Weil in New York*, by contrast, explicitly imagines Weil's encounters in New York with one of her prior students, a fictionalized version of one of Weil's actual correspondents, in a triangulation that allows Gordon to represent the frequent blend of admiration and concern for Weil, even horror at her evident anti-Semitism. *There Your Heart Lies* returns to a more distanced frame, this time imagining a young woman who, like Weil, travels to the Spanish Civil War as a volunteer and is confronted by the war's political and religious complexity. This most recent novel is less tied to Weil's biography than the previous two, but its notes name Weil as an instigating source, and in its insistent thematization of the tensions between public and private troubles and the deep ambivalences of violence and religion, the novel continues Gordon's long conversation with Weil over the place of religion in public and private life. In this way,

Gordon could be said to mediate between Adrienne Rich's perspective and Annie Dillard's: with Rich, she expresses deep concern over a gendered tendency toward self-erasure and the harms wrought by Christian institutions, but with Dillard she takes seriously the persistent role and even possible wisdom of religion. And alongside both Rich and Dillard, Gordon locates in Weil an ethics of attention both interpersonal and public that offers vital guidance even in a secular age.

PEARL

In her novel *Pearl*, Mary Gordon represents the challenge of interpreting self-sacrifice in a gendered and widely postreligious modern frame. Its eponymous protagonist is an American exchange student in Ireland who, horrified by a particular injustice—a death for which she feels responsible and the wider refusal to see this death as part of the Troubles of Ireland—embarks on an extended fast from both food and water before chaining herself in front of the American Embassy with a public written statement. In an uncanny echo of Weil, Pearl's ethico-political commitments lead her toward a death of self-starvation. Pearl's life is saved in the end by attention and forgiveness, but the discourse surrounding her political fast parallels debates that have followed Weil's death.

The question of interpreting a character who seems to "strain toward death," as Andrea Hollingsworth says of Weil, is at the core of *Pearl*, as Pearl's mother Maria and father-figure Joseph struggle to understand her choice.[7] The novel is also voiced by a mysterious and opinionated narrator who offers readers explicit interpretive instruction. "[Pearl's] act," the narrator admits early in the novel, "is full of contradictions, you might say. What is it: suicide or hunger strike, private act or public statement?"[8] Characters debate whether

Pearl suffers from anorexia—a medicalization of her refusal of food with gendered overtones—or seeks to be a political martyr, vocabularies complicated by Christian histories, secularization, and the particularity of place. These debates read back onto Weil and broaden to interrogate the possible value of sacrifice in a secular age and the way social expectations of women complicate this value.

Resonances between *Pearl* and Weil are present not just in the characters' parallel ethico-political fasting but in myriad subtle refrains: both Weil's writings and Gordon's novel insistently employ metaphors of hunger and thirst, eating and drinking; Maria and Weil share a favorite poet in George Herbert; and at one point Maria remembers an anecdote familiar to many through *Waiting for God*. Even the name and title Pearl nods toward one of Weil's favorite of Jesus's parables, in which a merchant gives up everything for a pearl of great price. Still more significantly, Simone Weil's philosophical vocabulary of force and attention is woven throughout Gordon's novel. Pearl's characterization also echoes Weil's biography. Both figures manifest sensitivity from a very young age to the suffering of others, a sense of the world's corruption by power. Pearl, we read, "from childhood had disliked and even feared the idea of force" (76). Two instances in which a young Pearl observed force used against vulnerable individuals persistently "come to Pearl when she's been tired or discouraged or just sad, and when they came they suggested to her that they were the truest things about the world" (82). In her letter to her mother, Pearl explains that she believes "this world" "to be a place of harm" and that she has "learned that [she is] capable of harming" (17), that this propensity to hurt others is in fact "the nature of the world" (18). To Joseph she writes, "I have lost my faith in the goodness of life. Replacing that belief: a belief in malignity. In the will to harm. And dismay that this impulse is in myself" (18).

In all this Pearl echoes Weil's sense that the will to harm, to use force against others for one's own benefit, is at the core of human nature. Weil begins "The *Iliad*, or the Poem of Force" by asserting that force is not just the "true hero, the true subject, the center of the *Iliad*" but at the center of human life, mangling both those against whom it is used and those who use it. Force, for Weil, again, is a phenomenon of power that destroys the human spirit and body, "that x that turns anybody who is subjected to it into a *thing*" and the primary cause of radical human suffering.[9] Weil is concerned with such suffering not just philosophically but personally. In one letter she admits, "I knew quite well [in my youth] that there was a great deal of affliction in the world, I was obsessed with the idea." All people, she repeatedly asserts, possess an "animal nature" of hurting those more vulnerable than they are; one of her favored metaphors for this phenomenon is hens pecking one of their wounded peers. Like Pearl, Weil includes herself in this description of human nature, admitting that she has not only suffered but caused suffering, writing to her priest friend Father Perrin of her "miserable faults" and insisting that we are all complicit in diminishing others.[10]

But both Pearl and Weil view the height of ethical response to this suffering and vulnerability and will-to-harm within the world as self-sacrifice: "Sacrifice is the acceptance of pain, the refusal to obey the animal in oneself, and the will to redeem suffering men through voluntary suffering."[11] Again, this sacrifice is what Weil means by decreation: "To listen to someone is to put oneself in his place while he is speaking. To put oneself in the place of someone whose soul is corroded by affliction, or in near danger of it, is to annihilate oneself."[12] Affliction, that bodily, social, and psychological form of radical suffering that makes people into things, naturally invites others to despise it, she claims.[13] The ethical act of *attending* to one who is afflicted thus is radically countercultural and counterintuitive, in that it requires of the subject absolute renunciation: "[The attending individual] must be ready to die of hunger and exhaustion rather than change his attitude." In fact, for Weil, to attend to an afflicted individual "is to consent to affliction oneself, that is to say the destruction of oneself. It is to deny oneself. In denying oneself, one becomes capable under God of establishing someone else by a creative affirmation. One gives oneself in ransom for the other. It is a redemptive act."[14] The biblical echoes in this claim are far from accidental: Weil's model, by the time she writes these later essays, is Christ, whose self-sacrifice she takes as exemplary. In Weil's life and in her writing, choosing to experience the suffering of others in solidarity, and further choosing to take on the degradation of another, emptying or limiting or restricting the self in order to bring the other life, is the height of ethical good.

In many ways, Pearl enacts Weil's ethical philosophy. First, she follows Weil in recognizing her own ethical failure, which is only slowly revealed to the reader over the course of the novel: angry at a risky and ridiculous feat of political protest undertaken by her Irish boyfriend and his peers in the so-called Real IRA, Pearl castigates her friend Stevie, the developmentally disabled teenage son of one of the group's ringleaders, for participating. After calling him "stupid," Pearl watches as "his face [loses] all its features: [goes] flat, white, like a plate" (168): in Weil's terms, Pearl watches as her forceful language renders Stevie a thing rather than a person. Not long afterward, Stevie is hit and killed by a bus; his mother Breeda, Pearl's greatest friend in Ireland, blames Pearl's words for the boy's death, and Pearl accepts the blame, horrified by her own impulse to pick on the weakest in a group and manifest "the will to harm" (169). She believes that her words "erased" Stevie (171), that "his blood was on her hands" (324). In her letter to Joseph, Pearl closely echoes Weil's vocabulary: "A boy died because of me. Because I rendered him as nothing in my self-righteous blindness in the name of an idea. I made a thing of him. I stole his faith and hope" (18).

Pearl also sees Stevie's death as a more-than-personal event, not just "private" but also the result of the Troubles in Ireland, and she refuses to accept that Stevie is not being mourned in these political terms (16). She seeks through her act of witness to retroactively establish him as a political victim and a figure worthy of the attention the world failed to give him. This is Pearl's first stated aim in her public document, but she also names her goal to "give [her] life in witness" to "the goodness of the peace agreement, and to protest the evil of continued violence" (16, see also 174). Pearl cannot bring Stevie back to life, but she believes that her death is stronger than her life—that in coupling her emaciated body with an explanatory statement in a public spectacle, she can *call attention* to his goodness, to the goodness of peace for Ireland, to the evil of violence. As the narrator claims, her statement (and her body) "invite[e] anyone's attention, everyone's" (17), even though she has had a lifelong distaste for public visibility. Pearl's particular self-sacrifice also aligns with Weil's ethics of decreation: repeatedly we read of Pearl "emptying herself," "turning from body to idea" (19, see also 102, 299), seeking a particular "purity" (174–75). Pearl literalizes a biblical metaphor of self-emptying, favored by Weil, through her empty belly, the concrete erasure of flesh, the diminishing space her body occupies over the six weeks of her fast from food and the six days of her fast from water. She seeks to become nothing for the sake of the other. Having lost faith in language (a sad irony, as one character points out, for a linguistics student), Pearl seeks to "[turn her] body into a sentence, a sentence everyone would have to understand" (238).[15]

Do they understand Pearl's body-text? Do we? And why does Pearl feel so sure that "the body is stronger than words" (238)? What compels her to turn so fully to the feminine side of the classic gendered binary of flesh and text? For Pearl, as for Weil, observers grapple not only with how to attend to the self-giving body and its ethical message. *Pearl* highlights the difficulty characters have accepting the young woman's self-starvation as a viable ethical statement, emphasizing the cacophony of possible interpretations. Pearl's mother Maria is perhaps the most mystified: repeatedly we read of her desire—and failure—to understand, to the point that the vocabulary of understanding becomes a refrain.[16] Maria's outlook on the world, with its powerful optimism and confidence, stands in stark contrast to her daughter's and leads her to insist on the impossibility of chosen death as an ethical good. Numerous times Maria repeats, "Nothing is worth your life." In this view, Pearl's *life itself* is the pearl of great price, the thing of greatest value compared to which all else pales.

Hazel Morrisey, the doctor who attends to Pearl after she is finally cut away from the flagpole and taken to the hospital, seems to fundamentally agree with Maria's valuation of biological life as the highest good, though Maria resists her explanations for Pearl's behavior. Dr. Morrisey's training equips her with compassion, but it also gives her a medical framework of interpretation. She insists, "Whatever else we call it, whatever she calls it, moral witness or political statement, we have to understand it's at least in part a suicide attempt" (249). But isn't it possible that "suicide," if "we call it" that, is the sort of term that privatizes and psychologizes, erasing the moral and political aims of Pearl's act? Maria and Joseph both question the doctor on this count. A parallel problem accompanies Simone Weil's death. As Sissela Bok notes, "The coroner's report added that 'the deceased did kill and slay herself by refusing to eat whilst the balance of her mind was disturbed'" and that newspaper headlines included claims like "French Professor Starves Herself to Death" and "Death from Starvation: French Professor's Curious Sacrifice." Yet the curious sacrifice resisted easy categorization: Bok claims, "Neither her parents nor others who knew Simone Weil would characterize her death so summarily as suicide."[17] Critics and biographers, including her friend Simone Pétrement and more recently Robert Coles and Francine du Plessix Gray, continue to wrestle with the question of whether suicide is a helpful category for understanding Weil's death.

They also struggle with the label of anorexia. Coles, in conversation with Anna Freud, problematizes it, whereas Gray assumes it.[18] If "suicide" diminishes the possibility of understanding starvation-witness in terms of political or moral agency, "anorexia" risks reducing the complex act to a rubric of gendered mental health. And yet mental health is an inevitable category for consideration, as the texts of Weil's and Pearl's lives both express the young women's unusually sensitive awareness of suffering in the world, their desire for an austere purity, their attraction to extremity. Pearl longs for death "as a kind of thirst," finds the "weakness" that accompanies her self-starvation to be a "sweet exhaustion" (15): her experience does align with Dr. Morrisey's description of the "hopeless passivity" and hypersensitivity of suicides (250). Weil, for her part, famously wrote to Fr. Perrin, "every time I think of the crucifixion of Christ I commit the sin of envy" and alarmed her friends and family with a passionate commitment to risking her life in a scheme to parachute nurses to the war's front lines.[19] Further, the category of disordered eating demands consideration on both counts, based not only on the emaciated bodies of Weil and Pearl but also in the fact that Weil's prose and Gordon's novel are both threaded through with images and metaphors of hunger and thirst, eating and drinking. The hunger-riven texts that enflesh these two characters for our imaginations, and the death-aimed bodies that signify their hunger for emptiness, demand an accounting—but it is a risky one, for how do we speak of eating disorders without reducing the women's acts to this one thing? Caroline Walker Bynum addresses a similar challenge in her groundbreaking book *Holy Feast and Holy Fast: The Religious Significance of Food to Medieval Women*: while the label anorexia nervosa may offer some explanation, it also risks robbing the remarkable fasts of medieval women of their spiritual and political significance. Bynum's work is also significant for reminding us that the sacred past/secular present binary oversimplifies a medieval era in which not all fasting was regarded as religious and a twentieth century in which not all fasters maintained secular motives. Simone Weil is her prime contemporary example.[20]

This challenge of interpreting Pearl's and Weil's refusal of food is vividly exemplified in the patronizing reaction of middle-aged American "Real IRA" ringleader Mick, who claims that his son Stevie's "death got all mixed up for [Maria's] daughter with politics and her eating issues, which is a big thing for young women these days" (291). Ironically, Mick echoes feminist commentators like philosopher Chris Cuomo, who compares Weil to "many earnest young women predisposed to hating their bodies."[21] Mick refuses to see Pearl's statement as a valid political act—valid political acts, for Mick and his pals, are exclusively performed by men—instead interpreting her through a social script of gendered stereotypes. Though a strong tradition of Irish hunger striking exists and is in fact one impetus for Pearl's act, Mick refuses to read Pearl in its terms.[22] Indeed, in choosing at points to call Pearl's act self-sacrifice, I go against Mick and the novel itself, which never applies the word "sacrifice" to Pearl but in three of its five appearances *does* apply the term to the men of the IRA. This gendering follows the fact that secular rhetorics of sacrifice most commonly refer to war: even Weil turned not just to Christ but to Alexander the Great's treatment of his soldiers for an exemplary case of self-sacrifice.[23]

Yet while Mick highlights the dangers that accompany the label "anorexic," he does accidentally draw one important link. In recent years, scholars have begun to recognize greater connections between the diagnosis of anorexia and ancient traditions of religious asceticism. Dr. Morrisey makes this connection in passing in the novel, noticing her patients' tendency to "burn up, consume [their bodies], with the avidity of the old saints" (198). Implicitly answering Bynum's frustration in the early 1980s that doctors expressed their interest in

"so-called female eating disorders . . . without the least awareness of
the religious context in which, until very recently, similar behaviors
occurred,"[24] in their article "De-medicalizing Anorexia: A New Cultural Brokering" (2008), Richard A. O'Connor and Penny Van Esterik
argue that contemporary anorexia shares with ancient religious
asceticism a strong emphasis on values, on *virtue*. Socially contextu-
alizing anorexia, they argue, results in a view of anorexics as "mis-
guided moralists" rather than "cognitive cripples," reframing people
with anorexia as individuals who take a cultural emphasis on "good"
eating to an unhealthy extreme.[25] Importantly, such a stance is not
limited to women, though the diagnosis is still often gendered even
in clinicians' approaches.

Per O'Connor and Van Esterik's view, "Today's anorexics are secular ascetics whose austerities come to control them," as they no longer tend to inhabit the "traditions [that] control religious asceticism."[26]
In this, they echo Bynum's claim that extreme medieval fasting practices developed as the Church moved away from communal understandings of fasting and feasting.[27] The idea of "secular asceticism"
aligns provocatively not only with commentators' views of Simone
Weil as a secular saint and Weil's own calls for a new kind of saintliness, but also with the questions of martyrdom and secularization
threaded through *Pearl*. Both Weil and Pearl were raised in postreligious households—Pearl by the daughter of a Jewish convert to
Roman Catholicism who rejects religion altogether, Weil by parents
who had abandoned their parents' Orthodox Jewish practice in favor
of the bourgeois values of a secular-Catholic France. Gordon's novel
is insistent in its exploration of this generational dynamic, mining the
religious histories of Maria and Joseph and highlighting Pearl's dis-
coveries of the religious and political traditions of martyrdom. While
at first it seems that Pearl stumbles across the possibility of self-
sacrifice as a *political* activity, it becomes clear that even the political
examples she learns from have their foundations in religion—and that

Pearl herself is better versed in such religious foundations than those around her assume.

First, we read of her model of the "Irish hunger strikers of the 1920s and the 1980s" (19): "Heroes were called *martyrs*. Her spine thrilled when she heard the word; she'd discovered it secretly, on her own, as other children might discover the term *sadist* or *coprophilia*" (27). Pearl's attraction to this unspoken word is immediately linked to Maria's Catholic childhood, full of the word, and the narrator questions, "So would you say that it was part of Pearl's background even if it was silenced, rendered invisible? Maria Meyers was raised Catholic, but she was determined that her child would not be" (27). Reading as a young adult of Bobby Sands, the Irish Republican hunger striker, introduces Pearl to the concept of "the strength of offering up your life," but this awakening to the possible good of self-sacrifice holds for Pearl none of the religious significance it would for Irish Catholics, who would have viewed him "as a figure of the suffering Savior, Christ on the road to Calvary beneath his cross" (30). Indeed, Pearl's IRA friends of a younger generation transfer their veneration from Christ to Sands, from religious to political martyrs, as well, participating in the generational shift away from the faith of "their parents and grandparents" (72).

Still, for Pearl and her peers, the secular, political martyrdom they idealize is culturally traceable to the Christian tradition. And it becomes clear through the narrative that Pearl is more familiar with the Christian tradition than her mother realizes. Significantly, this familiarity comes through texts:

> Pearl knew many of the things that [Maria had] kept from her. Knew saints' lives, the lives of martyrs, because she'd found her mother's childhood book, *A Girl's First Book of Saints*, by Jerome Lowery, OSB, the letters cut in gold into the purple spine. Reading her mother's book, she had to understand that some deaths were said to be a good thing.

It went against everything else in her life to think that a death might be what your life was leading up to all along. She had never had the slightest hint that death might be a good thing. What would Maria say if she knew Pearl's first thought about the death she is pursuing now came to her from a book with Maria's childhood signature on the flyleaf[?] (71)

Though Pearl was not raised within a context of religious devotion, her access to the books of her mother's Catholic upbringing continues to shape her imagination. Contemplating Pearl's act, Joseph believes that she "would not have the word *atonement* in her vocabulary" (104); engaged in similar thoughts, Maria "remembers now: *martyr* means witness in Greek. Pearl says she is a witness. Does she think she is a martyr? Maria can't imagine where she could get such an idea" (131). But Pearl's ideas come from both the quasi-religious fervor of the IRA and also from the Catholicism her mother sought to keep from her. For all Maria's attempts to raise her daughter in a postreligious context, Pearl nevertheless discovers the teachings that shaped her mother's early years. The vocabulary, the imagery, the *values*, even, seem harder to escape or erase than Maria and Joseph themselves believe.

In fact, at points it seems as though Pearl's lack of a full knowledge of the Christian tradition her mother has tried to protect her from actually causes her more trouble. In this regard, the text suggests an observation similar to the one O'Connor and Van Esterik make that asceticism grows especially problematic when it is divorced from the religious traditions that once contained it. This status outside the religious community is significant both for how characters interpret Pearl's act and also how she comes to choose it. She seems terribly surprised by the evil within the world—and within herself—when its full extent finally reveals itself to her; the post-Catholic humanist worldview provided by Maria has not adequately accounted for the presence of both good and bad, hope and despair. Similarly, Simone Weil's extremism seems to have resulted at least in part from her self-directed and frankly partial study of theology. For both Pearl and Weil, reading Christian texts and participating in radical politics in young adulthood, outside robust communities of interpretation and traditions of practice, results in a troublingly hyperbolic, private ethic that mystifies those around them.

Not surprisingly, it is the character in *Pearl* who is most willing to understand the young woman's act in terms of the Christian valuation of sacrifice who is most sympathetic to her project. Joseph, though he views Pearl's behavior as deeply troubling, also seeks to understand her in her own terms when he believes others do not. He resists Maria and Dr. Morrisey's shared assumption that physical life itself must be the greatest good: "The basis of their connection, he realizes, is this: they have both rejected, quickly and automatically, the concept of martyrdom as a useful idea." Joseph "is not so ready to throw it out. Again he wonders if we must necessarily believe, before we can begin to speak with the assumption of a common language, that nothing is worth dying for. . . . What is it to be human if you are unwilling to give up your life?" (245). In this way, Joseph echoes Weil's readers who seek to understand Weil's decreative impulses rather than dismissing them outright as neuroses.

Joseph is self-aware enough to recognize that this impulse to value sacrifice may have its source in his religious upbringing, even though he is no longer a practicing Catholic. His mental process expresses his deep desire to understand Pearl; he hates both the thought of her death and the thought of "a world in which the possibility of dying for something is automatically considered sick and ridiculous" (246). Joseph's status as the sole character who seems in any way sympathetic to Pearl's project and his explicit considerations of Christianity as the source of such a mode of valuing life (and death) perhaps most strongly demonstrate how uncommon such an interpretation can be in contemporary society. His recognition that others see Pearl's act as "sick" and "ridiculous" points to Pearl's lack of religious and political context as a young woman in the late twentieth-century West: without a shared religious valuation of martyrdom, and without a place within the masculinist political movement to which she is tangentially connected, Pearl can only be interpreted in the privatized terms of medicine or madness. This approach reads back onto Weil through her association with Pearl's character.

But the narrative's characters are not the only subjects responsible for interpreting Pearl's self-starvation; readers of the novel are also held responsible, not only by virtue of our role as readers but also through the narrator's direct addresses. At points, the narrator is even explicitly directive, insisting "you must understand" (23, 42) or suggesting alternate interpretations. We read the various competing perspectives from a privileged point of view, with access to characters' thoughts as well as their dialogue. But we also experience the unique position as coconspirators with the narrator, who has a distinct perspective of his or her own. Early in the novel, for instance, the narrator directs our interpretation of Pearl's self-starvation and of the public statement and letters we have just read, long before Joseph and Maria have access to them in the temporality of the narrative:

> I want you to understand that although you may think of her death as a suicide it is also more than that. She wanted to die to be out of this life, but she also wanted to use her death. Her death was the vessel of her hope. She could use her death as she could not use her life. Her death would be legible, audible. Her life, she believed, was dim and barely visible; her words feeble whispers, scratches at the door. (19)

The narrator's direct address here establishes several important dynamics at this early point in the narrative: First, that readerly understanding will be difficult but that it is also a crucial undertaking as the text unfolds. Second, that complexity, realized in part in the novel's heteroglossia, will be key to the interpretive puzzle: the narrator doesn't insist that the death *isn't* a suicide but rather that it is *also* more. (This statement also stands as a nearly direct inversion of the doctor's claim that "whatever else we call it," we must also recognize Pearl's act as a suicide attempt.) Third, the narrator's direct address here calls attention to the novel's thematization of interpretation, not just of written texts but of the body-text through which Pearl seeks to communicate when she loses faith in her own language. In this thematic concern with interpretation, the text also follows Simone Weil, whose concept of reading extends to both texts and people: "We read," she writes in *Gravity and Grace*, "but also *we are read by*, others."[28]

At points Joseph seems to be an exemplary reader, unique in his capacity to understand Pearl on her own terms and in his willingness to go with Pearl and Weil into a realm of ethics that values even ultimate self-sacrifice. To a somewhat lesser degree, both Hazel Morrisey and Maria also exemplify elements of a Weil-inspired ethics of attention, in scenes that wink in the direction of Weil's writing. *Pearl* alludes to Weil's Holy Grail passage, first, when the medical student "watcher" assigned to prevent Pearl from harming herself tells her to rest until Dr. Morrisey arrives, as "she'll want to hear what you're going through" (236). The fact that Pearl latches onto this language, wondering about its literal meaning, draws even more attention to it. And only a few chapters later, when she meets Pearl's boyfriend Finbar and feels compassion for the ordeal he has undergone, Maria recalls "something she read once" about a knight who "asked another knight, 'What are you going through?' And this was the right question, the one that unlocked magic" (275).[29] The novel's ethics of attentively reading others is clearly in conversation with Weil.

Yet Joseph's reading of Pearl ultimately goes terribly wrong, and his missteps dramatize an element of Weil's ethics that Pearl herself has been trying to express throughout the narrative: in order to attend in a life-giving way to a suffering other, one must consent to self-diminishment. Love, for Weil, requires "distance."[30] Maria's all-encompassing sense of maternal unity with her child has precluded her really seeing Pearl as other from her. Joseph's manic sense that he and Pearl are utterly alike in their view of the world has a similar effect of forcefully erasing Pearl and re-creating her in his own image. According to Weil, however, true love, true friendship, "is a miracle by which a person consents to view from a certain distance, and without coming any nearer, the very being who is necessary to him as food."[31] In other words, an ethics of attention requires both risking looking at the suffering other *as she really is* and also withstanding our hunger to fully comprehend and possess: both seeking to understand and recognizing that we cannot. Pearl herself learns this lesson from the receiving end at the novel's conclusion, when she is confronted with Breeda's inscrutable forgiveness ("I also am other than what I imagine myself to be. To know this is forgiveness," writes Weil).[32] Imagining Breeda's face, Pearl "understands that you cannot see a whole face at once, even in memory" (343): we are constrained to partial sight, partial understanding. We are responsible, not only to attend to others in a way that does not reduce them to *things*, but also to rest with Pearl in the "incomprehensible" (342). In a fragment titled "Readings," Weil writes,

> Justice. To be ever ready to admit that another person is something quite different from what we read when he is there (or when we think about him). Or rather, to read in him that he is certainly something different, perhaps something completely different, from what we read in him.
>
> Every being cries out silently to be read differently.[33]

Pearl seems to learn Weil's lesson about justice most fully in the attentive care she receives and particularly in the surprise of Breeda's forgiveness. Following this surprise, Pearl contemplates her mother-daughter relationship in the novel's final pages by musing on the phrase, "My mother is my mother and I am I": a vivid instance of the distance Weil attributes to true friendship and good reading, and a provocative inversion Joseph's stance and the phrase from the Song of Songs, "I am my beloved's and my beloved is mine."

There is a circularity to this ethics, an endlessness. Those who would seek to help Pearl in her starvation must learn *from her* to metaphorically look instead of eating; Simone Weil's witness offers pearls of compelling wisdom, even if in the words of Henry Finch, "We may find ourselves unable to enter into her thinking."[34] Weil's (and *Pearl*'s) ethics of attention collapses back into itself, rife with hungers. As Rich echoes in her poem "Hunger," again and again Weil represents the sufferer as one who is hungry or thirsty. The ethical imperative, on paying attention to that other, is not only to ask "What are you going through?" but also to provide food or drink: "It is an eternal obligation towards the human being not to let him suffer from hunger when one has the chance of coming to his assistance."[35] At the same time, Weil asserts that part of loving an other means resisting *our own hunger*, "loving a human being *for his hunger*" rather than as "food for ourselves."[36] Hunger and thirst become overdetermined signs, at points literal, at points metaphorical, both an ethical good when chosen and a sign of the utmost suffering when unchosen.

But what happens when, as in the case of Pearl, one chooses to abstain from food and drink, to literally annihilate oneself, for the sake of an other—and in so doing becomes the sufferer that others recognize as needing help? Are those who attend to Pearl not then obligated to feed her? The literalization of Weil's philosophy in Pearl's body (and in Weil's own) highlights its inner flaw: if one values life to such an extent that one is willing to give one's own life in ransom, why should one's own life not be treated with the same degree of value? Or maybe the literalization highlights the philosophy's holistic logic *when practiced in a community*: within the connections of relationship, none need offer themselves up to the utmost degree. The circle of attention spirals, endlessly, as each recognizes the suffering of another, as each chooses to forgo a meal but not life itself. It is telling that for both Pearl and Weil, hunger-unto-death only took shape when they were far from the parents who loved and cared for them. As Ann Loades writes, "Without [the context of love], life may be eaten away by metaphor."[37] It is also important that Mary Gordon's fiction offers a dramatically different ending for the would-be ascetic than Weil's own story's ending, imagining her family showing up in time to pull her back from the brink, even if the lessons in attention and distance they must learn still align with Weil's insights.

In her influential essay on Simone Weil in 1963, Susan Sontag describes Weil as a saint by whose example of secular sacrifice we are "moved" and "nourished" rather than a hero we should emulate.[38] Ironically, Sontag renders Weil a source of spiritual, or at least ethical, food for malnourished moderns—a contemporary Christ, even, whose sacrificed body is present in the bread and who is also known as the Word, or a prototypical woman who feeds others with little thought of herself. It is easy to read a similar suggestion in Mary Gordon's novel: Pearl is the daughter of single-mother Maria and surrogate father Joseph, the story's narrative action beginning on Christmas Day; Pearl is the young woman whose self-renouncing act those around her can't help but interpret in gendered terms. Reading *Pearl* with Weil reminds us, however, of the dangers of such an attributed gendered or quasi-religious sainthood. If it is unjust to refuse to read Pearl or Simone Weil in the ethical, political, and even spiritual terms they request, it is also unjust to idealize them so wholly that there is no room for question or criticism.

Pearl offers us a contemporary reworking of Weil that both honors the philosopher-mystic-activist and also highlights the dangers of sainting her, the importance of recognizing hyperbole, the difference between rhetorical flourish in a text and the impassioned sacrifice of cells and synapses. Perhaps some degree of self-sacrifice is necessary, some restraint in favor of the other, some risked action in the face of the incomprehensible, but must Pearls and Simones relish the terrible purity of their hunger in order to render their bodies sentences? Is this really their only way for women to be read as witnesses to ethical extremity?[39]

In the end, I am arguing, Gordon's novel answers *no*. Pearl's story radically departs from Weil's in that she chooses life, chooses to be saved by the "incomprehensible," chooses to live into the mystery of the world, a mystery she ultimately recognizes not in ascetic sainthood but in forgiveness. She recognizes that she need not atone with her life but will struggle, instead, to trust again in the incomplete, impure, imperfect world of words and relationships: restored by Breeda's forgiveness to friendship and "the work of memory," a meaning for the life she thought only meaningful in death (343), and also to relationship with her mother. The narrator closes the novel by "leav[ing] Pearl and Maria to themselves" in a reimagined Pietà, and in a last instance of directiveness, with the final statement, "We will hope for the best" (354).

SIMONE WEIL IN NEW YORK

If *Pearl* explicates the troubles of gendered martyrdom in a secular age, the novella *Simone Weil in New York* interrogates the inconsistencies of Weil's life and work, including her social oblivion, her turn to Christianity, and most especially her anti-Jewish outlook. The novella's protagonist Genevieve is an imagined former student of Weil's, a French woman who now lives in New York, where she cares for her brilliant disabled brother and her infant son while her Jewish husband is away fighting in the war. After a chance encounter with Weil, Genevieve reluctantly enters a renewed acquaintance. Constructing this fictionalized cast of characters around a deeply researched depiction of Weil herself, Gordon triangulates the challenge of interpreting the French writer not through a chatty narrator reminiscent of *Pearl*'s but through Genevieve, who grapples with a blend of admiration and distaste. This character's difficulty acts as a double for readers'—and perhaps for Gordon's own—mix of attracted fascination and repulsion to Weil's work and its points of troubling paradoxes.

Weil's presence in Gordon's text is rooted in her presence in the texts she left behind: the narrative is full of unattributed passages from letters, essays, and published lecture notes, particularly in scenes of dialogue. Genevieve's focalizing psyche, however, is fictional, and its framing of Weil's presence complicates any illusion of biographical verisimilitude. In my discussion I follow Genevieve—and Gordon—in referring to this literary representation of the historical Simone Weil as Mlle Weil.

Genevieve's stance toward Mlle Weil is one of strongly remembered love and admiration but also frustration and even distaste. She admits to herself that Mlle Weil's reminder of her girlhood nine years hence is deeply painful in how it calls to mind her life before her mother's death, which required Genevieve to give up further education and become Laurent's primary caregiver, not to mention the war. Mlle Weil represents "the whole of what has been lost."[40] Further, Genevieve finds Mlle Weil "ridiculous" in appearance and behavior—the word is a refrain throughout the text—even as she admires Mlle Weil's greatness; she wars with her own impulse to evade her former teacher. She finds herself frequently frustrated by Mlle Weil's inconsistencies, including the number of small social lies required to protect Mlle Weil in her avowed pursuit of the real, like her mother's subterfuge to feed her filet mignon and call it horse meat due to her

daughter's finicky palate. That Mlle Weil, prime advocate for attention to the truth, is oblivious to these tricks, exposes a discrepancy
that Genevieve finds perplexing at best and at points deeply disap-
pointing. Mlle Weil's eyes, Genevieve believes, see "everything"—
"except what she doesn't wish to see" (70). Genevieve can't decide
whether this blindness is more than others see or less, "the real, true,
deep, high reality" or "careless": "Not seeing what is being done for
you, what people are doing for you so that you can see only what you
want to see. Rather than trying to get the truth of what is there" (78).

Genevieve's difficulties with Mlle Weil are personal and particular: Mlle Weil reminds her of better days and of the distance between
her current life as wife, mother, and caregiver and her earlier hopes
of higher education. She wonders if her life lives up to her teacher's
high standards, never quite realizing how this concern parallels her
question of whether Mlle Weil lives up to the teacher's *own* standards.
Genevieve also shows a strong impulse to protect her, a desire for her
approval and love, in numerous situations where she tries to save Mlle
Weil from embarrassment or social hurt. In recollections of her
schoolgirl past, Genevieve remembers Mlle Weil as a "hero," a "saint
of the mind," one who called forth her students' love through "her
extreme purity of mind, her extraordinary learning, her extreme devotion to them, her students, and her clumsiness," which aroused their
desire to protect her (73–74).

But layered atop its particularity, Genevieve's experience of Mlle
Weil also acts as a sort of double for other readers of the historical
Weil. The blend of admiration and perplexity is a recurring theme
in commentators' discussions. As E. Jane Doering writes in *Simone
Weil and the Specter of Self-Perpetuating Force* of Weil's contemporaries,
"Her dogged work for just causes alienated many who were on the
receiving end of acerbic comments when they ignored her requests."[41]
Other commentators extend these admissions to the personal, like
Adrienne Rich engaging with Weil's work even while commenting,

in the 1977 interview with Valerie Miner, on how she was "so full of potentialities and yet still so unfulfilled."[42] Robert Zaretsky summarizes many readers' feelings in the conclusion to his *The Subversive Simone Weil* (2021) when he echoes Simone Pétrement's sentiment, "Who would not be ashamed of oneself in Simone's presence, seeing the life she led?" Zaretsky writes:

> This has often been my experience with Weil. Reading her is always a revelation and a reproach. I have never met, and will never meet, the expectations she had of herself and others. But, to be honest, I have also felt at times the irritation and impatience that many who met her also felt, exasperated by her extreme character, confused not just by some of her philosophical ideals, but also by her insistence upon enacting them in our lives. "What I cannot stand," she told her students, "is compromise."[43]

As one of these imagined students, Genevieve struggles to hold together her admiration and her criticism. This is due, in part, to the many ways in which what is most troubling in Weil is precisely what is remarkable: her moral seriousness and lack of compromise, for example. Even in the realm of vision, Mlle Weil's evident unawareness of certain workaday realities also undergirds her extraordinary capacity to attend to "the afflicted." Here is another point of influence in the novella, at least partly explained by its focalization through one of Mlle Weil's former students: her vocabulary of "affliction," along with "force" and "attention," is insistently present across the novella's scope. "Affliction" here appears, in particular, to describe Laurent, whose cerebral palsy interrupts others' capacity to see his brilliance as a professor of psychology and as a man. Genevieve refers to her brother as "one of the afflicted, his body broken from birth" and admits that she "can only love people who are able to look at Laurent without looking away." She recalls that Mlle Weil, who tutored

Laurent in that earlier time in France, "seemed to have the least trouble looking at him" (76). Unlike others who had to control their initial impulse to "recoil," Mlle Weil seemed not to see Laurent's body but only his mind, and for this Genevieve owes her "fealty" (77).

Genevieve is capable of this kind of attention to her brother, although it seems to demand more conscious effort for her than it does for Mlle Weil: "An important part of her life is pretending she is not seeing what she sees" of Laurent's tremors and challenges (90). However, she struggles to afford the same attention to Mlle Weil. Not only is her teacher "ridiculous" in appearance and behavior, Genevieve finds her physically repulsive. In a later encounter, when Mlle Weil asks Genevieve to cut her hair, "A bubble of nausea forms behind Genevieve's lips. She doesn't want to wash Mlle Weil's hair. She doesn't want to be touching Mlle Weil's body, particularly knowing how much she dislikes being touched. And the truth is, she does not smell good. The truth is: Mlle Weil stinks. But Mlle Weil is a hero. So how can Genevieve not do this thing, this exceedingly simple thing?" Genevieve wonders, "What is there about this woman, so devoted to the truth, that requires the telling of so many lies?" (118).

This characterization of Mlle Weil as unwashed echoes the biographical account of a farm family Weil visited who were perplexed at her personal hygiene even as she patronized them with questions about their poverty.[44] Although it appears in Jacques Cabaud's biography and several others, as well as some of the poetry-biographies I discuss in the next chapter, one doesn't run into accounts of Simone Weil's personal hygiene in most of the scholarly criticism. Gordon's fictionalization of it here could seem almost indecent, a moment where the narrative itself diverges from Genevieve's strong impulse as an insider to protect her teacher from ridicule. But the scene's earthiness—its description of Mlle Weil's scent, of her hair the shampoo will not penetrate due to its thickness or its dirtiness (119)—vividly depicts the philosopher's humanness, her frailty. That frailty is further emphasized in Genevieve's realization of how thin and breakable her former teacher's bones are and how "vulnerable" her eyes are without glasses, a realization echoed in a later scene in which Genevieve's neighbor Lily cries after trying to take Mlle Weil's hand: "When I felt the bones in her hand, even for a few seconds, I could see how frail she was. She won't live long" (128).

Mlle Weil's vulnerability stands in contrast to her "force" (68), her imperiousness, her evident genius: it humanizes her. It's also telling that Lily recognizes it, given Genevieve's frantic efforts to protect Mlle Weil and her neighbor from each other. Lily is mistress to Joe, a middle-aged hair salon owner devoted to beauty and gustatory pleasures Genevieve worries may be sourced on the black market, given wartime rationing. The narrative's moments of humor arise in these encounters: Joe explaining spitballs to Mlle Weil, for instance, while Genevieve listens, horrified, wondering, "Do you know who you are speaking to, Joe?" (98). Genevieve worries Mlle Weil's moral principles will be offended by the couple's infidelity and black-market dealings, not to mention their priorities, while worrying Mlle Weil will offend them with her tactless lack of care for social niceties. The former teacher does cause an awkward moment when she asks Joe to read a poem she carries around in her pocket, George Herbert's "Love": he reads the theologically dense poem, one long metaphysical conceit, but it's clear he doesn't understand it, and Lily is "embarrassed to be in the same room with poetry," at least according to Genevieve's perception (101). Angry after the encounter, she complains to Laurent, who sees the encounter from another angle: Joe "will remember this time, remember meeting her, remember what she allowed him to think, what she allowed him to say. Lily, I think, will especially remember it. Remember how the workers she taught loved Mlle Weil" (101). Laurent's interpretation holds up in the later scene when Lily cries. Genevieve assumes her tears are due to Mlle Weil's abrupt pulling back, that she's hurt Lily's feelings, when in fact Lily has perceived something true: Mlle Weil will follow the historical Weil in succumbing to tuberculosis within the year.

As the narrative progresses, these moments of dissonance accrue. The Herbert poem—"Love bade me welcome, yet my soul drew back"—hints at another revelation soon to come, as Mlle Weil reveals to Genevieve her turn to Christianity. Observing a tree in the park, Mlle Weil asserts, "The presence of beauty in the world is the surest sign of the presence of God" (104). "The words," we read, "are shocking to Genevieve," who recalls her teacher's agnosticism. Mlle Weil, for her part, guesses her former student will be surprised and goes on to recount her mystical experience in Solesmes, further shocking Genevieve with her claim to have been "pierced in my soul" and felt God "take possession of my body" (105). These accounts follow closely Weil's "Spiritual Autobiography" and other writings posthumously published in *Waiting for God*, but as Doering notes in *Simone Weil and the Specter of Self-Perpetuating Force*, "Aside from her conversations with a limited number of confidants, Weil kept her mystical experience and her attraction to Christianity very private."[45] The character Mlle Weil admits to such privacy when she tells Genevieve, "I don't speak to people about these things. I'm always afraid people will misunderstand, purposely misunderstand, out of a mysterious desire I arouse in people to do me harm" (105–6). Mlle Weil's articulation of this risk highlights some later commentators' difficulties with Weil's religious turn. For her part, Genevieve is "repelled, but at the same time fascinated. She both does and doesn't want to hear more" (106)—but this reaction seems to be more to Mlle Weil's description of others' will to harm her, not her newfound faith.

This mixture—repulsion and fascination, both wanting and not wanting to hear more—echoes Zarinsky's description of revelation and reproach, his combined attraction and irritation with Weil. This scene is an example of what I am calling the narrative's triangulation, where Genevieve acts as a double for other interpreters of Weil. For

ultimately, as in *Pearl*, the narrative's primary conflict is one of interpretation. How ought Genevieve understand Mlle Weil? Is she ridiculous or great? Is her blindness to everyday reality inconsistent with
her pursuit of the real, or is it a necessary condition of that pursuit?
Is her turn to Christianity a betrayal or an extension of her genius?

Genevieve has an important realization in a later conversation with
Mlle Weil about the philosopher's headaches, for which she expresses
gratitude. Glad for how the experience helps her "understand suffering," Mlle Weil admits that "there was a time when the pain and
exhaustion were so great that I was uncertain whether or not death
was my imperative duty" (116). Genevieve asks about this—how death
can be a duty—and Mlle Weil speaks of her self-hatred, self-repulsion
in this experience of affliction. But when Genevieve imagines Laurent overhearing Mlle Weil's thoughts on affliction, she believes they
would harm him: it would be "dreadful" to imply to him that others'
"revulsion" toward him would be internalized, "to suggest that the
afflicted might consider it their duty to take their own lives" (117).
This is the moment in the text when Genevieve

> suddenly understands, in a way that she knows will be permanent, that
> it is possible for Mlle Weil to be wrong. Grievously, dangerously wrong.
> Including but not limited to a category that could be called mistaken.
> She knows it because she knows her brother. He loves life. He doesn't
> want to die. He would never imagine that it is his duty to die. He has
> struggled with everything in his power to keep alive. This is his
> greatness.
>
> Is it possible that her brother is greater than Mlle Weil? And she
> wonders: Which is greater, to be willing to die, or to fight death in the
> name of life? (117)

The passage reads back powerfully onto *Pearl* and its conclusion,
Pearl's decision to live in a sharp deviation from Weil's example. It

offers a sort of primer to interpreting Simone Weil from Mary Gordon's perspective, a suggestion that her absolute principles don't always hold up in the face others' experiences, that these principles are at points quixotic and even deadly.

Laurent himself makes a similar case in a later conversation with Genevieve about Mlle Weil's description of her misery at factory work. They've had a conversation with Mlle Weil about these experiences, and the former teacher's description of the "affliction" it caused, the way it marked her as a "slave"—descriptions, again, drawn from the historical Weil's accounts—has troubled Genevieve. In the moment, again, the protagonist is of two minds that echo other commentators on Weil, both starting to "resent being lectured at" and yet aware "she is in the presence of great thought" (127). Later, Laurent explains that Mlle Weil's experience does not truly allow her to theorize about all workers' experiences: "We have to understand what Mlle Weil doesn't understand, that her experience in the factory wasn't typical": "her story is not a worker's story, but the story of an intellectual in a factory" (129). The conversation adds to the narrative's implicit primer of how to interpret Weil: not only recognizing that she can be grievously wrong but also recognizing that in order to read her well, at points we must understand in her work and experience what she herself does not understand. We must do this, Gordon seems to be saying, even as we recognize with Genevieve that despite her teacher's limitations, she did "put her body on the line" in ways others have not, some by choice as free moral agents, and others, as in Laurent's case, cannot (129).

The climax of this interpretive learning—and of the novella—occurs in a scene very near its end, when Mlle Weil pays her last visit and announces she's arranged for a "very intelligent priest to come and speak to you in order to arrange for the baby's baptism" (131). Genevieve's perplexity at Weil's relation to her own Judaism, hinted at in the earlier discussion of her turn to Christianity, becomes explicit

here. Mlle Weil opines about how such a baptism can bring benefit—
including social benefit—and do no harm, since the baby won't
choose it for himself, echoing a letter Simone Weil wrote to her
brother advising his daughter's baptism.[46] This letter gives the novella's imagined Weil the phrase "fanatical Judaism" (131), and Genevieve
is taken aback: "This cannot be Mlle Weil speaking." Marshalling
uncharacteristic boldness, she claims that such a baptism would be a
"betrayal of his father's people, particularly now, when they are under
threat of extermination" (132). But Mlle Weil simply insists that given
these threats, baptism could be "of great advantage."

Once again, even in the moment this time, Genevieve recognizes
that Mlle Weil is deeply "wrong." But when she claims, on the spur
of the moment, that she and her husband have decided to raise the
baby as a Jew, their own irreligious outlooks notwithstanding, Mlle
Weil goes still further, speaking not just of convenience but of her
critique of the entire "tradition of the Hebrews," which she claims
has been "disastrous for the mind of Europe. It is a tradition of bloodshed and exclusion. Yahweh, like the Roman gods, is a god of punishment and force" (132).

Laurent—speaking in the voice of many of Weil's later readers—
gently reminds Mlle Weil of her own Jewishness, her current flight
from Hitler, and in response she avers not to consider herself a Jew.
Again, this claim derives from Simone Weil's writing, particularly a
letter she famously sent to Jérôme Carcopino, the French minister of
public education, when Jewish teachers were no longer permitted to
work for the state. "I am a Frenchwoman, not a Jew," she concludes
(133). And Genevieve feels "afraid of what has entered the room. A
darkness greater than the dark created by the blackout shades" (132).

Of all the points of tension in the reception of Simone Weil's
life and work—her ideal and literal self-decreation and relation to
embodiment, her lapses in logic, even her Christian turn—the most
tenuous and terrible is her anti-Jewishness. Like Gordon's imagined

characters, scholars struggle greatly with this evident betrayal of her otherwise compelling ethic—and of her people in their time of greatest modern affliction. Weil's early commentators criticized it soundly: as early as 1952, philosopher and Talmud scholar Emmanuel Levinas wrote in "Simone Weil Against the Bible" of how Weil's "anti-biblical passion could wound and trouble Jews" (by Bible, here, Levinas clarifies, he means "what the Christians designate as the Old Testament"). He critiques Weil's insistence on an absolutely pure Good that she sources anywhere—and almost everywhere, given her otherwise nearly universalist approach to religion—except Judaism, "while Evil is specifically Judaic."[47] Ultimately, Levinas accuses Weil of bad reading in her conception of "Jehovah" as unremittingly violent and the idea of a chosen nation problematically exclusionary.[48] Martin Buber, in *On Judaism* (1967), likewise addresses Weil's reading of Israel as a tribalistic and idolatrous "Great Beast": "Everything that was hateful to her in modern history," Buber writes, "was ascribed by her to the influence of what she called the 'totalitarianism' of Israel." He concludes, "Seldom has it been so evident as in this instance how a half-truth can be more misleading than a total error. (As far as Simone Weil is concerned, scarcely a quarter-truth.)"[49]

Scholars generally agree that Weil's trouble with the Hebrew scriptures is a problem of poor reading and a lack of familiarity with the living tradition that would have shared her critique, as Levinas does, of accounts like the violent destruction of the Canaanites. David Tracy echoes her earlier critics of what he calls her "narrow, willful, and ignorant reading of Judaism": Why, he wonders, didn't she find resonance with the Hebrew prophets, whose calls for just treatment of the vulnerable prefigure her own? He concludes, "Her reading of Judaism is a sad exercise in a life and thought otherwise driven by a sense of justice and a demand for compassion": these readings are not "the real Simone Weil."[50] Doering follows Tracy's perplexed line of questioning: "One must ask here why Weil was so unwilling to treat the Hebrew sacred scriptures, in all their complexity, with a fairer, more scholarly attitude." As Doering notes, it's not just the prophets that bear such powerful resonance with Weil's work, but also elements of Hasidism, including the concept of *tsimtsum*, which many scholars have noted—alongside Annie Dillard—uncannily prefigures Weil's writing on God's self-removal in the process of creation.[51]

Doering's approach to the conundrum is to read how Weil's anti-imperialist stance, her commitment to calling out force wherever she saw it, led to both her deeply flawed—because radically incomplete—reading of Hebrew scriptures and also, perhaps paradoxically, her criticism of Hitler.[52] Sylvie Courtine-Denamy follows a similar tack in her reading of Weil alongside Edith Stein and Hannah Arendt, criticizing "Weil's profound misunderstanding of the Jewish religion" and "unfair treatment of it" but also naming the contradictions at the heart of her work: how her anticolonialism stood in contrast with her lack of concern for the Jewish people, particularly given her historical moment; her misunderstanding of the Jewish tradition but admirable principle of countering force; her wrong theory but ultimately good action in the resistance efforts.[53] These nuanced readings, which seek, like Gordon's Genevieve and Laurent do, to hold in tension Weil's scholarly and moral genius with her deep imperfections, stop short of imagining the psychological mechanisms that would motivate Weil not just to reject her own heritage but to willfully misunderstand and blame it for many of the world's wrongs, particularly at a moment when that very identity threatened her life. Michelle Cliff does, however, drawing a parallel in her essay "Sister/Outsider: Some Thoughts on Simone Weil" between her own experience of internalized anti-Black racism as a mixed-race woman from Jamaica and Weil's evidently internalized anti-Jewish racism. "I am not Jewish," Cliff admits.

I was not a Jew in Europe during the thirties or before or since. I feel presumptuous passing judgment on someone who may have internalized the anti-Semitism around her; on someone who was trying to survive. . . . But I do know about the effects of internalized racism on the life and heart of a Black person. I know about people who cut themselves off from their pasts and their identities and so internalized racism that they ended by hating their pasts and identities, and deeply hating themselves.

Cliff expands on this reading with a few biographical details: tellingly, she relates the story of the farm family that noted Weil's endless talking—especially about "the coming martyrdom of the Jews"—and her lack of personal hygiene, her refusal of food when colonized people were hungry. Cliff reads anti-Semitism as either in the farm wife's account of Weil—as obsessive and dirty—or in Weil's own expressed fears and their manifestation in her lack of care for her own body. Neither of these dynamics is unfamiliar to her as a woman of color and lesbian, Cliff writes: self-hatred "can make you feel crazy," and self-protection can lead to extraordinary isolation.[54]

In *Simone Weil: Portrait of a Self-Exiled Jew*, Thomas R. Nevin goes still further to suggest that Weil was more Jewish than she realized: "Much that is most positive in both her life and her writing suggests an *anima naturaliter Judaica*."[55] He argues that like other "catastrophic Jews"—Jews pushed into their identity as such by Hitler's regime— Weil was Jewish not "racially" or "religiously" but historically, shaped by forces beyond her control and at points beyond her ken. Reading Weil in the context of postrevolutionary France's assimilationist policy and anti-Semitic nationalism even before the collaborationist Vichy regime, Nevin seeks to both document the extent of Weil's troubling anti-Jewish writings and also to nuance it. Her apparent Marcionism, the refusal to recognize the God of the Hebrew scriptures as consistent with the one Jesus called Father, Nevin reads as not so different from liberal protestant distinctions between "law" and "grace." In this way, Nevin establishes Weil as less unusual in her outlooks than some commentators have suggested, yet still culpable. Sounding much like Gordon's characters, he concludes, "That a mind of abundant energy, a mind that has cast brilliant lights on some of the abiding problems of this century, could do itself harm and give hurt to the Jewish people must be reckoned one of the intellectual and moral catastrophes of a dark age. It should also serve as one of the saddest of cautionary tales, perhaps, for those who go looking for saints."[56]

As they struggle to understand their last visit with Mlle Weil, Genevieve and Laurent come to similar conclusions. "I don't know how to speak about it, how to understand it," Genevieve admits to her brother, again echoing so many of Weil's commentators. "What is the right way to describe what she said: mad or evil?" Laurent replies, again, as many commentators do, "It would dishonor her to call her mad. And the way she lives shows she cannot be evil. No, she is a person terribly wounded, yet possessed of extraordinary gifts" (133). Laurent refuses to fall into the trap of a graduate professor Michelle Cliff describes, who commented on a seminar presentation she gave on Weil, "You do realize she was insane, don't you?" (323). Echoing Doering, Courtine-Denamy, and even Levinas, Laurent further insists that Mlle Weil's life contradicts her prejudice. Instead, like Cliff, he sources her anti-Jewishness—and perhaps her other lapses—in her vulnerable humanity, her woundedness, and holds this fact together with her gifting: she is a "maimed genius." He refuses to look to her biography for causes but instead reads her as "deformed" in her own way, manifesting both the greatness and the "poisons" of French culture (134). The very frailty of her body—her evident near-ness to death—exposes the fact that she is not above imperfection, that she is in need of attention herself.

In the novella's final pages, a year has passed and Mlle Weil has died as Laurent and Lily predicted. Genevieve continues to contemplate her former teacher's legacy in terms that echo the eighty years of commentary that have followed Simone Weil's life: "She is not ridiculous. She is many things. Great? A saint? A madwoman?" Purposing to bake a cake for Mlle Weil's parents—a symbol of everyday kindness for the grieving, of tethering to the material that would have doubtless made little impression on the teacher herself—Genevieve wonders, *"How do I understand her? How do I understand everything she was?"* She concludes, *"I will never understand. I will never understand"* (135). But she knows Laurent *will* understand her use of their butter ration—a sacrifice of his dearly loved pleasure—for the cake. And so the narrative concludes, much like *Pearl*, with an intimate scene of relation, of quotidian sacrifice, honoring Mlle Weil's life by caring for those she left behind. This denouement confirms the narrative's status as a sort of primer for reading Simone Weil in all of Mary Gordon's work—and perhaps for reading Simone Weil in general, a reading that holds together both her extraordinary gifts to the world and her catastrophic mistakes while seeking to honor goodness not just at the hyperbolic limits but in the everyday.

THERE YOUR HEART LIES

An undercurrent in *Simone Weil in New York* is Genevieve's relation to belief: repeatedly she describes herself and her family as "unbelievers," yet more than once in the brief narrative she experiences the urge to pray. This undercurrent of relating to belief after the social or familial rejection of religion, so prevalent in *Pearl*, continues to flow through Gordon's novel *There Your Heart Lies* (2017), which again imagines a generational movement away from the Catholic Church and its concurrent freedoms and challenges to cross-generational understanding.

There Your Heart Lies also continues Gordon's long literary conversation with Simone Weil by riffing on the story of a young woman's departure from her privileged family to serve in the Spanish Civil War, as Weil herself did. The differences are not insignificant: Gordon's protagonist Marian is American rather than French, her parents Roman Catholic rather than agnostic Jewish, her beloved brother one of many rather than just one. She's younger than Weil was at the time of the war and sails to Spain with a husband—although the marriage is in name only, and Marian does not, like Weil, succumb to a vat of boiling oil but rather works in field hospitals and eventually meets a Spanish man, remarries, and has a child, spending years in Spain before returning to the States. But the young women share an excitement over moral clarity and connecting with the working class and sensitivity over both the horrors and beauty of the world, and both ultimately find themselves horrified by the violence committed on both sides of the conflict.[57] In the acknowledgments following the narrative, Gordon thanks a robust list of historians whose work on the Spanish Civil War informed her fictional approach as well as a number of conversation partners, but she also explicitly names Weil: "When I try to remember why I felt the urge to write this book, inevitably I return to the work and life of Simone Weil, her letter to George Bernanos, and his searing *Diary of My Times*" (320).

Weil's letter to Georges Bernanos—French novelist and Roman Catholic Monarchist—is collected in *Seventy Letters*, originally published in 1965. In this letter Weil admits that in general she thinks fan letters to writers are presumptuous, but after reading his *Les Grands Cimetières sous la Lune* (1938; published in English as *A Diary of My Times*) and its condemnation of the Nationalists' violence in the Spanish Civil War, she had to write to him. "I have had an experience which corresponds to yours, although it was much shorter and was less profound; and although it was apparently—but only apparently—embraced in a different spirit."[58] Weil here refers to the fact that although she and Bernanos traveled to Spain to aid opposing sides of the conflict, he the nationalists and she the anarchists, both became disillusioned by their side's behavior toward vulnerable people, including priests and children. After telling several stories she heard and witnessed, Weil concludes, "One sets out as a volunteer, with the idea of sacrifice, and finds oneself in a war which resembles a war of mercenaries, only with much more cruelty and with less human respect for the enemy." She claims Bernanos is the only person she's found who has been "exposed to the atmosphere of civil war and has resisted it. What do I care that you are a royalist, a disciple of Drumont? You are incomparably nearer to me than my comrades of the Aragon militias—and yet I loved them."[59]

As Gordon notes in the acknowledgments for *There Your Heart Lies*, the Spanish Civil War is "rocky territory" (319). Her one-page preface, which offers the barest outline of its historical events, begins, "In July of 1936, the Fascist army, led by General Francisco Franco, launched a coup against the democratically elected Republic of Spain." This preface explains international relations around the conflict, including the decision of the United States, England, and France to remain "neutral," the Communist commitment to the Republican side, and the support of Hitler and Mussolini for the Fascists, who ultimately won in 1939, allowing Franco to rule Spain as dictator until 1975. These historical details help explain why volunteers from the United States and France would travel to participate in the conflict.

What the factual preface doesn't address is the Roman Catholic Church's contentious role in the conflict—one of the tensions at the heart of Bernanos and Weil's concern: this is a tension that the fictional narrative opens up. Gordon does not hesitate to depict harms wrought in the Church's name, the first of which is Marian's family's treatment of her beloved brother Johnny once they discover him to be gay. They institutionalize him, subjecting him to treatments so horrifying that he takes his own life. This religiously motivated betrayal layers atop the family's classism and racism to the point that Marian marries Johnny's partner Russel—a Jewish doctor—to escape them, joining him to volunteer with the Communists in Spain and carrying with her a "rage-filled aversion for the Church as an institution" (75). Her father believes "the reds hate all that is good and beautiful and valuable and true, everything that the Church keeps alive in the world" (17), but Marian can only see the harm the Church has caused. She recognizes "that a whole category that, without her knowing it, had been important to her—the sacred, is quite useless now, entirely gone" (76): an explicit representation of a certain mode of secularization, secularization as the rejection of the sacred altogether.

Yet, as with others among Gordon's characters, Marian finds her religious roots hard to shake. Her years of parochial education and religious training arise as "flotsam of an old, violently discredited life," evoking verbal associations like "the Passion of Christ" from a hospital's name (65), vague unease at seeing a church building used as a hostel (75), and the impulse to cross herself when she sees a cross-shaped stain on a sheet (92). Though she never returns to the Church, much later in life, in conversations with her granddaughter Amelia, Marian will use implicitly Christian language (165) and wonder whether Amelia can understand her grandmother's life story without understanding the history of the Church, the religious stakes of the fighting in Spain (170), or the experience of losing faith (199).

These problems are problems of meaning and understanding within secularization. How can we access the past, including the past of our loved ones, when we have no access to the life-and-death, eternally significant frameworks that motivated them? By extension, how can we understand a figure like Simone Weil—her politics as well as her spiritual affinities—without reference to these framing systems of meaning?

But the novel's problem also extends to the Church itself, for while Marian rejects it on solid grounds, she's also horrified by the glib violence with which her compatriots treat priests and even church buildings. The Spanish Civil War confronts Marian with violence on all sides. In a drunken conversation with Randall's anarchist lover Eugenio, she asks why they burn down churches, and he explains that it's because "they were so bad to the poor people, the ordinary people; they were always on the side of the rich" (81). This argument—that the Church sided with the wealthy and ultimately the Fascists—compels Marian until Eugenio admits that the violence extends to priests: "I didn't feel I was really a man until I got my own priest," he boasts. Taking a page from Weil and Bernanos's descriptions, Eugenio relates how he and his peers let the priest and other powerful men of a town run, shot them from behind, and then went to a café to celebrate with beers. Later they hung the priest's stripped body in a butcher shop window. Eugenio "is laughing, and he expects them to laugh" before recognizing they're "horrified" (82). Marian wonders how a "person whom I know to be basically decent can do something like this and laugh about it" (83), echoing Weil's horror at both those who perpetrated such "useless bloodshed" and those "peaceable Frenchmen, for whom I had never before felt contempt," who "savored that blood-polluted atmosphere with visible pleasure."[60]

Joining the Republican side fighting against fascism, Marian initially feels "the most wonderful feeling in the world: to know that you're doing exactly the right thing" (5). The Church in Spain *is* incontestably corrupt. But her original excitement to be "with people who look closely at the suffering of the world, with people who take the ideas she had, the vague ideas of a privileged girl, and make them real, turn them into actions" (37)—another echo of Weil's embodied commitments—wanes in light of her own side's gleeful use of force.

At the same time, when she tries to claim to her lover Ramón that she understands the war more than most Americans because of her Catholic upbringing, he resists, telling her she "can't possibly understand" because she's not grown up under the Church in Spain. "You can't possibly understand the absolute power they had, not just over your spiritual life, but over the bread in your mouth and the earth under your feet" (98). The particularity of the Church's power in Spain, Ramón asserts, renders it another problem altogether, including the Fascist requirements of religious observance under threat of execution and sights like "a priest with a rifle in his hand saying, 'Shoot, shoot the animals, all reds are animals,' calling from the altar for a massacre, for the holy sacrifice of shedding blood for the great cause, God's cause, God's cause against the devil's" (98). He goes on to describe priests urging poor young men to kill in the name of the Virgin, to shoot pregnant women, standing calmly by while prisoners are burned (98–99). These public instances of violence seem to outweigh Marian's private losses, leading her to contemplate one of the novel's—and Gordon's—persistent themes, namely, the tension between public and private "horrors" (99) and the ethics of witnessing these horrors and choosing how to act.

In Marian's experience of the Spanish Civil War, as in Weil's, no party escapes with clean hands. The Church is responsible for grievous wrongs in its participation in Fascist force—as in *Pearl* and *Simone Weil in New York*, Weil's term for the violent workings of power runs throughout the novel—but the Republican side is likewise prone to force's corrupting influence. Many years later Marian will tell her granddaughter, "What I want you to understand, Amelia, what I want you never to forget, is that there is a malign force in the world, the desire to humiliate, which you must always be on your guard for, which you must always resist" (174). In the aftermath of the war and Ramón's death, Marian is stranded in Spain with her infant son and in-laws, whose triumphalist religious observance—and Franco's requirements—mandate her presence at Sunday Mass. Deep in post-partum depression—or what she later learns to have been her pharmacist mother-in-law's furtive drugging with sedatives—Marian in her "numbness" begins to see that public and private pain, rather than competing, "shed a garish light on one another" (106). Her losses of Johnny and Ramón, and the loss of the war and rise of fascism, are mutually illuminating and overwhelming.

What eventually helps Marian is, in classic Weilian form, the "attention of curious strangers" who help her when she falls and hurts her leg in the street as she runs, sickened, from her own son's first communion party (157). The care of these women leads her to convalescing at the local doctor Isabel's house, where she learns she's been sedated for years and meets Isabel's brother Tomas, known locally as "the wounded priest" (212). Tomas complicates the novel's otherwise dim picture of the Catholic Church and offers yet another striking parallel to Weil.

Marian learns Tomas's background gradually from Isabel, who admits after a full year of friendship to her role in his story: Tomas had become a priest but was studying botany in Ireland during what Isabel calls "the madness" of Spain. She began to write to him letters telling him of all the terrible things "the Church had done in the name of God": priests fighting as Fascists, archbishops extolling violence, priests laughing at the desecration of executed bodies and encouraging soldiers to shoot women (232). Isabel blames herself for what Tomas did next, which she relates to Marian by having her read Tomas's letter confessing to an extraordinary act he'd "deliberately" (233) undertaken to "witness" to justice (234). Guilty for having been safely away during the war, and for believing for a time that the Church was in the right, Tomas admits in his letter that he's carried out an "accident" with a friend's combine harvester, cutting off the two middle fingers of his right hand and thereby disqualifying himself from performing his Eucharistic priestly duties: "You

know—perhaps you don't—that in canon law a priest can only con-
secrate the host if his right hand is intact. He must have a proper
thumb and middle finger, or he is considered unfit to touch the
Host" (234). Observing how the "Church was triumphing" in the
Spanish Civil War, he writes, "I had to put my body on the line as
you and so many people I loved had done" (234–35). Tomas's act is in
some senses senseless, a personal and symbolic attempt to relieve his
shame, but it is also an act of concrete divestment of the power to
serve in the central rite of the Church he still admits to loving. He
commits to returning to his hometown and living with Isabel to
"bind up wounds," not in a spiritual sense—she is not a believer—
but in solidarity and shared love.

Like Pearl's, Tomas's act echoes Weil's own self-divestment, her
literal decreation of the self in ostensible solidarity. In none of these
cases does the destruction of the body have a practical helpful out-
come. As with those seeking to understand Weil and Pearl, Marian
struggles to interpret Tomas's act and letter, "the justification of an
unjustifiable action; the explanation for what must be inexplicable."
Like the coroner after Weil's death, Tomas's bishop uncle reads his
nephew as "not in [his] right mind," but Marian "doesn't know how
to name an action such as this. Madness? Heroism?" Ultimately,
"what comes to mind is a word from a way of life she will no longer
allow into her understanding: martyrdom" (236). Like Joseph interpreting Pearl, Marian has to resort to her Catholic upbringing to find
a category, but unlike Joseph, she chooses to reside in the realm of
the unknown—"She will not name" but instead dwell in a "physical
sensation she calls understanding," a wordless intuition that there is
a logic to Tomas's actions even if she does not share his outlook (237).

Tomas does not just echo Weil's personal decreative impulse: he
literalizes her desire for a humbled Church willing to "say openly that
she had changed or wished to change" and priests of good faith even
"during the periods of the most atrocious abuse of power committed

by the Church."⁶¹ His status as wounded priest prevents him from presiding over the central sacrament and leaves him with the primary role of confessor, listening for hours each week to the horrors perpetrated by *both* sides of the war and honoring the anonymity of the confessions, never divulging them but holding them within himself. "Forgetfulness," he claims, "would be the greatest betrayal. I must remember" (240). In attending to the suffering on all sides, Tomas realizes Weil's ethics of attention, not just as a man but as a priest, in some sense seeking to do justice through the institution, even though it is a passive sort of justice. As Weil writes, in the case of "pure" attention that receives the other and releases one's own power and control, "one gives oneself in ransom for the other. It is a redemptive act." And it is, for Weil, modeled in Godself.⁶²

Weil's own attraction to the Roman Catholic Church was complicated, like Tomas's, by horror at the Church's participation in injustice, its triumphalism and imperial power. She admitted to being frightened of "the Church as a social structure," and "Church patriotism," of the number of good and beautiful things Christianity has historically excluded, and above all of "the two little words *anathema sit*," the Church's authority to excommunicate those whom it judges heretical.⁶³ This authority, she further argues, led to the "totalitarianism" at play in the Inquisition and other violent historical movements of the institution. She recognizes on a smaller scale that some individuals "develop a hatred and contempt for religion because the cruelty, pride, or corruption of certain of its ministers have made them suffer."⁶⁴ Yet for all this, Weil still hungers for God and even specifically the bread of the Eucharist, as she confesses in her letters to her friend Fr. Perrin and in the essay "Forms of the Implicit Love of God." She understands the Church to be in its truest form not the religion of the powerful but "the religion of slaves," of the humble, including herself. She believes the self-emptying Jesus to be "the Incarnation of God" even as she holds a more universal understanding of God's manifestation. But because of her identification with outsiders and the excluded, Weil committed to remaining at the "threshold of the Church": "The love of those things that are outside visible Christianity keeps me outside the Church," she writes. And so despite her keen hunger for the Eucharist, Weil imagines that "the desire for and deprivation of the sacraments might constitute a contact more pure than actual participation."[65]

Weil sought to purify the Church by denying herself full participation in it, to witness to what it could be by refusing to participate in its corrupted form. Tomas, already inside the gates, witnesses to the atrocities his beloved Church perpetrated and suffered—the moral muddiness of the war—by denying himself full participation, as well, prioritizing like Weil attention to those who suffer. The paradox in both cases is that rather than abandoning the institution—which both Weil and Tomas admit may be a fully necessary course of action for those most wounded by it—they witness to what it could in fact be, the possibility, as Weil wrote, "of a truly incarnated Christianity."[66]

As Marian, ill and nearing death, tries to explain her past to Amelia, she struggles to express Tomas's importance in it: "There was no one like him," she thinks. "There never will be again. He was the best of his kind, and his kind will not be seen again. Perhaps this is a good thing; no one should suffer as he suffered. But it isn't good for the rest of the world that there should be no more like him. People were better for having known Tomas. Of all the things she has questioned in her life, this she has never questioned" (265). This is one of the narrative's key representations of the struggle to help younger generations understand abandoned religious worldviews, for Marian's admiration of Tomas is senseless without the label "saint," even in her own postreligious imagination: she worries that without reference to these old "categories," Tomas will be "incomprehensible" (265). Implicitly echoing Susan Sontag's famous vocabulary for Weil, she decides to translate into the familiar language of "hero" but then resorts to "saint," causing in Amelia a sense of "panic" that she hasn't studied for this exam (266). They work together to come to a definition of saint as one without "strategies," and Marian uses this characterization to explain Tomas, who, again, sounds here very much like Weil: "It's as if he was missing a protective skin that kept him separated from people, from their griefs, as if the layer separating him from other people was completely porous. He would absorb other people's sorrows, he would become saturated with them, and somehow the grief was lessened for the other person; he had taken it in, it had become his" (266). For her part, Weil wrote: "The affliction of others entered into my flesh and my soul. Nothing separated me from it."[67]

Halfway through *There Your Heart Lies*, Amelia, grappling with what it means to be the second generation raised "without faith," realizes that while she believes in social, economic, racial, sexual, and gender justice, "She has never been able—this has been the problem—to connect these things with any actions that she thinks can change anything at all." Instead, she submits to a sort of nihilism, believing "there is darkness underneath everything, stronger than everything," that the earth is "doomed," humans hateful and selfish, and "nothing, nothing she could ever do is as strong as all of that" (200). This, to Amelia, is what it means to be without faith. But in the later scene, Marian explains faith was not what Tomas had, not faith as optimism about "things turning out well in this world" but rather hope in an ultimate trajectory of redemption for all (266–67). Yet again, like Weil, Tomas didn't require this hope of others or try to convince them of it. Marian explains, "He knew that for someone like me, who had no faith, who had lost all faith, or had renounced it deliberately, what he believed in was ridiculous. He admitted it was ridiculous, and he never tried to make anyone believe anything that he believed." Given both the public and private wounds perpetrated by the Church—in the war, in Johnny's death, in "unbelievable suffering"—Marian says she could not believe in God, but she believed "in Tomas," or "in something he had access to that I refused to call God." This "something," she claims, acted for Tomas as a source of strength, a depth that allowed him to give "his utmost" to others and still carry on (267). Marian's description of Tomas—and the goodness she could recognize in him—echoes Weil's claim that for those too wounded by Christianity to believe it, "the love of our neighbor and the love of the beauty of the world, if they are sufficiently strong and pure, will be enough to raise the soul to any height."[68] Again, Weil even went so far as to claim that atheism may in fact be a necessary purification of Christianity: "Those who do develop an idolatrous attachment to the mysteries or to the Church as a collective society need to undergo purification by means of atheism and incredulity: that is, by doubting their beliefs," she writes in *First and Last Notebooks*.[69] Tomas seems to have recognized a similar dynamic in those who lost faith. As Marian explains it to Amelia, his self-mutilation blocked his public participation in "communal celebration" and moved his work as a priest into the private realm of hearing confession, offering consolation by taking on everyone else's suffering in a way that "nearly killed him" (271).

Amelia doesn't quite understand the story, but she understands that it is deeply sad. She understands that even without belief in God, her grandmother received genuine consolation from Tomas, and that this consolation only makes sense in the language of her abandoned faith. In the events that follow, Amelia tries to find redemption for Marian by secretly traveling to Spain to find her long-lost son, only to be confronted by the fact that Tomas was right: on this earth, stories often hang open-ended, without happy conclusions. The novel ends with Marian nearing her death and the two women talking about how much they wish they could believe they would see each other again (317). They end in a space not of faith or belief but of longing and possibility: "One day, you know, Meme, I will be among the dead"—"So it's possible we'll see each other again. You must admit it's at least possible" (318). "Yes," says Marian in the novel's final words, "it may be possible. Yes." There is no triumph here, no false comfort or faith or hope in the sense of belief but instead hope in the sense of desire: the consolation of the *possibility* of Tomas's long view.

Again, Gordon ends her narrative in the space of unknowing. As a negotiation of faith after faith, *There Your Heart Lies* is paradigmatically (post)secular, unremittingly honest about Christianity's failures even as it explores the good it makes possible. There is no denying the Church's heinous partnership with fascism and destruction of Johnny, even as Tomas—like Weil—paradoxically seeks to purify the institution from its edges, not through power but through divesting of power. Gordon also seems to suggest that even though Marian herself abandoned her faith, it provided her with a framework for acting in the world—seeking justice by volunteering in the war and advocating, even in her old age, for local community causes. Similarly, Amelia's disillusioning trip to Spain, including an encounter with her religiously bigoted uncle, seems to have grown new moral courage in her. She has become "a person who will refuse some things. Will refuse to allow them to go by while she keeps silence": having risked standing up to her uncle, she has determined "to be a person of faith"—not in the sense of believing in God or expecting happy outcomes, but in the sense of saying yes and no, "not counting the cost," standing up to evil with moral seriousness (315). This is faith after faith: faith purified of corrupt institution and even perhaps its language of God, but sourced in the kind of moral courage Weil advocated for and claimed to be divinely empowered, whatever it was called. Such purified faith goes hand in hand with her newfound hope that the love she and her grandmother share does not simply end with death.

The religious vision of the novel is multivoiced, secular in the sense of plurality: Tomas's integrity keeps him within the Church;

Marian's takes her outside it; Amelia's doesn't return her to the institution but to the purest form of any goodness the earlier generations found within it. This is a keenly secular vision, not in the sense of rejecting religion but in the sense of criticizing what must be criticized, abandoning what must be abandoned, and opening oneself to the mysteries of love and the mysteries of the unknown. In this it is also a keenly Weilian vision.

4

(DE)CREATION

Simone Weil Among the Poets

The entire universe is nothing but a great metaphor.

—Simone Weil, *First and Last Notebooks*

In the essay "Decreation: How Women Like Sappho, Marguerite Porete and Simone Weil Tell God," collected in her volume *Decreation* (2005), the poet, translator, and classicist Anne Carson addresses a central challenge of Simone Weil's literary afterlives and, indeed, of Simone Weil's own writing. This challenge is the implicit tension between Weil's concept of decreation—the "shift away from an egocentric perspective toward one where the 'I' disappears," as Yoon Sook Cha summarizes in *Decreation and the Ethical Bind*—and what Carson calls "the brilliant self-assertiveness of the writerly project."[1] In other words, the writer who seeks to "disappear from herself in order to look" (169) nevertheless manifests herself in the very act of recording what she sees. She may seek, as Weil did, to absent herself from her prose, choosing to record ideas and observations over personal narratives, choosing a style that is strikingly impersonal. But the very fact of the writing records a trace of the writer, reestablishes a perspective from which she observes.

The tension persists in texts *about* Weil, be they biographical, scholarly, or literary. Weil didn't just theorize decreation; in Carson's words, she "arranged for her own disappearance on several levels," not just through the "self-starvation" that has troubled so many who admire her but also through her attempts to share her work without establishing her legacy (173). Weil published in her lifetime under pseudonyms; she left eleven notebooks with her friend Gustave Thibon with the expectation he might digest their ideas and share them as his own. His choice to arrange and publish excerpts not in his own treatise but as *Gravity and Grace*, ostensibly "by" Simone Weil but inescapably shaped by his editorial choices, thwarted Weil's desire to disappear into her ideas' influence on others. Thibon's choice both recenters Weil in her work and also occludes the "true" Weil through editorial or authorial shaping of her story. The same could be said for any literary representation of Simone Weil as paradoxically both a creative refusal of her drive toward decreation and a substitute of an imagined Weil for the real human person.

These literary attentions to Weil persist in contemporary poetry: Carson is one of a number of late-twentieth- and early twenty-first-century poets fascinated with Weil. For example, M. NourbeSe Philip, the Toronto-based writer and lawyer born in Tobago, speaks openly of Weil's influence in interviews and weaves a possibly Weilian vocabulary of roots and rooting in her collection *She Tries Her Tongue, Her Silence Softly Breaks* (1989).[2] Fanny Howe writes of her long-standing interest in Weil in her *The Wedding Dress* (2003), and Gjertrud Schnackenberg memorializes Weil in her poem "The Heavenly Feast" (1985), as does Edward Hirsch in "Simone Weil: The Year of Factory Work" and "Away from Dogma," collected in *Earthly Measures* (1994).[3] Mary Karr includes a poem on Weil called "Waiting for God: Self-Portrait as Skeleton" in her collection *Sinners Welcome* (2006), and Jorie Graham alludes to Weil in several poems in her collection *Overlord* (2005), including the poem "Praying (Attempt of June 6 '03)," which names Weil and her concepts of obedience and necessity.[4] Christian Wiman quotes Weil in *Survival Is a Style* (2020) and *Joy: 100 Poems* (2017).[5] Jan Zwicky's *Wisdom and Metaphor* (2003) incorporates Weil as well, and so do Nathalie Stephens's *Touch to Affliction* (2006) and Rita Mae Reese's *The Book of Hulga* (2016), a series of poems suffused with Weil's influence as they imagine a character Flannery O'Connor did not live to write.[6]

Another group of poets joins Carson in going still further in their engagement with Weil, however, devoting entire sequences of poems, even entire books, to imaginative renderings of the philosopher-mystic herself. Joining the titular opera in Carson's *Decreation*, these include the sequence "Hunger and the Watchman: For Simone Weil" in Maggie Helwig's *Talking Prophet Blues* (1989); Stephanie Strickland's *The Red Virgin: A Poem of Simone Weil* (1993); the sequence "The Testimony of Simone Weil" in Kate Daniels's *Four Testimonies* (1998); Sarah Klassen's *Simone Weil: Songs of Hunger and Love* (1999); and the sequence "Songs for Simone" in Lorri Neilsen Glenn's *Lost Gospels* (2010). These sequences and volumes are at points biography-by-poetry, at points philosophy-by-poetry, rendering and responding to Weil's life and thought in verse. They participate in the paradoxical creation and occlusion of Weil through their imaginative figurations. They also represent new generations of writers engaging with Weil, demonstrating that her legacy prevails beyond the first decades of her popularity—especially the 1970s moment when so many writers, like Michelle Cliff, Annie Dillard, Sigrid Nunez, and Mary Gordon "found" her—and extends beyond the East Coast literary scene.

Introducing a special issue of the journal *Biography* in 2016 on the subgenre of the verse biography, Anna Jackson explains that the form had risen to popularity over the past twenty years—a span that roughly corresponds with the surge of longer-form versified approaches to Simone Weil. Verse biographies, which can range from single poems to full collections, are in many ways like traditional prose biographies: "Like all biographers, verse biographers must make selections, portray character, and construct a narrative; must balance aesthetic considerations with considerations of accuracy and completeness; must decide on how much interpretation to offer, what sort of transitions are necessary, what structure best organizes the material. Like all biographers, too, the verse biographer is inevitably involved, more or less deliberately and consciously, with the representation of self." At the same time, verse biographies also uniquely involve "interesting points of tension between the demands of biography as a genre and poetry as a form," and, following the lyric tradition, they are often written in first person, a much less common phenomenon with prose biographies that raises its own questions of representation and verisimilitude. Another consequence of the poetic form is that verse biographies tend to be significantly shorter than prose biographies.[7] Perhaps an even more striking difference is that of source material: prose biographers tend to rely on archives and, when history allows, interview, whereas verse biographers tend to draw primarily on the published prose biographies and perhaps published letters. In the case of anglophone verse biographers of Weil, this tendency is likely further motivated by the fact that the Weil archives are in French, adding the complication of language to the question of accessible materials. At the same time, many of these archival materials—letters and journals, for example—have been translated and published in English, in a sense making much of the archive available to the anglophone reading public. In the case of the six Weil verse biographies I discuss in this chapter, all but one cite sources in introductions, afterwords, or notes. The vast majority of these sources are written in or translated into English, although Anne Carson appears to have worked with *Gravity and Grace* in French. Indeed, *Gravity and Grace* is the most often cited, with four references among the six poets. Simone Pétrement's biography is cited three times, as is the *Simone Weil Reader*. Other than that, however, the poets cite a notably wide array of *different* biographies and edited collections of Weil's work, suggesting a dizzying array of different paths to reading—and then writing—Weil. And none of the poets cites earlier verse biographies: there is no clearly intentional conversation to trace among them.

This preponderance of poetry sequences devoted to Simone Weil raises a series of questions: Why are so many poets drawn to write about Weil? And why are they drawn to memorialize her life in verse when so many prose biographies already exist? As I note in this book's introduction, at least a dozen prose biographies of Weil have been published in English, from memoirs of her close associates to later tomes drawing on interviews and extensive archival work. What are the poems meant to do that the extant prose biographies cannot do?

In part, I think, these poetry sequences participate in what Jessica Wilkinson characterizes as a "sense of feminist urgency" that impels poets to versify the lives of earlier women.[8] As Carolyn G. Heilbrun articulates in her classic *Writing a Woman's Life* (1988), the late twentieth-century outpouring of life writing by about women seeks to undo the long-held assumption that "anonymity . . . is the proper condition of woman."[9] Many of the poets who versify Weil seem to participate in this project of reclamation, joining Helen Rickerby in "revisioning the lives of women" in part because like her they are "looking for heroines and role models of my own gender."[10]

But what is it about Weil, in particular, that provokes such an abundance of lyric afterlives? And what are the risks and benefits of enlivening her through verse? In this chapter, I read the sequences and books chronologically, tracing patterns and distinctions among the poetic renderings of Weil. I find in these poems, as I find to varying degrees in Rich's more diffuse poetic treatment of Weil, in Dillard's nonfiction, and in Gordon's fiction, an attraction to Weil's moral seriousness, a wrestling with her religiosity and self-sacrifice, and an enactment of her ethics of attention, turned back on Weil herself, that manifests both the challenge and the possibilities of the creativity involved in attending to a suffering other: again, the tension between creation and decreation, between Weil's multiply distant self and the self one can grant a historical figure through imaginative verse.

These texts also participate in other themes and tensions highlighted by Carson's essay, including a propensity to address shared interwoven motifs of hunger, spirituality, love, and sexuality; to situate Weil among other thinkers, depathologizing her by demonstrating how her evident extremes participate in traditions of thought and practice; and to metatextually and sometimes self-referentially struggle with the question of how "we"—poets and readers—approach Weil. In focusing on these six longer-form poetic engagements with Weil, this chapter considers her continuing importance to poets and the drive to memorialize and grapple with her life and thought in lyric form, especially given the challenges of knowing a historical figure through textual figurations in the context of shifting ideals around gender, embodiment, religion, and love. This comparative reading ultimately recognizes a shared mournful tenderness in the poets' approaches, a passion to introduce Weil to new communities of readers, and a desire to correct the biographical record, in part through insisting on a respect that refuses hagiography but instead embraces imperfection, ambiguity, and paradox in ways uniquely possible in the distinctive form of poetry.

"WHO SEES YOU?" MAGGIE HELWIG'S "HUNGER AND THE WATCHMAN: FOR SIMONE WEIL"

Maggie Helwig's book *Talking Prophet Blues* consists of three sections: the first, titled "Hunger and the Watchman: For Simone Weil," is a thirteen-page lyric sequence. The second is a longer homage to the renowned Canadian pianist Glenn Gould, and the third section, which shares the book's title, ends the collection with another thirteen pages of lyrics devoted to the early church fathers. These latter two sections suggest a community in which to understand Weil, one characterized by aesthetic, bodily, and spiritual intensities. Unlike many of the poems in the latter two sections, the pieces making up the Weil sequence are untitled.

These poems open in London, where Simone Weil spent the last months of her life in 1943, with occasional flashbacks and recollections of earlier experiences from childhood and adulthood, including the Spanish Civil War, the factory and farm work, and Trotsky's visit to the Weil family. The poems are threaded through with Weil's keywords: necessity, attention, waiting. Like many of the other poets who take up Weil's life, Helwig threads together themes of hunger, love, and faith—a threading that follows Weil herself. At points Helwig quotes small sections from Weil's writing without citation; indeed, she's the only poet of the six I discuss in this chapter who includes no paratextual material like foreword or endnotes to name her sources, but the poems clearly derive from familiarity with both Weil's writings—*Waiting for God* and the *First and Last Notebooks*, at least—and biographies.

Helwig participates in the decreation-creation paradox—and metatextual commentary thereon—in part through a heady blend of pronouns: the initial poems address a "you" walking through London, flâneur- or flâneuse-like, that may be an imagined author-persona or may be Weil, which seems most likely by the sequence's second page, which describes this "you" as "coughing," "too pale and far too thin, living/on cigarettes and headaches."[11] The next poem introduces a first-person plural "we" who "weep for you" (11), suggesting an audience of compassionate observers—perhaps the speaker and readers—who sorrow for the Weil figure, with her headaches and passion for Greek tragedy. In a sense, Helwig dramatizes one of the rhetorical functions of all the poetry sequences about Weil, which is to invite a broader range of readers who attend to Weil. The pronouns complexify still further in the next poem, which moves stanza by stanza from naming "you" in Portugal, the site of Weil's first mystical experience, to "we," to an "I" who seems to be Weil, describing the women in Portugal singing their hymn. The first-person persists in the following poems as Weil's apparent voice addressing a "you," at points more poetically and at others quite conversationally, with some sections in prose. Near the end, the poet persona interjects in a first-person poem wholly bracketed by parentheses, locating herself "in a Toronto restaurant, crying, Simone, Simone" (16). The self-representation of the speaker's (or author-persona's) mourning offers explicit metatextual commentary on the relationship between creator and Simone, whom she casts (without using the word "affliction") as a suffering, starved, and lonely one in need of compassionate attention in a direct, if implicit, application of Weil's own theory of attention and the obligation to attend to those who suffer. The remaining poems shift back into the Weil character's first-person voice, describing love and hunger, before ending on a poem that again borrows the "I" for the poet persona and addresses "Small one, Simone-Adolphine" in her death.

One result of these shifting pronouns—"I" as both author and subject, "we" encompassing author and readers, "you" as "Simone" and also perhaps a more general "one" at points—is a performance of the instability of characterization that marks all biographies but is perhaps heightened by the generic flexibilities of a collection of poems. If "I" is both the author-persona and also the imagined Weil, rendered in the condensed language of lyric, neither "I" can be a natural, straightforward mimesis. The form itself reminds readers that the voice of Weil is a literary fabulation. Further, the poet persona's "I" and "we" stage the act of watching this Weil, even as she watches others. The opening poem thematizes this trouble of watching as it represents the "you" wandering alone through London's cold streets, seeking to "see / a thing entirely," to "see / a man entirely." The first section of the first poem seems to describe Weil's decreative theory when it ends, "If someone asks your name, you can only say / here is the point I watch at" (9). The idea of attending to another as a self-erasure that brings the other into being is at once a spiritual ideal, an ethical ideal, and an aesthetic ideal. As Weil writes in her notebooks, "A painter doesn't draw the place where he himself is. But looking at his painting, I know his position in relation to the things he has drawn. On the contrary, if he represents himself in his painting, I know with certainty that the place he shows himself to be isn't the one where he is."[12] Helwig imagines Weil refusing to give her name as a marker of her presence and identity, instead pointing to her self-absenting function as a watcher, what Weil elsewhere describes as her role as an "intermediary."[13] But although Helwig is also a "watchman" of sorts, watching Weil and constructing a community of readerly watchers through the occasional "we," the Weil figure's watching is profoundly lonely, the line between necessity-as-responsibility and unhealthy compulsion very fine indeed, her death predicted in the very first poem.

Yet while "Hunger and the Watchman: For Simone Weil" watches this Weil character with sorrow for her many hungers and impending death, the sequence also participates in the strategy of several Weil poetic sequences—and some biographies and scholarly works—of situating her within a discourse within which she did not situate herself, thereby demonstrating that her proclivities are neither entirely unique nor entirely pathological. In addition to the book's larger-scale company of Gould and the Desert Fathers, Helwig's sequence is rich with intertexts and allusions: to Achilles, to the book of Isaiah, to Gerard Manley Hopkins, to Christina Rosetti's *Goblin Market*, perhaps even to Stevie Nicks. Against a reading of Weil that renders her solitary in her asceticism, whether this solitude is taken as saintly exceptionalism or lamentable sickness, understanding her within a discursive context renders her more extreme hungers part of a broader conversation. So, for example, the line "Eat me, drink me, eat me," which arrives at the end of a prose-poem section in Helwig's poem given over to contemplation of hunger for food, for love, and for God, echoes Rosetti's *Goblin Market* and its line "Eat me, drink me, love me."[14] The line is spoken by a character, Lizzie, who has sacrificed herself to save her sister Laura from a highly allegorical illness brought on by her giving into the temptation to eat "goblin men's" forbidden fruits. Lizzie is an obviously Christic figure, Eucharistic in her decision to risk the goblin men's abuse so that she might return to her sister covered in the fruit they have pressed on her, bearing on her body the antidote to her sister's ailment. Christ is a shared model for both Rossetti and Weil, but Rosetti's poem opens still further into implications about other kinds of gendered and sensual hungers as well as the kind of love and care made possible by a refusal to eat. The Rossetti allusion, just one line long, reminds readers that Weil is by no means unique in her approach to hunger, to self-denial, and to sensual pleasure more generally. She participates in a complicated and storied tradition.

These associations are complicated still further by the next poem's layering of the horrifying hunger of concentration camps atop the "Jewish girl in London, the French child / far away from home, coughing / staring through windows, skinny, exhausted, unknowing" and still further "the world's death body" (18). The poem's abrupt shifts in perspective and startling juxtapositions trace connections among Simone Weil's emaciating hunger, both embodied and relational, and the world's immense sufferings. The images contribute to a picture of Weil as suffering and lonely but far from unique, a picture still further corroborated by another of the sequence's uncanny intertexts, Franz Kafka's short story "A Hunger Artist" (1922).[15] In addition to bearing striking similarities to Weil's life, the story also includes three watchmen in its limited cast of characters, a resonance highlighted by Helwig's title and her repeated use of the word "watchmen." In Kafka's story, the hunger artist is a caged performer whose long fasts audiences love to witness. His trouble is not the caged fasting but the fact that he wishes to fast longer than the imposed forty-day limit. Three watchmen, often butchers, are tasked with observing the hunger artist to guarantee he never breaks his fast during its forty-day period, but even the watchmen themselves do not believe he doesn't secretly eat sometimes.

After a time, the European societies lose interest in the hunger artist, and he is relegated to a zoo and forgotten, allowed to fast beyond the forty-day limit. But few attend to him, and the staff ceases to keep track of his fast's duration, diminishing its pleasure. At long last they realize they have forgotten him where he lies dying in the straw at the cage's bottom. He confesses to the zoo supervisor, asking forgiveness and admitting that he wanted admiration but didn't deserve it: the fast had been not a burden but a necessity because no food tasted good. It had been no real deprivation to refuse what he did not desire. The hunger artist ultimately dies of starvation and is buried with his soiled straw, then replaced in the cage by a prowling panther.

The story's resonances with Weil's life are difficult to miss: her lifelong self-restrictions, the prevalence of hunger and eating as metaphors throughout her writing, and, of course, her death suggest strong parallels with Kafka's hunger artist. So does Weil's commitment to attention to sufferers and theorizing about how difficult it is for observers to really pay attention to a hungry person. Helwig amplifies these resonances with repeated descriptions of Weil as "too pale and far too thin" (10). The prose section describing Weil's factory work in first-person is interrupted abruptly by the line "The question of food remains a difficult one" (15), just one of many instances of food and hunger's insistent presence throughout the poems. The penultimate poem, voiced by an imagined Weil at the end of her life, likewise echoes the hunger artist's end-of-life confession: "I have attained a degree of detachment, but it is a result of exhaustion and is a purely biological process. As such, it has no value." The piece ends, "I should very much like to eat a piece of chocolate, but one must not, of course, be absurd" (20). This is the question: Is Weil's self-diminishment valid as a mode of self-sacrifice, of spiritual or aesthetic practice, if it is motivated by illness rather than a free choice?

The resonances also extend to the figure of the watchman in Helwig's poem, from its title to its first poem's thematizing of sight and watching. To the "you" who walks through London's streets feeling the necessity of attending to others for the sake of their "salvation," lonely, emaciated, and in pain, a watchman of sorts, the poet persona asks, "Who sees you as you walk / the geometric streets?" (9). The "we" Helwig constructs watch Weil not with admiration but with compassion: "we weep for you" (11). The poet persona's parenthetical poem, interrupting the sequence just past its halfway point, similarly constructs herself as "crying" for "Simone, Simone" (16). This watching threatens to shade into condescending pity, but the poems' ambiguities complicate such a stance. The poet persona sitting in Toronto, mourning "Simone, Simone," describes her life not as "poetry" but as "the demon Hunger," mourning her "torture." Yet she also admits that "Here now, we are dying / of needing each other," an apparent embrace of Weil's own claims about the importance of human responsibility for each other. Whether the "we" who are "dying / of needing each other" is general contemporary society or Helwig and Weil—Helwig in need of Weil's insights, Weil in need of Helwig's saving attention—Helwig honors Weil's wisdom while bearing witness to her pain. This "we" as poet persona and imagined Weil arises again in the sequence's final poem, which imagines Weil's grave and ends with a figuration of mutual gift and need: "Sister, I give you what I can. / Pray for me, sister" (21). After the evident gift of watching, manifested as a poetic rendering not just of Weil's glory but of her pain, the poet persona asks, in turn, for Weil's own attention in the form of beyond-the-grave prayer. Calling her "sister" implies a gendered intimacy; asking for her prayer perhaps surprisingly returns us to the realm of sainthood and religiosity the rest of the sequence seems to resist, ending the sequence with a postsecular openness to faith that the previous pages have mostly refused and offering a link to the later sequence on the Desert Fathers.

Weil emerges in Helwig's elegiac vision as a tragic victim of her own unsatisfied hungers: not a triumphant saint or a genius of ethics or politics but a mourned absence, a "small one," a "sister," a "beautiful child." The poems' allusive fragments of her biography and ideas present Weil as lonely and longed-for, as elusive as the poems themselves. The poet-speaker's task is to enact Weil's own ethics of attentive compassion upon her, in some sense creating "that which does not yet exist" by representing the very act of noticing her vulnerability and pain.[16]

"COME TO HER / YOURSELF": STEPHANIE STRICKLAND'S *THE RED VIRGIN: A POEM OF SIMONE WEIL*

Stephanie Strickland's *The Red Virgin: A Poem of Simone Weil*, published four years later in 1993, at points echoes Helwig's elusive style while offering a more robust biographical and textual picture. Strickland's book offers an introductory note naming several primary and secondary sources on Weil and a two-page chronology of her life before moving into its forty-nine lyric poems, which are arranged in rough alphabetical order by title. The poems are a blend of insistently self-aware musing on the problems of approaching Weil, quotations and paraphrases of Weil's writing (all italicized), and attributed quotations from others, including Simone de Beauvoir, Weil's brother André,

Gertrude Stein, and Gustave Thibon. The result is a sense of documentary collage with an overlay of the poet persona's soul searching.

Strickland explains her motivation for this approach in an interview with Devin Becker in 2014: "When I was first reading Simone Weil I was very upset about the way people responded to her, because either they couldn't stand her religious side or they couldn't stand her political side. . . . No one would see her as like one person—that one person could have these sides, and she could come from that."[17] Strickland goes on to explain that she found some writing about Weil "unbearably reductionist" and decided that in her own approach, she would correct others' "polarized assessment" by including "lots of materials," "documentary materials," and Weil's "own language." This commitment clarifies not just Strickland's strategy, which follows the collage-like modern biographical practice scholars often trace to James Boswell's *Life of Samuel Johnson*, but also an impetus evident in many of the Weil verse biographies, which through both content and form complicate the oversimplifications of not just earlier prose biographies but also scholarly conversations about Weil.

Strickland's collection begins and ends with Weil's italicized words in two untitled poems that stand outside the alphabetized pieces. The first begins with Weil's commentary on the joy and pain of different cultures' poems and the acts of communication and love. The poem's second half shifts out of italics after a stanza break into the voice of the poet persona:

This is how she talks, too focal, too close
to the tension in her thought. I would descend
lower still, bring her near me, gossip
about her, paraphrase. If I distort,
I don't abandon.
    Come to her
yourself: we each build our own scaffold.[18]

This initial poem sets up the tensions and themes in the book's approach: first, in its ostensible documentary quotation of Weil's own voice, and then in its poet persona's commentary, which places some distance between the two. The speaker triangulates between her own perspective, Weil, and the "you" explicitly addressed and invited in the poem's last line, offering not just an introduction to Weil's verbal style ("This is how she talks") but also a judgment of it ("too focal, too close/to the tension"). The poem introduces the collection with a sense that the poet persona is no blithe admirer or hagiographer, but one critically engaged with Weil's work and life. The phrase "I would descend/lower still," though, shows the degree to which the speaker is willing to engage: not just at a critical distance, but, borrowing Weil's own vocabulary of the mind's descent from the poem's first half—"*the mind becoming relaxed/descends a little, from its greatest/concentration*" (3)—shows Weil's influence and interpolation into the poet's language: the poet persona learns from Weil, even as she questions. Still, this descent may be of a different sort than the attentive openness to which Weil refers: the speaker's "I would," which is perhaps conditional or perhaps an expression of desire, suggests the "lowness" of nearness, gossip, paraphrase, all of which stand in tension with Weil's own exacting moral code, particularly her sense of friendship as distance.

The speaker's self-awareness continues with the reference to distortion. This claim, which I read as an admission that any book's engagement with Weil carries an inevitable risk of imaginative misleading, is further complicated by the fact that the poem's first six lines, italicized to indicate Weil's voice, are in fact not quotation but paraphrase.[19] To be fair, Strickland indicates clearly in the introductory note that italics signal "Weil's actual or paraphrased remarks" (ix). The author never explains why, given her commitment to attribute every other quoted source, she does not differentiate between Weil's actual and paraphrased words or name the sources of Weil's words. The result is disorientation, an uneasy uncertainty about how the poet's power to paraphrase functions in the text. Unless one traces down the source texts—a challenge even in a digital age, given Weil's voluminous notebooks and the posthumous edits, selections, and remixes—one is never quite certain whether one is reading Weil's own words or Strickland's rearrangement of those words or what difference such rearrangements might make. And while the other poets I discuss in this chapter write imaginatively in Weil's voice, Strickland's use of italics for both quotations and paraphrases—as apart from her own, nonitalicized poems in Weil's imagined voice—further complicates the distinction.

The result is twofold: not just a disorienting uncertainty about which of Weil's italicized words are actually her own sentences but also an implicit commentary on the inevitable power of the poet. For even if Strickland exclusively italicized direct quotations, problems of authorial interpretation would still arise: questions of inclusion and exclusion, organization, perspective, and the meanings that develop through juxtaposition, not to mention the looming instability of translation. Rather than burying these tensions, Strickland's first poem amplifies them, noting that the solution to the risk of the poet's inevitable distortion is for the reader to "Come to her/yourself" (3). In this sense, perhaps the blurred distinction between quotation and paraphrases is a further provocation for readers to seek out the original sources, to "build [their] own scaffold."

The poems that follow craft a biographical sketch, although they are frequently interrupted by metatextual commentary along the lines of the untitled prefatory poem. So "Absent from Dances, 1925," which describes Weil's "awkward" personal appearance at sixteen and quotes (or paraphrases) her despair at fourteen when she compared herself to her brother's mathematical genius (5) is followed by "Agent," a meditation on Weil's first and last names, both the gender tension in her propensity to sign her letters home "Simon" and the pronunciation of "Weil," with its "oversound of woe" (6). The next poem, "At Home," returns to Weil's childhood, with italicized sections about pain and family trees (7–8), and the following, "Bench-Hand: 'The Famous "Real Life,"'" imagines Weil's later factory experience and her resulting reflections on labor (9–11). The poems proceed in this manner, jumping around chronologically and thematically, with occasional interruptions from secondary sources, like Simone de Beauvoir's recollections of Weil in "De Beauvoir, from *Memoirs of a Dutiful Daughter*" (12) and quotations from André Weil's interview about his sister, printed in *Gateway to God*, in a poem titled "Consent" (21–22). The found nature of these fragments, and their apparent submission to the order of alphabetized titles, again belies their provocative juxtapositions.

Weil emerges from the collection as a complicated figure with nuanced ideas. Strickland's interactions with Weil's biography and thought are wide-ranging: true to her interest in disrupting others' "unbearably reductionist" and "polarized" approaches to Weil, Strickland shies away from neither the political nor the religious aspects of Weil's life and thought. The tone throughout follows the prefatory poem's willingness to critique, yet the sustained engagement—indeed, the *attention*—also manifests Strickland's respect and even admiration for her subject.

Against those who favor Weil's religious turn over her politics, Strickland writes insistently about her experiences of industrial and farm labor and political philosophy, in poems like "Airdrill" (14), "Dignity" (25), and "Revolution: Simone at 27" (57). In "On the Wireless" (52), she goes so far as to name Weil's insistent anticolonialism, a core tenet in *The Need for Roots* and even *Waiting for God* that commentators have been surprisingly slow to discuss, a dynamic I reflect on in my conclusion. Yet Strickland also shines light on Weil's attraction to Christianity in poems like "Excused for Illness" (26), "How Imperatives Enter the Body" (34), and "Revelation" (55).

These poems tend to emphasize Weil's status "on the threshold" of
the Roman Catholic Church as Strickland puts it, borrowing from
Weil, in "Past Centuries" (53) more than, say, her cruciform theology
and ethics, and to read Weil's interaction with the faith tradition as
one more experience of rejection, as in the depiction of her conversation with Father Perrin in "Comic Progression" (18). But while they
don't go in depth into Weil's turn to Christianity, they take this turn
seriously.

Similarly, the poems address Weil's Jewishness—and notorious
anti-Jewishness—with sensitivity and nuance. With characteristic
concern for how observers and commentators have seen and treated
Weil, several of these poems highlight the degree to which her rejected
Jewishness nevertheless colored how she was perceived. For example,
in "Gustave Thibon, *How Simone Weil Appeared to Me*," the poetically rendered Thibon attributes Weil's "hardness to her racial
origin—// she was, indeed, the daughter of that People / whom the
prophets sought to unbend" (29). But he goes on to attribute "her passionate anti-/ Semitism" to this very racial typing. Similarly, the
poem "How Imperatives Enter the Body" describes the priest who
comes to Weil in the English hospital as "annoyed" by her thought
as both "too 'feminine'" and "too 'Judaic'" (34), echoing Jacques
Cabaud's biographical account.[20] "Interview with André Weil, 1973"
quotes a BBC interviewer opining that Weil's "deep respect for learning and education" was "something of a Jewish trait" and quotes
Weil's brother's insistence that their parents would have "disliked it
entirely" had his sister been baptized into Christianity in her youth
(37). Yet André also notes the degree to which their shared childhood
deemphasized their Jewishness. The following poem, "Jews," provocatively rereads the quoted interview through juxtaposition—one of
Strickland's organizational strategies—quoting or paraphrasing
Weil's assessment of "*Them*" as

that people held together
by a terrible violence,

by massacres
they carried out—
those, inflicted on them. (38)

Strickland here highlights Weil's sense of Jewish people as both *harming* and *harmed*, tracing the internalized dissonance into Weil's own person:

she indicts *them*,
pushing *her* food away,
blocking *her* baptism. (38)

Echoing novelist Michelle Cliff's and biographer Robert Coles's assessments of Weil's internalized anti-Semitism, the poem suggests that Weil's critique of her own people manifested most powerfully in her self-diminishments. Yet the next poem, "Justice," complicates this reading still further by representing with frank respect Weil's philosophical ideal of justice as a divestment of power, another lens through which Weil's refusal to allow herself both food and baptism could be read (39). The condensed nature of poetry, including the myriad juxtapositions, allusions, and multiple meanings it allows in a short space, illuminates the tangled complexities of Weil's relation to Judaism in a way prose discussions of the topic have struggled to adequately express.

Later, the poem "Revelation" notes Weil's critique of the Old Testament's "sanctioned/genocide" as parallel to the "Inquisition" (55), and the poem "Unregarded Source" returns to this theme, relating her friend Maurice Schumann's recollection of a conversation about her concern with Old Testament records of God's mandated "geno-cide" (63) in the destruction of the Canaanites after the Exodus, for example. "They had not heard of the concentration/camps, yet, Schumann said": the poem ends with Weil's haunting question, "*How can we/condemn a holocaust, today*" . . . "*if we do not// condemn all holo-causts in the past?*" (64). The collection's whole engagement with Weil's critique of Judaism follows this paradigm of honesty about her troubling outlook paired with complicating contexts in a way that complements Mary Gordon's approach in *Simone Weil in New York.*

On the subjects of gender, relationships, and food, the poems con-sistently manage to present the tensions—Weil's signing a boy's name, her apparent blocking of her own beauty, the cultural and familial pressures of femininity, her refusal to eat, her dislike of being touched, her death—without pathologizing or fetishizing them. The poems often implicitly interpret Weil's famous aversions to touch, food, and femininity in terms of cultural pressures, as in "Letters from Mme. Weil to Mlle. Chaintreuil, André's Tutor," in which Weil's mother admits to "esteem[ing] boys much more" (41), or the follow-ing poem, "Love Affair, Fourth Century," which repeats the ques-tion "Is sex debasing?" in a three-page conversation with the Desert Fathers. The poem concludes by adding *Simone* to their number, admitting, "Sex is/debasing—they are not wrong/about this" spe-cifically when "women/are subordinate" (44). The problem, in other words, is not about a universal spiritual law—matter versus spirit—but the degradation that arises from social inequity, recalling Weil's position, scandalously taught to schoolgirls, that the French institu-tion of marriage was legalized prostitution.[21]

Strickland takes a similar approach in numerous poems devoted less to Weil's biography or person than to her ideas: unafraid to chal-lenge the philosophical concepts, these poems also accord them the frank respect of careful attention. "Defilement," for example, draws a metaphoric parallel between the transition of "Ice to water, to steam" and the transition from "hurt" to "*affliction*" (23). This poem, as do others in the collection that focus on Weil's ideas, suggests a speaker that may be Weil (in a voice imagined rather than quoted or paraphrased, as the poem is not italicized) or a sympathetic commentator. These poems offer strikingly poetic explications of Weil's concepts. "Defilement" ends with questions:

> *Why*
> of all things in the world is affliction
> given power
> —to eat
> into souls? To possess them? (24)

This question resonates more with the voice of the poetic persona than the historical Simone Weil, whose commitment to accepting "necessity" typically precluded such questioning. The poem also emphasizes its implicit conversation with other poems in the collection through the telling enjambment in the short lines: the break between "to eat" and "into souls" resonates with other poems' concern with literal food and eating. In this way, Strickland's poem joins other poets' work in echoing Weil's own overdetermined use of the figures of food and hunger, which stand for friendship, love, injustice, and divine communion.

"Necessity" is another of the powerful "idea" poems in the collection, a spare lyric meditation on the sea, beauty, and the obedience of a boat wholly submitted to "infinitesimal pressure of wind, water, light" and thereby moving those who watch it with its beauty (49). The poem, again, explicates Weil's difficult concept of necessity, of the good of obedience to what *is* as superior to particular divine interventions, and in explicating the concept with such control and poetic loveliness in a sense advocates for this view. It is a stark contrast to Annie Dillard's bewilderment at how the absence of divine mercy here below could in fact evince divine mercy; instead of a confrontation, this poem functions as an apologia.

But grappling persists throughout the collection, particularly in the poems that offer metatextual commentary on the act of attending to, interpreting, and writing about Simone Weil. One such poem is "How You Are Withheld from Me," in which Strickland pictures Weil "raised / on some banner," known through textual scraps, "Coming to me / soured, brought by the distaste / you cause some man or woman" (35). Here as elsewhere in the collection, Strickland emphasizes the degree to which Weil's presence to contemporary readers relies on others' observations and opinions—and the frequency with which these observations and opinions are partial at best, supremely prejudiced at worst. The implication, of course, is that Strickland here seeks to do something like justice to Weil through the form of poetry. Yet the poem sources Weil's withholding not just in others' approaches but also in Weil's own lack of self-awareness at points ("no one // saw what you were doing, not even / you") as well as her secretiveness and chosen silences (35). In the poem "Mathematics: Galois," Strickland similarly explores Weil's hiddenness in one of her pseudonyms and reacts strongly to the persistent dialectical thinking throughout Weil's work and life: "well, I'm tired / of contradiction, tired of riddling, / Simone" (45). The poet persona's casually phrased frustration, however, stands in tension with the collection's commitment to naming the philosopher's many contradictions. Like the prefatory poem, "Mathematics: Galois" highlights the degree to which the poet persona can both admiringly engage with Weil's life and work and also admit bewilderment and frustration. "Xmas Pudding," the collection's last titled poem, ends with a similar sentiment: meditating on Weil's death and her last notebook entries, which addressed both food and teaching, the poem ends with a section of Weil's italicized voice and then a response:

Bearing my scrutiny
First. My adoration. And then
To withdraw . . .

she said of God.
It was also true of André.
True of us all. *(73–74)*

Here Strickland employs strategies she has used throughout, not just the quotation or paraphrase followed by the poet persona's meditation, but also the widening of the application—and indictment—to a general "we." Weil might have claimed God withdrew from her after her scrutiny and adoration, the speaker insists, but so did her brother, and so do we. Like the many rejections documented throughout the collection, we readers participate in withdrawal from Simone Weil: in refusing to join her on the bridge too far of her thought and life; in failing to understand her fully; and finally in closing the book and setting it aside. We cannot perpetually attend.

The final untitled poem, all italicized save the opening "She said," speaks to the "*silence/of God*—" and ends on the collection on the word "*silence.*" It is at once a fitting conclusion to a haunting documentation of Weil's complexity and also arguably a misnomer, for the book's indexical form—much like the organization of so much of Weil's writing in books like *Gravity and Grace* and *Gateway to God*—invites a reading and rereading that picks up anywhere in the middle and disrupts linear or chronological modes of reading and understanding. The *silence* at the end does not suggest a final disengagement. It does, however, highlight the mystery of a Weil who, even in a thick collage of her own quoted words, others' observations, and a poet's imaginary construction of her voice, still somehow, inevitably, escapes our attempts to "come to her."

"EDIT OURSELVES / OUT OF THE PICTURE": KATE DANIELS'S "THE TESTIMONY OF SIMONE WEIL"

Kate Daniels's *Four Testimonies* (1998) is threaded through with Weil: the first section, twenty pages long, is titled "The Testimony of Simone Weil," but the following three sections—which give voice to imagined victims of a bridge collapse, the mother of a daughter whose abusive husband has died by suicide, and the experiences of a young poet mother—are all preceded by epigraphs from Weil's writing. Daniels's epigraph for the initial Weil sequence draws a sort of implicit connection to Strickland's work in that it quotes Weil's statement about "the silence of God" that Strickland turns into her collection's final found poem.

Yet Daniels and Strickland sharply diverge in their poetic approach to Weil: in contrast to Strickland's unremitting complexity, documentary collage, and metatextual commentary on the challenge of approaching and representing Weil, Daniels eschews distance between poet and subject by composing her entire sequence in Weil's imagined voice. Strikingly, Daniels is also the only poet of the six here who spends no time imagining Weil's death or London hospital bed. But perhaps the most unique feature of the approach to Weil in *Four Testimonies* is Daniels's choice to write Weil through the lens of Weil's imagined responses to another historical figure whose life overlapped with hers in Paris, the photographer Eugène Atget. As Daniels explains in her introductory note, Atget was an "early documentary photographer" committed to preserving "the visual remains of Old Paris and the emergence of the modern city."[22] "His style," she writes, "is noted for its elegant austerity, the eerie absence of human subjects, and extraordinary technical effects," including "extreme lighting conditions" like "shooting directly into the sun." Daniels concludes her introductory note, which offers brief paragraphs on both Atget and Weil, with the frank statement, "There is no evidence that Simone Weil and Eugène Atget ever met" (4). Daniels explains in an interview with Ernest Suarez, however, that studying both Weil and Atget and starting to compose poetry about them brought her to realize "there was some kind of correspondence between their visions, both so characterized by the void, by self-negation, by a kind of austere elegance. Atget's photos image Weil's thought, in a way."[23]

Thus, Daniels's sequence translates Weil's story through Atget's work. The opening poem begins, "I was born in Atget's Paris" (5). Certain resonances emerge as Daniels constructs a Weil persona who insistently turns and returns to Atget's photographs and artistic practice: the dissonances of class privilege in early twentieth-century France; the absence or erasure of humans in Atget's aesthetic and Weil's ethic of decreation; approaches to beauty, pleasure, pain, and sex. These resonances participate in a series of overlapping themes that dominate "The Testimony of Simone Weil," namely, Weil's wrestling with social class, beauty, gender, sexuality, and God. Daniels's approach distinctively layers these concerns, taking a markedly psychoanalytic approach—likely influenced by biographer Robert Coles, whom she names along with Simone Pétrement in the book's endnotes. The result of these strategies is a sequence that relies on Atget as a sort of aesthetic foil, and the combined first-person voice and psychoanalytic angle produce a persistent imagined autoanalysis that offers a distinctive and more obviously fictionalized Weil, given that Daniels occupies her constructed voice to offer aesthetic and psychoanalytic comments Weil herself never made. This is the paradox of the first-person voice in verse biography: it is both more intimate and more inescapably fabricated, an imaginative effort to bring the subject to life that by its very nature implies its distance from the subject occupying her own original space in the world.

The sequence opens with the Weil-persona's description of "Atget's Paris" as a "city of smoke and shadow and mysterious light" in which people "dissimulated themselves" to allow the photographer to capture unpeopled images (5). The imagined Weil describes seeing Atget at work, how "People shoved each other/to the sides of the square until a curious emptiness—/a deep, still hole of angles and light—completely split/the afternoon in two" (6). Daniels's Weil attributes to this experience a revelation about absence, implicitly connecting Atget's photographic practice to her concept of decreation, which is not named here but appears later in the section:

> I saw, then, that we were nothing—or *thought*
> we were nothing—that we would edit ourselves
> out of the picture in favor of art. (6)

This self-erasure is not Weil's ethical ideal but rather an aesthetic practice, a comment on human nature. It is striking that Daniels sources Weil's insight not in her own philosophical process but in her observation of a male photographer.

The first half of the sequence is one long series of recollections, untitled, divided by asterisks. Following this initial meditation on Atget, the Weil speaker goes on to describe her bourgeois childhood, the strong presence of her Papa and Maman filling the house with beautiful objects to which the young Simone objects in solidarity with the impoverished, "those disenfranchised/by Atget's images" (7). Daniels draws on biographical material to construct these recollections of a young Weil eschewing luxury and even food out of concern for "*les misérables*" (8). The next section moves back even further to a "first memory" of breastfeeding. "Perhaps it all began right there," the speaker observes in the poem's first explicit act of autoanalysis, "buried/in my mother's bed, the breast offered/so churlishly and secretly. // The enigma of food was quite severe." The imagined Weil interprets her trouble with food as perhaps arising from her early experiences of nursing and further describes—following textbook articulations of anorexic agency—the "pure emptiness / and order" and "radiance of self-control" that follow not eating (8). The poem next connects not-eating to an Atget image of hard-boiled eggs and to the speaker's initial menstruation, her resistance toward gendered expectations for "a daughter's life," her early "yearn[ing] to be a boy" (9), a secretive childhood observation of her parents engaged in sex (10), and her own sexual awakening and refusal (10–11).

This series of pages reads like a poetic psychoanalytic précis. It leads to the poem's first of many references to the tension between mind and body, as the Weil-persona describes abstracting herself from sexual desire to return to her proper self, "a brain in a school-girl's uniform" (11). This section also voices an imagined revelation—also based on an Atget image—that the "agony of pleasure" and "orgy of pain" evinced in a photographed singing statue could also appear in "a saint," drawing one of the poem's many connections among pain, pleasure, beauty, sex, and faith (11).

The themes continue. Daniels's Weil recalls her delight at the Bolshevik revolution, summarizing her perspective: "The politics of deprivation flourished / in me—an antidote to the opulence / of my privileged life, it mitigated my guilt" (12). Here the speaker's self-assessment reads her philosophical commitment to "deprivation" as political and also deeply personal, given her bourgeois upbringing. This section reads Weil's Leftist politics as a refusal of her background and also a romanticizing of labor as she dreams of "A perfect beauty / in working-class life, an harmonious balance / of body and brain" (12). Again, the Weil figure associates her philosophy with personal longing and Atget's work:

As Atget longed to erase the poor,
I longed to erase *myself* to assume my rightful place
With those unnoticed in the margins of the world (12)

This self-erasure carries with it, here, both a refusal of femininity and a rejection of embodiment:

> Instead, I would think. *Je penserais.*
> Ignore
> > my body
> Become
> > my brain. (13)

These are, of course, not the terms with which the historical Weil wrote about decreation or her experience more generally. Nor are the imagined Weil's insistent interrogations of femininity strictly biographical; they are their author's creation, a poetic interpretation of an inner life to which even Weil's voluminous notebooks do not give full access. This authorial creativity continues in the sequence's extended musings on gender and femininity ("Inside, / full of tenderness as any / woman, soft at the core" [13]) as well as sexuality in the later titled poems "Inventory" (18–20) and "Love" (21). "Inventory" takes stock of all the speaker's possessions, ending with an extended metaphorical meditation on Weil's "sex, / that fragrant, celibate / garden I cultivate for God" (20). "Love," which begins with Weil's characterization *"Decreation: To make something created pass into the uncreated"* from *Gravity and Grace*, translates her mystical experience into a sexual encounter: "It must be this to love / someone, to *faire l'amour* [make love]" (21). Daniels returns to this theme in the later poem "Epiphany 1938," in which the imagined Weil speaks of her mystical experience at Solesmes, "I found God, the son of God, the unimagined man / of my dreams" (23).

This approach to Weil, again, stands in contrast—and tension—with Strickland's indexical documentary sources. In fact, one reviewer of *The Red Virgin*, writing anonymously for *Publishers Weekly*, pans

Strickland's book for precisely this characteristic: "Biographical poetry, if it is to succeed as poetry, must reach beyond mere biography. Poet and subject must merge to express insights that might not be historically documented but are all the more valued for that very reason. Strickland . . . falls short on all counts."[24] If this union of subject and poet is the rubric for success, where Strickland fails, Daniels achieves, although even a quick reading of Strickland's book will recognize "insights" beyond the historical, not just in Strickland's purposeful inclusions and juxtapositions but also in her commentary poems. The reviewer's comment raises broader questions, however: Is there such a thing as "mere biography" to begin with? Can any biographer, poetic or otherwise, be truly objective? In any case, Daniels's consistent first-person approach, which leaves no room for Helwig's interrupting "I" or "we" or Strickland's metatextual commentary on how to approach Weil, paradoxically both performs its own fictionality by admitting Weil may not have known Atget's work and elides the distance between author and subject.

Nevertheless, like Helwig and Strickland before her, Daniels approaches Weil with sensitivity and respect. She minimizes neither Weil's political nor her spiritual concerns. The challenge of "Testimony of Simone Weil" arises not from its poetic interpretation of Weil, which in all cases involves distance from the actual, but, I think, in this combination of fictionalization and first-person. Unlike Mary Gordon, who rewrites Weil time and again in fictional alter-egos living in different lives and places, or imagines the historical Weil from a fictional character's perspective, opening up the safety of distance, Daniels's liberally fictionalized and autoanalyzing Weil threatens to collapse onto her historical self. Rather than the distance Weil advises between those who love, Daniels proceeds with an authorial intimacy that, as Weil warns in her discussions of friendship, threatens to occlude the object of her affection. The irony, of course, is that in making more of Weil than Weil made of herself, supplying what is absent in the record, Daniels in a sense decreates Weil by erasing the historical figure in favor of the fictional one.

Daniels is by no means unaware of these risks. The sequence's final poem, "Dialogue/Epilogue," highlights its own status as an aesthetic object through its form, which stands in contrast to the earlier poems. A series of brief lines run down the left side of the page in plain text, while a series of even briefer, italicized lines, are right-justified, every other line. One can read either side on its own as a sort of list poem, or read the two interspersed as a single voice or as a dialogue, as the title suggests. The poem comments on aesthetics—Atget's and Weil's—and on politics and embodiment, including "the aesthetic desirability of distance" (25). In Weil's writing, distance is desirable not just aesthetically but relationally, in friendship or love a consenting to allow the other to be. She writes in *Gravity and Grace*, "To love purely is to consent to distance, it is to adore the distance between ourselves and that which we love" (58). Yet this distance Weil desires stands in contrast with the impulse—arguably present in Daniels's sequence—"To invade a scene with artistic consciousness" (25). How does one negotiate the degree to which "accepting one's vision"—whether that vision be Atget's, Weil's, or even Daniels's—*"annihilates the self"* (25)? These are the poem's, and the collection's, final lines, a commentary on decreation, which Daniels earlier portrays as both an aesthetic ideal and a troubling aspect of Weil's religious turn, that also reads back onto the entire sequence and its authorial control over the Weil character, the risk of full occlusion. The inevitable question, though, is whether Daniels's approach to Weil is unique in this respect. "Testimony" may prove the most explicit instantiation of this risk, but is this not a risk any poetic imagining of Weil wagers?

"LIFT MY EMPTY ARMS / TO GOD": SARAH KLASSEN'S *SIMONE WEIL: SONGS OF HUNGER AND LOVE*

Sarah Klassen takes up the challenge in part by remaining painstakingly close to the source materials. Her collection *Simone Weil: Songs of Hunger and Love* (1999) comprises forty-two lyric and prose poems devoted to Weil's life, arranged mostly chronologically and exclusively in a first-person imagined voice. The poems are all titled, several of them divided into numbered sections. They rely heavily on Weil's own vocabularies of force, attention, affliction, gravity, and grace, and they seldom stray from the record of Weil's writings and her biographers' accounts. As with Kate Daniels's use of first-person, Klassen's composition in Weil's voice disallows metatextual commentary on the challenges of approaching Weil of the sort Stephanie Strickland and Maggie Helwig engage in. Klassen's own poet persona does not speak for herself. Yet the book's frequent use of an obliquely defined "they" in the poems suggests the Weil character's awareness of how others perceive her, and this strategy accrues throughout the book as a sort of implicit metatextual commentary on the challenge of reading and interpreting the historical Weil.

Klassen's approach is less explicitly feminist in its grappling than many of the other poets who elegize Weil: like Dillard's, it does not impose feminist analysis on Weil's relationship to embodiment, desire, or God. It is also distinctive in its engagement with Weil's religious turn, not just to God but specifically to Christianity, and the cruciformity of her later thought. This approach is signaled even in Klassen's selection of epigraphs: the page before the first section boasts two quotations from Weil, one from the gospel of Matthew, and one from the Stoic philosopher Seneca. The Weil quotations— from *On Science, Necessity, and the Love of God* and *Gravity and Grace*, although these sources are not named—are on the collection's titular themes of hunger and love. Klassen quotes Weil insisting that "we must only wait and call out" into the void "that we are hungry and want bread," and that "in the end we shall be fed."[25] She also quotes the brief claim, "Love is not consolation, it is light" (7). The passage from Matthew interposed between these two statements from Weil is the familiar assurance, "Blessed are those who hunger and thirst for righteousness, for they will be filled" (Matthew 5:6), which confirms Weil's reflections on hunger as linked to the Christian tradition. But the final epigraph quotation from Seneca—"There is no great genius without some touch of madness" (7)—complicates the initial resonances of the first three quotations, its perhaps surprising turn a conclusion that opens the book with a degree of critical distance or dissonance. The suggestion of a "touch of madness" signals to readers that the poet responsible for the poems that follow is not unaware of the difficult challenge of her subject. Again, we see here the strategy of triangulation, in which the poet invites her audience into an implicit "we" who together observe the figure of Simone Weil with at least some critical distance.

The book is divided into three sections—"Hunger," "God exists because I desire him," and "We can only cry out"—suggesting a thematic organization overlying the chronological. The opening poem, "Beginning," continues the book's persistent biblical engagement by starting with an allusion to Genesis 1:1: "In the beginning the world bursts open,/a shimmering opal" (11). The creation narrative persists in the reference to the Luxembourg Gardens, the grass, the sea, the stars, and birds, which will prove another persistent theme throughout the collection. The poem recollects an infancy of union with this creation, in contrast to Weil's later experiences and theories of distance "(What do I know/of distance?)" (11). In this early childhood vision, the world's beauty can be touched and is proof of both "truth" and "love" that precede the verbal realm, signaling yet another theme that will occupy the following poems, of language and its limitations. The poem ends by returning to its creation framework, with an image of the cosmos that reads back onto the epigraphic commentary on love and light:

> The madly spinning
> and expanding universe
> holds for one fragile moment
> only light. (11)

This layering of Weil's infancy with the creation account establishes Weil's life story in cosmological terms at once biblical and evolutionary. It also suggests implicitly that a creator is at work, a subtle reminder of the fact that the Weil who speaks here is made by another.

The next poem, "Hunger I," envisions Weil's early hunger not as arising from a deprivation of "mother-milk" or fatherly provision but rather an inborn "voraciousness" for beauty, both natural and cultural, "a sudden harmony of curved light, an organ chord" (12). Unlike Daniels's psychoanalytic approach to her early life, this poem roots Weil's "unseemly thirst" and "unearthly appetite" not in psychosocial infant development but in the mysterious inner life, nature rather than nurture. Klassen's next poems of childhood do consider context, however: "At the piano" images a Russian grandmother remembering wealth and violence (13), "Eiffel Tower" conveys the formative fear arising from Weil's early surgery (14), and "A reading list" explicates the influence of Weil's early and later reading, her immersion in history, philosophy, and literature (15). The sources listed here—"Stories by Larousse," "Marx," "Descartes," "Sanskrit and Greek," the *Bhagavad-Gita*, Dante and the *Epic of Gilgamesh*, among others—are not just childhood reading but a lifetime of influences, and the poem characteristically renders Weil's reading in terms of hunger. "Refusing food I consumed tragedy / and comedy," the speaker admits, the enjambed line complicating tragedy's initial weight. The conceit carries through the language: the speaker "sampled," "tasted," "became/sated," "craved," but all in relation to books, not food. Against the austerity of her refusal of food—which, again, in contrast to other approaches is never discussed in the book in terms of anorexia—Weil's imagined voice here admits to being a "glutton" for literature, from "the Iliad" and "Plato" to "the hard gospel/stories" (15).

"A reading list" also offers the collection's first engagement with the problem of Weil's anti-Judaism, echoing Strickland's honesty on this challenge, explaining her parallel distaste for the violence of "*the Romans*" and the "Hebrew scriptures" as an influence of her reading (15). The later poem "Jew" also addresses this tension and reads as a sort of self-justification, though one Weil herself would never have voiced. The poem opens with and repeats the phrase, "It wasn't fear" to explain why the speaker chose to "refuse/absolutely to let anyone accuse me/of Jewishness" (41). She goes on to detail family connections to Judaism—"one grandfather/sometimes entered the synagogue" and "one grandmother may have/kept a kosher kitchen"— but insists on her parents' secularism, their "cured ham," "Pascal and Racine." The speaker points out that she openly criticized Hitler and sought truth, ultimately sourcing her critique of Judaism not in fear or internalized anti-Semitism but in her unflinching rejection of oppression:

How could anyone claim the murderous God
who commanded armies to slaughter
his own warm creation
fathered Jesus who was betrayed, nailed
innocent to a Roman cross? (41)

The imagined Weil concludes by rejecting the title of "betrayer" and insisting she was instead "betrayed" by "their cruel statutes" and "refusal" to let her act out her risky pursuit of justice and truth. Yet the poem ends with an admission, after all this insistence that she was neither afraid nor a betrayer, that she recognizes she has also not been understood: "the sum of my most reasoned logic / served to convince no one / except myself" (41). Again, with Strickland and Gordon, Klassen offers a frank attempt to understand Weil's grave error in her relation to Judaism.

The "they" who reject the Weil persona's desire to "speak out" and even "die" among them in the poem "Jew" seems, on the plainest reading, to be the Jewish community. But given the scope of her life and thwarted attempts at involvement in the French Resistance efforts, also pictured in "Memos to a government in exile" (66–67), the rejecting "they" also suggests a broader reading, "they" as her compatriots in general. And at the widest scale, this unspecified "they" who misunderstand, disallow, and reject the Weil figure can also extend to the community of those who comment on her life and work. This layered "they" functions in several of the collection's poems, suggesting, as I've argued, an implicit commentary throughout the collection on Weil's readers, biographers, and critics. This commentary positions Weil's perspective as manifested in and allied with the poet-creator's project of seeking to do her justice, against these naysayers and misreaders. For example, the prose poem "Adolescence," which comments on both Weil's appearance as she grew older and her headaches, ends with the statement, "They noticed none of this [growing pain], diverted by the turbulent shock of my hair, my spectacles' thick lenses and the poor fit of my overcoat" (17). The most immediately suggested "they," which has no grammatical antecedent in the poem, is Weil's peers. But the emphasis on her hair, glasses, and clothing is also present in much of the posthumous commentary about the historical Weil. The voiced experience of being misunderstood—and of having one's pain unattended to—is both an expression of a lived isolation in adolescence and also a criticism of scholars and biographers hung up on Weil's appearance, an example, I think, of the poet's effort to do justice to Weil in a way the prose biographies haven't always managed.

A similar layered "they" functions in the poems "Character" (24), "Defence" (30–31), "Grief" (77), and "Outside the gate" (79). Like "Jew," these poems deal not just with how Weil was understood in her lifetime but also how she has been interpreted since. In "Character," the Weil persona imagines an old age of mystical cronedom, one in which she becomes rather like Annie Dillard's imagined horrific nun in *Holy the Firm*, with hair hanging "grey and matted / to my shoulders like an ancient unused wedding veil," one about whom an unspecified "they" will "tap their foreheads / wink and motion to me," suggesting they think she's mentally ill (24). "Defence" takes up the question of Weil's sexuality with its opening line, "They said because I wouldn't open my legs / or give my body for pleasure / I wasn't loved by men. They were wrong" (30). The poem goes on to detail the men who loved Weil in various ways, including miners and a priest, again defending against an undefined "they," although of course the choice to defend against this accusation suggests that it's important to prove the speaker *was* loved by men. Klassen's approach here, and throughout the book, is inescapably sensual—the priest "touched my soul everywhere / with the flaming point of his love" (30)—but much less explicitly so than Daniels's poems, and somewhat less invested in interpreting the spiritual as sexual.

In "Grief," the Weil speaker describes how at the end of her life "They've brought me broken beyond mending / into a room silent and pure as a mountain" (77). This "they" is likely her caregivers, but it opens further in the next stanza: "They believe I'm dying of hunger, not knowing / hunger is the kind of grief leaves you sterile / as stone." The hint of commentary here on the dissonance in interpreters' discussions of Weil's death extends in "Outside the gate," which speaks generally of mourners from a voice beyond the grave:

Why do they weep?

They will learn how I fed on light

and became fire. (79)

Again, like "Jew," this poem opens by rejecting certain readings,
in this case of Weil's cause of death: "It wasn't despair or fear/not
lack of nourishment nor lack of consolation" (79). Such an insistence
subverts, to a degree, the suggestion in "Grief" that the speaker's
death was hastened by sorrow; it also contradicts many biographers'
and scholars' assessments of Weil's death, and even her own coroner's
report with its claim that "the deceased did kill and slay herself by
refusing to eat," insisting instead on death as a sort of inevitable necessity,
"Something I had unwillingly foreseen" that overtook her body (79).

The ultimate result of all these references to "they" is, again, a
sense of the book less as elegy than as apologia, a (self)-justification.
The poetic voice speaks mostly simply; the lyrics are lithe rather than
showy. The voice is consistent, threaded through with Weil's vocabulary of attention, affliction, force, gravity, and grace. Its full book
length allows the collection to address a remarkable range of episodes:
Weil's teaching in "Lyrics from a *lycée*" (20–23), her factory and farm
work in "Idealist" (18), "On vacation" (32), and "Making the rate (factory journals)" (33–37), her visit from Trotsky in "Sanctuary" (43), her
time in Spain in "Revolution" (45), her visit with her imprisoned brother
in "Places of abandonment" (55–57), and her trip to the United States in
"Exile" (63–65) before her ultimate return to Europe as depicted in the
final poems. Klassen's research is also evident in her references to
details like Weil's interest in Lawrence of Arabia (as reported by Pétrement) (29, 63), the prologue from her journals in which she writes an
allegorical mystical encounter (referenced in "Credo" [39]), and her so-
called Terrible Prayer alluded to in the poem "Exile" (65).[26]

Like Strickland, Klassen also at points interrupts her poems about
Weil's biography with poems about her thought. Unlike Strickland,

however, Klassen maintains the Weil persona's voice throughout, and so these thought poems are in the form of "*Pensées*": the title and form are used for one poem in each section (25, 51, 68). These are not found poems, unlike some of Strickland's italicized works or, as we shall see, Lorri Nielsen Glenn's "*Trouvées*." Instead, the poems are written in a style that amalgamates Klassen's imaged poetic voice for Weil and Weil's gnomic notebook entries. For example, the first "*Pensées*" poem begins

> Everything is circumscribed.
> The frail body has its constant
> limits and the mind beats
> and beats and beats
> the cruel air earth fire
> and water
> the way the bird beats
> wings against the memory
> of sky (25)

This is not a modified quotation of Weil but an imagined note-book entry that interweaves the historical Weil's themes of body and mind, creation and limits, with the poetry collection's characteristic slim lyric form and recurring images of birds. Birds appear in the second "*Pensées*" poem as well (as they do in both the first and final poems of the collection), suggesting one reason for their suitedness to a book concerned with the desire to both accept and transcend the earth: "Nor can imagination / fill the emptiness, command growth of wings, / defy gravity" (51). This second poem titled "*Pensées*," as well as the third, also takes up the explicit imagery of Christ, echoing Simone Weil's later fascination with the cross in a way most of the other poets who write Weil shy away from. The result is a voice closer to the voice we find in *Waiting for God* or the last notebooks, thick as they are with interrogations of Christianity and suffering, and another reminder of the postsecular range of approaches to faith—and comfort levels with Weil's own religiosity.

Klassen minimizes neither Weil's political nor her religious leanings, joining the chorus of poets keen to correct for the imbalance, but doing so in a way that is particularly resonant with Weil's religious sensibilities. In hewing so close to Weil's own writing, Klassen amplifies some of the through lines in Weil's work that undermine a rejection of either her politics or her turn to Christianity, as when Klassen quotes Weil's claim about factory work that it made her "a slave" (36) and then quotes again Weil's claim to have realized, observing Portuguese fishermen's wives, that Christianity was "the religion for slaves and therefore/I would have to stay" (47). Klassen's integration of Weil's own words highlights the repeated vocabulary, drawing the line between Weil's class politics and her awakening to Christian faith: the two are cut from the same cloth. The poems in which the Weil persona grapples with the historical Weil's difficult theological positions, such as God's "infinite distance" (39), the necessity of waiting (51), and "the severe mercy/of affliction" (60), do not exoticize Weil's difficult religious vision but instead present them with straightforward respect.

Klassen participates in the strategy of situating Weil in company. The prose poem "Pilgrim of the Absolute," which borrows its title from a documentary on Weil in 1973, spends most of its time imagining not Weil but George Orwell, William Carlos Williams, and James Agee, three contemporaries of Weil who, as Robert Coles notes in his biography, also attended to the deprivations of the poor. The poem, which immediately follows the five-page sequence "Making the rate (factory journals)," with its unflinching interrogation of the risks and degradations of factory work, describes how all three of these writers, experiencing their subjects' deprivations, experienced "the collapse of words." "Grief left [Orwell] mute" after Wigan, the speaker observes. Williams learned "the open language of sores, syntax of wounds, the imperative mood of desperate wanting" in his tenement patients' homes to the degree that he "tongued pain." Agee, observing sharecroppers' lives of "constant hunger, unspeakable thirst," was "branded" by "a grammar in his brain fierce as the burning of a factory furnace" (38). In the two paragraphs that follow, Weil's imagined voice comments on her shared experience of "traveling light across dark borders," working in the factory and then coming home to write, comparing all their wounded, wordless attention to the mythical Philoctetes, "staring with incredible despair, speechless, into his empty hands" (38). The poem aligns Weil with a wider tradition of writers seeking out the experiences of those suffering in their (British, American, and French) economic structures. It also highlights the way grief enters a body—not just Weil's—and the way language fails in the wake of such recognitions. This poem situates Weil, one who "wept for the whole world" (78), as part of a tradition, not an aberration.

Weil's weeping for the world, coupled with the hunger for beauty, truth, and God that marks so many of the book's poems, carries through its end, which imagines Weil's death and voice beyond death still suffused with "mystery" (80). This Weil reassures her mourners that she, recalling one of Annie Dillard's favorite stories of the Desert Fathers, "fed on light / and became fire" (79). The final poem, "Dirge," ends not with a statement but a question thick with Weil's favored words:

> Who's there to tell us
> the afflicted (if attentive
> and motionless and mute)
> will catch above time's cruel transience
> above the swallow's flight
> an echo of the absolute? The unmistakable
> breath-taking wingbeat of grace. (80)

Returning to the persistent motif of birds, with their fragility and their flight, the collection's final words wonder who can bear witness to the hope of the absolute, to the hope of grace. The implication is not that Weil can offer this assurance from beyond her death but a reminder of the historical Weil's quoted claim in the book's epigraph that "in the end we shall be fed, and then we shall *know* that there is really bread" (7). Klassen's quietly confident approach to Weil's complexities and hungers resolves, here, in the mystery of the philosopher-mystic's confident words, notwithstanding her "ill-cut body" (79) and its final frailty. For Klassen, the spiritual wisdom persists in the text, even as the text itself proves inadequate and the task of interpreting justly fraught.

"UNDO THIS CREATURE": ANNE CARSON'S "DECREATION (AN OPERA IN THREE PARTS)"

In contrast to the mostly lyric verse form at work among the other poets I discuss in this chapter, which tends toward earnest self-searching and a sincere approach to Weil, the Simone Weil sequence in Anne Carson's collection *Decreation* (2005) takes the form of a philosophical essay followed by a tragicomic opera. In this essay-opera pair, Carson, known for her wide range as a poet, classicist, and translator, situates Weil alongside the Greek poet Sappho and the French mystic Beguine Marguerite Porete, crafting yet another tradition for Weil of women writers and seekers. Like Klassen's list of Orwell, Williams, and Agee, Daniels's comparisons with Atget, Strickland's appeal to the Desert Fathers, and Helwig's frequent literary allusions, Carson's choice to read Weil alongside others rejects the frequent treatment of her as a one-off eccentric. Her exuberantly creative approach in the form of operatic verse similarly joins the earlier poets in seeking to find a different angle of approach to Weil's perplexities than the prose biographies' conventional narratives.

The tripartite essay and opera in which Weil features arrive 154 pages into a book full of personal and topical poems and essays that address subjects as diverse as the speaker's mother, Samuel Beckett, sleep, ekphrastic meditations, and a sequence on "Gnosticisms." The forms include not just lyric and essay but also an oratorio, screenplay, and documentary. Within this cacophonous variety, "Decreation: How Women like Sappho, Marguerite Porete and Simone Weil Tell God" takes its place. In both this essay and the opera that follows, Carson divides her subjects into parts: part 1 of the essay establishes its attention to "spiritual matters" in the first line (159). The readings that follow interpret a poem fragment by the seventh-century B.C. poet Sappho, the mystical book *The Mirror of Simple Souls* by Porete (who was burned at the stake for its heresy in 1310), and the writings of Weil, particularly those collected in *Gravity and Grace*. In all three writers, Carson locates a search for—and speech about—God, a tendency toward triangulation in love, and a move of the self to "leave itself behind" (162). The theorizing of self-annihilation in pursuit of love expands as the essay proceeds, culminating in Weil's vocabulary of decreation, a neologism to which, Carson notes, Weil "did not give an exact definition nor a consistent spelling" (167). To clarify the concepts, Carson quotes Weil: "We possess nothing in this world other than the power to say 'I.' This is what we must yield up to God."[27] This idea of rendering the self back to God echoes Porete, Carson notes, drawing careful parallels between the two.[28]

Carson characterizes Weil's relationship to God and self as a sort of fraught love tangle, an "erotic triangle" "involving God, herself and the whole of creation" (168). The reading may at first seem like a stretch, but the long quote Carson follows it with from *Gravity and Grace* in fact demonstrates that the metaphor originates with Weil: "I must withdraw so that God may make contact with the beings

whom chance places in my path and whom he loves. It is tactless of
me to be there. It is as though I were placed between two lovers or two
friends." Later in the quoted extract, Weil concludes, "If only I knew
how to disappear there would be a perfect union of love between God
and the earth I tread, the sea I hear. . . ." (168). Explicating Weil,
Porete, and Sappho together, Carson ends this section by meditating
on their approach to presence with and absence from God, the paradoxical necessity of self-exclusion. These musings powerfully exemplify the often overlooked affinities between postmodern and religious modes of discourse, a feature of postsecularism illuminated in
the work of philosophers like John Caputo.[29]

In characteristic self-subversion and humor, Carson appends a part
4, which she opens with the note, "Inasmuch as we are now entering
upon the fourth part of a three-part essay, we should brace ourselves
for some inconsequentiality" (171). But this "inconsequentiality," she
insists, is not her own doing but arises from the three writers themselves, who present the inescapable paradox with which I introduced
this chapter: they write of the death, annihilation, and decreation of
the self, yes, but they *write* of it, and their writing involves a "brilliant self-assertiveness." The problem is baked in: "To be a writer is
to construct a big, loud, shiny centre of self from which the writing
is given voice and any claim to be intent on annihilating this self while
still continuing to write and give voice to writing must involve the
writer in some important acts of subterfuge or contradiction" (171).
Weil reads contradiction as itself illuminating and necessary, as Carson notes, but this writerly problem is not just contradiction: "it is a
paradox" (172).

Still, it is a paradox the writers themselves recognize and tease out,
Carson insists, each of them seeking to produce work in which "the
teller disappears into the telling" (173). She begins with Weil, narrating Weil's attempted self-erasure, thwarted by Thibon, which Carson reads as "a serious effort to force her back into the center of

herself": "the degree to which she nonetheless eludes this reinstallation is very hard for readers like you or me to judge from outside" (174). Carson here addresses the problem at work in so many of the scholarly, literary, and popular approaches to Weil: her efforts at self-erasure are undermined not just by her own powerfully present personality but also by her editors' and commentators'—not to mention poets'—propensity to emphasize her person.

Carson moves into a personal meditation on eating and books, with passing references to Weil's "problem with eating" (which, she notes, "lots of women" share). Echoing Klassen's work, among others, Carson notes that "food and love were analogous contradictions" for Weil (175). Dipping back to Porete and the "FarNear" presence of God, Carson returns to Weil to discuss her complex relation to Christianity and her meditation on the "unintelligibility" and "impossibility" of the Incarnation (177).[30] But, reading Weil with Sappho, Carson wonders, "Why should the truth not be impossible?" (178). This "zone of absolute spiritual daring" (179) joins all three women, who undergo decreation to arrive at a truth the rest of us can only read as "fake" (180). Carson summarizes so much of the commentary on Weil, and echoes Susan Sontag's influential 1960s approach, when she writes, "it is hard to commend moral extremism of the kind that took Simone Weil to death at the age of thirty-four; saintliness is an eruption of the absolute into ordinary history and we resent that. We need history to remain ordinary. We need to be able to call saints neurotic, anorectic, pathological, sexually repressed or fake. These judgments sanctify our own survival" (180).

Yet while Carson calls these interpretations a "need," she does not join in them, instead asserting, "What I like best about the three women we've been studying is that they know what love is" (180). The essay ends enigmatically with a warning that it's important not to be "fooled" by these women because you will likely "spend the rest of your days in terrible hunger" (181). For Carson, though, such hunger doesn't seem to be a problem. Her approach to Weil in this essay, alongside Sappho and Porete, is at once erudite and narrow, admiring and mildly sarcastic. Calling them "fake women," as Porete's accusers called her, highlights the degree to which gender constraints shaped their lives and reputations. Naming both the cultural "need" to read their intensity as beyond the pale and also the provocative insights of their passionate "telling God" allows Carson to implicitly expose her own (and her readers') likely attraction and repulsion. This is a common theme in the poets I discuss in this chapter and the writers I discuss throughout the book, the blend of admiration and bewilderment, often (though not always) accompanied by the feminist conundrum of how to understand Weil's self-absenting impulses.

Carson's essay ends with a long list of works cited, and this double-paged column of citations acts as a sort of buffer before the abrupt formal shift from philosophical essay to "Decreation (An Opera in Three Parts)." While I focus here on the third part, which imagines Weil, the first two are also threaded through with Weil's themes and vocabularies. Part 1, "Love's Forgery," imagines a love triangle among Hephaistos, Aphrodite, and Ares, along with a "Volcano Chorus" of "7 female robots" (187): it begins with the song "Hunger Tango" (189), a nod to Weil. Part 2, "Her Mirror of Simple Souls," includes a cast of Marguerite Porete, God, and "Quidnunc Chorus: 15 papal inquisitors" and in its one-paragraph introductory argument provides a historical overview of Porete (207) before moving into seven songs that interweave English and Latin, meditating on God's annihilation of the self but also the tension between Porete and her inquisitors in experimental forms (for example, a "Chorus" composed of numbered letters, nonsensical to sing [219], which is of course the point).

Part 3, "Fight Cherries," is sung by "Simone Weil," her parents, and "Chorus of the Void: 10 transparent tapdancers."[31] The opera's Argument characterizes Weil's life as "caught in the net of her parents' care," despite her efforts to escape into philosophy, labor, theology, and "the arts of hunger." Carson emphasizes not just Weil's relationship with her parents and her hunger but also her struggles with gender and existence: "She did not want to be a woman. She wanted to disappear" (223). The six songs present a "Simone" committed to decreating herself, in tension with her parents' attempts to pull her back from the brink into a comfortable material reality.

The opening song, *"Duet of What Is a Question avec Papa,"* unfolds in the two characters' voices persisting in their own themes on the question of the void. M. Weil begins, "What does she mean, void?/What about shoes and fruits and winecorks, many things exist,/they have colour and duration, they bear down on us" (225). Throughout the song, M. Weil appeals repeatedly to the material: to mundane objects, to art, to episodes from Weil's life like the Trotsky visit and her distaste for "anything flawed" like "fruit/with a spot on it" and "poor meat" (227). Simone's voice interrupts these comments with her own rejections of the material and biographical concerns in favor of philosophical topics. Her interruptions all follow the same form: "Winecorks are not a question./Power is a question"; "Football is not a question./Imagination is a question" (225); "Trotsky's night is not a question./Hatred is a question" (226); and so forth. The result is a seesaw between the trappings of the Weils' bourgeois life and Simone's insistent urge to theorize about metaphysics, as she follows each rejected and substituted question with a characteristic philosophical statement, such as "The world must be somehow a void to have need of God" (226). These statements read very much like Weil's notebooks. They also participate in a tension in the other poets' approaches to Weil between her life and her ideas. Yet while "Simone" here clearly emphasizes her philosophy over her life, the opera continues to navigate both together.

The next song, "Chocolate Chorus," weaves line by line back and forth between Simone Weil and the Chorus of the Void, with an absurd interrogation of how many chocolates various figures human and inhuman eat. These include a hero, a heretic, an anarchist, a whirlwind, Karl Marx, Adam and Eve, George Herbert, a Jew in occupied France, and (repeated four times) justice. Simone Weil cycles through a repetitive series of rhyming replies "Not many," "Hardly any," "Even in summer," "No big number" (228), implying a rejection of chocolate among all these subjects. The final verse turns the question, and the form, on its head, as the chorus asks, "And how much justice does chocolate eat?" Weil replies, "Chocolate eats till it feels complete" (229). The song implicitly invokes Weil's struggle with food and her refusal of luxuries. But its nonsensical juxtaposition of serious political figures with the question of their consumption of chocolate elevates the refusal of chocolate to the point of banality and absurdity. Chocolate itself suffers from no such self-limiting compunction: it eats justice and possesses plenty of itself, in stark (and frankly bathetic) contrast to Weil's quest to divest herself of herself (229).

"*Duet of the Sleeveless Sports Blouses* avec Maman" echoes the form of the duet avec Papa. The staging instructions describe Simone and Madame Weil "waltzing in an empty factory while the Chorus of the Void do calisthenics in slow motion" (230), tinging the piece with further absurdity before it even begins. The two women's voices appear to represent letters back and forth. Mme Weil's are all full of anxious reminders and practical advice: "Do not forget to watch the stove. / Do not forget to eat some meat. / Do not forget your eyeglasses when you go to war" (230). The reminders about preparing to go to war grow increasingly ridiculous, from bringing eyeglasses to taking a nap before leaving (231) to sending a card when she's arrived "at the war" (233). Simone's initial lyrics report on her life, as the historical Weil wrote to her parents as she was dying to hide her dire situation. The song begins,

Simone: *Chère Maman* I have bought two sleeveless sports
blouses Today a street fight between Nazis and

Communists No I was not there! Please send
me *special post* what I asked for last
letter (the Hegel) Kisses (230)

Simone's later lines toggle back and forth between increasingly scrambled iterations of this stanza and meditations on the importance of work and how it helps free her of "desire," "disorder," and even her "I" (230), how work is a cyclical necessity (231) and the site of the body's encounter with "hunger," "thirst," "joy," and other abstractions (232), and how work allows her to "create" herself and avoid "panic" (233). The chorus periodically interjects as well, variously describing a "saint" as "sad," "easy," and "out of tune." Several of these choral interruptions end with "Not really!" in a way that calls into question their attribution of sainthood to Simone. The others end with the phrase "Saints are never left altogether/in place/are they," yet another enigmatic claim that reads as both a comment on Mme Weil's meddling and Simone's movements out of her various settings. The song, which again relies on true-to-history depictions of Mme Weil's care and her daughter's devotion to her work, further emphasizes the parental pull and the philosopher's attraction to both decreation and self-creation through her work—her commitment to which, of course, also led to her destruction.

"*Decreation Aria,*" "sung by Simone alone in an empty place," is a sparse and desperate plea for self-erasure, encapsulated in the twice-repeated line, "Undo this creature!" (235). Simone describes herself as "excess" in her body and mind, and in the song Carson returns again to the historical Weil's triangulating vision, her sense of how she "blocks God's view of his beloved creation/and like an unwelcome third between two lovers/gets in the way" (235). Her plaintive request for self-undoing here is located not in some anorectic quest for control or gendered self-disgust but in her desire to love God by allowing God to love creation without her imposition. Unlike Adrienne Rich's insistence "and you are part of it," part of the creation God loves, Carson doesn't interject here but allows the agony of the singer's longing speak for itself. The sense may in fact be the same, though, as Carson's rendering of the tragic loneliness and desperation of Weil's longing implies its own sorrowful critique.

The humor returns in the next song, *"Parental Interlude,"* in which M. and Mme Weil sing a repetitive rhyming duet about geometry and colors, how "Nonagons are not useful"—"But a triangle is true!" (236). The song is frankly obtuse, but given the opera and essay's prior concern with triangulation, it suggests the value of both the triad of Weil and her parents (the opera never mentions her brother André in its familial drama) and the value of Weil's God-world-self threesome. The absolute uselessness of the parents and their song stands in stark contrast with the prior aria and the final song that follows, *"Aria of Last Cherries,"* which Simone sings "from a hospital bed" while "the Chorus of the Void tapdance around her" (238). In this song, the chorus repeatedly interrupts Simone to call cherries close to "tingle" and "tease a saint," while Simone's verses meditate on affliction and insist, "Take all my food away." She sings of working on a letter to her parents "about the blossoms" in London, as the historical Weil did, and contemplates on her need to know whether her request for baptism "would be granted or denied," though she interrupts her wondering with the insistence, "Yes you may bless me but *take that water away!*" (239). She finally admits she might like some cherries but then describes "lay[ing] back in Lethe," a reference to one of the rivers of Hades associated with forgetfulness or even untruth. The song ends not with her voice but with the chorus yet again inviting the cherries to "Come" (240).

The result of the strange opera form is a mix of pathos and bathos, a tenderness toward Weil's serious desires only amplified by the previous part's serious engagement with Marguerite Porete's similar spiritual longings and theories. Mme and M. Weil, in a sense, stand in for commentators who would have Simone Weil exist on a more palatable everyday plane, attempting, as does the chorus at points, to pull Simone back into the realm of comfortable bodily life. Yet Simone's lines maintain their seriousness: despite the absurdity with which they are interwoven in the operatic form, despite the duets and interrupting chorus and nonsensical staging directions, Weil persists in her pursuit of divine love even to the point of self-erasure. The final aria, set in the place of the historical Weil's death, may imply her end, but her voice within the songs persists in its integrity, standing in stark contrast to the comic excess that swirls around her.

Carson's work ultimately achieves a seriousness despite its participation in the absurd: it exposes absurdity not in Simone Weil's life and work but in the forces that would resist and undermine it. While "Decreation (An Opera in Three Parts)" is in many ways an anomaly among the other sequences I discuss in this chapter, it has many features in common with them, too, including a lyric approach (in this case, literally the form of a lyric opera), obviously careful research, attention to both ideas and biography, and a focus on Weil's relationship with her parents and her hungers. Carson also joins the other poets in a stance that is both admiring and critical, using her form to project a degree of distance from her subject and highlight the constructedness of this representation of Weil. Indeed, Carson's choice to introduce Weil as "the twentieth-century French classicist and philosopher" (157)—a description that renders Weil in Carson's own classicist image—reminds us that for all their attempts to decenter themselves in their depictions of Weil, these versified biographical approaches inevitably manifest the poets' own varied hopes and hungers as much as they do Weil's.

"HOW FAR CAN I TRAVEL WITH YOU?" LORRI NEILSEN GLENN'S "SONGS FOR SIMONE"

Lorri Neilsen Glenn's Simone Weil sequence "Songs for Simone," published in the center of her collection *Lost Gospels* (2010), carries through many of the themes in other poets' engagements. Like Maggie Helwig and Stephanie Strickland, Glenn grapples explicitly with how to properly approach Weil as a subject. Also like Strickland, she constructs found poems of Weil's own writing, signaling Weil's voice in italics. With Helwig and Anne Carson, Glenn renders Weil in explicit comparison to and conversation with music, from opera to jazz and hymns. With Kate Daniels and Sarah Klassen, she wonders over Weil's romantic life, and she joins Klassen in embroidering the poems with persistent motif of birds. Glenn's approach also insistently renders Weil within certain contexts: in the context of the poet persona's attraction to and difficulty with Weil; in the context of Weil's biography, as one poem offers an explicit chronology; in Weil's historical moment and other figures' experiences of that moment in the varied locations of western Canada, Eastern Europe, and the United States; and in a "chorus" of other thinkers and spiritual guides. In so doing she participates in the widely repeated strategy of rendering Weil not a saint or an inhuman or abstract figure but a participant in traditions, conversations, histories.

The nine poems follow a pattern, with three repeated and numbered series of three titles: "*Trouvé 1*," "*J'offre 1*," and "*J'imagine 1*" give way to the same three titles numbered 2 and 3. The "*Trouvé*" (found) poems give Weil's italicized words (supplemented, in "*Trouvé 2*," by a dated brief chronology suffused with Weil quotations). The "*J'offre*" (I offer) poems give the poet persona's intense struggle with Weil's ideas, mostly directed to "Simone" herself. The "*J'imagine*" (I imagine) poems extend this struggle to context, putting Weil's thought and life into conversation with happenings in the war and in other famous and anonymous lives, or into conversation with imagined peers. The lines are mostly long, extending to the end of the page in stanzas that frequently blur the distinction between prose poem and long-lined verse. The effect is at least twofold: first, it conveys a conversational, speakerly voice whose attraction to and struggle with Weil's ideas exceed slim lyricism; second, it echoes Weil's own notebook style of meditative paragraphs, some brief and some long, and perhaps participates in Joan Dargan's sense that Weil's most poetic writing was in fact her notebook prose.[32] Yet at the same time, these are densely allusive and searching lines, their long lengths not loose but tightly woven with images and repetitions.

"Songs for Simone" opens with two epigraphs: the first quotes Weil and the second a traditional hymn, the four lines of which also close the poem:

> *Through all the tumult and the strife*
> *I hear the music ringing;*
> *It sounds an echo in my soul—*
> *How can I keep from singing?*[33]

The hymn's reference to singing through "the tumult and the strife" signals the sequence's concern with song as a manifestation of beauty despite the world's difficulties. The Weil quote signals its concern with decreation: *"We possess nothing in this world other than the power to say I. This is what we should yield up to God, and this is what we should destroy"* (45). The epigraph, in both form and content, stands in contrast to the poem that follows, *"Trouvé 1,"* which is composed of Weil's italicized words as well, mostly taken from *Gravity and Grace*. These phrases are inescapably poetic, and so Glenn's added lyric form only serves to emphasize the imagery and rhythms already there. For example, the poem opens with an enigmatic image to which Glenn will return: *"The egg is the world we see, the bird/in it is Love"* (45). Weil's conceit continues to discuss the breaking shell, spirit, space. As the poem unfolds, the lines Glenn lifts from Weil offer further images: a tree "rooted in the sky"; a buried pearl; workers needing poetry more than bread; falling petals (45). The themes are vision, sensation, friendship, beauty, light. Weil's words in the prose epigraph appear as philosophical and theological governing challenges, but in the poem Glenn constructs, they read as poetic provocation.

Glenn responds to the provocations of both the epigraph's challenge to yield and destroy the power to say I and the poem's startlingly beautiful images in the following pages, which turn more to the poet-speaker's own voice while incorporating words and images from the first poem. She invites "Simone" to "travel" with her in *"J'offre 1,"* narrating the experience of rail and air travel, driving through downtown Winnipeg, visiting her mother, and returning home to find a bird has eaten seeds she left out (46). Weil's words and ideas (which are "a lens, sharp, hard, trapping light in anything//that moves") are threaded throughout: gravity, erasure, attention, detachment, prayer. "Your fingerprints are everywhere on my imagination," the speaker observes as she describes the sky, the city, the panhandler and aging mother who raise questions of responsibility (46). The poet persona grapples with this influence, however: "I want your ideas to rip at the flesh of my comfort," she insists, but later, reflecting on Weil's desire to "destroy//your power to say 'I,'" the speaker wonders, "Tell me, how to speak of you or for you without offering/the food of your creed, bread for the bellies of pilgrim spirits wandering/alone and far behind? How far can I travel with you?" (46). The poem's final question suggests a tension between Weil's appeal and her troubling legacy of self-erasure through starvation, which the poet connects to her writings on humility, attention, and prayer. What does it mean to engage with these ideas, write of these ideas, without offering "the food of [Weil's] creed"—an ambiguous phrase that could mean either inviting others into Weil's troubling self-diminishment or filling them with comfort when they should remain empty. Having begun the poem asking Weil to travel with her, the speaker reverses her initial question to wonder how far she can go with Weil into these difficult realms of thought and action.

This grappling, reminiscent of Adrienne Rich's "For a Friend in Travail" or "A Vision," continues throughout the sequence. Glenn begins "*J'imagine 1*" with the line, "I read you and read you, but cannot understand the ferocity of your will" (47), which she connects to Weil's attachment to Catharism's "austerity" and Plato's suspicion of artists. Imagining Weil on her deathbed, "smothered by hunger," the poet persona wonders, "In your state of decreating bliss are you now fully emptied? Is such perfection worth the price?" (48). These questions echo concerns raised by women writers since at least the 1960s: How do we reconcile Weil's enormous strength of commitment with her self-diminishing drive? Writing five decades after Susan Sontag's original review, Glenn's struggle highlights Weil's persisting appeal and challenge.

For despite these concerns, the speaker also clearly articulates her attraction to Weil: "I find direction in your words"; "To be pierced with wonder in the everyday is what entices me. It empties me and it fills me" (49). "I realize I am reading you because I am blind, feeling for the walls of belief. I too want belief so deep it will swallow me" (50). In this image of a blind self feeling for the walls, the speaker references Weil's concept of *metaxu*, a Greek word she found in Plato for the in-between. Weil writes of *metaxu* as like walls that both separate and link, and Glenn quotes the word in an epigraph to her book's first section: "*The true earthly blessings are metaxu . . . the temporal seen as a bridge*" (9).[34] The concept functions throughout "Songs for Simone" in its persistent dealing with contradictions and connections: "Every separation is a link, you say" (47). Imagery of bridges also persists: "I think of all the bridges we cross," she speaker reflects, going on to list literal bridges ("The Brooklyn Bridge. The London Bridge. The Ponte Vecchio.") and also figurative bridges that link disparate lives and experiences (50).

These links include histories and communities Glenn constructs. In "*J'imagine 1*," she pulls together stories from "August, 1943," the month of Weil's death, imagining Peggy Wemyss—better known as Margaret Laurence, one of Canada's most famous writers—as well as Duke Ellington, the Allied forces in Japan and Tripoli, uprisings in the Warsaw ghetto, a young woman making her wedding dress from German soldiers' abandoned parachutes, and another young woman named Grace in Winnipeg, accidentally killing a bird and dancing on a first date (48). Weil's death occurs in the broader context of human death and life. Later in the poem, in the paragraph beginning with the literal bridges, the speaker references Billie Holiday and Nina Simone, also making music in 1943, making beauty for the world while they suffered in the background and insisted on racial dignity (50). In "*Trouvé 3*," the speaker quotes Weil's poetic lines in concert with other wise voices—"Chuang Tzu, Lao Tzu, the Desert Fathers, philosophers, poets" (51).[35] In all these cases, Glenn is locating Weil within a context: historical, discursive, artistic. She is refusing a sense of Weil as otherworldly or timeless: others lived and died in 1943 and made their difficult negotiations with pain and beauty. Glenn treats their lives as *metaxu*, walls or bridges that both divide and connect across difference and similarity.

These juxtaposing bridges of comparison help Glenn address one of the struggles at the center of the poem, which is whether Weil's insistent ethical, political, and spiritual call to an uncompromising self-emptying allows for joy and beauty. Does such a passionate austerity, rooted in attention to the world's suffering, leave room for music? Does love for the divine leave room for earthly love? Implied in all the talk of song is the metatextual question of whether such close-honed ethical, political, and spiritual focus leaves room for poetry itself: "Can I slice my complacency to the bone, as you have, and still sing?" (49). The bridges offer tentative insights: Billie Holiday's "pure and perfect 'God Bless the Child,'" for example, a song that "supported the young woman born Eleonora Fagan Gough, descendant of slaves, raped at the age of ten" (50), both suggests musical beauty and calls out the complacency in the biblical justification for poverty, "Them that's got shall have / Them that's not shall lose." The bridge joins and separates Holiday from Weil: differences of country, of race, of place in the world, but a unity of concern with injustice and religious excuses for it. The bridge likewise joins and separate the song's form and its content, its gentle invitation to dance and its deep-down critique of structures of poverty.

The speaker builds another bridge between Nina Simone's "I want a little sugar in my bowl" (50) and the question of Weil's refusal of romance. Like Kate Daniels and philosopher Chris Cuomo, Glenn wonders about Weil's love life and her loneliness, imagining the advice she'd give an imagined lover: "Simone belongs to no one"—"Dismantle the possessive, unhinge the transitive." Trying to imagine Weil in love, the poet persona ends up defending and explaining how "her heart is a subject that needs no object" (51). The appeal of dreaming up a love life for Weil—a life with the satisfactions and softened edges of relationships enjoyed by others of the characters with whom Glenn populates the year 1943 in the poem, making wedding dresses and dancing on first dates—leads the poet to speak with tenderness not to Weil but to the imagined lover: "O dear imperfect soul, you can't take this woman, and you can't have her" (51). It's hard not to read this advice as doubly intended for both the dreamed-up lover and the poet persona herself, or perhaps the reader, all of us who want more of Weil than she wants to give.

Yet, again, Weil is not alone. "*Trouvé 3*," the poem that imagines her voice "in a chorus of others,'" immediately follows this reflection

(51) and leads to the brief wondering in "*J'offre 3*": "What if the search for the divine *is* a search for song?" (52). Seeking not precisely to resolve the tension between ethics and aesthetics, philosophy and art, suffering and joy, but rather to follow Weil in holding the evident oppositions together, the speaker presses the image still further: "Hermes hollowed out the tortoise shell to create the lyre. Simone, you hollowed out yourself to be with God. You became the song" (52). The emptied self *is* the music, in a figure that recalls Annie Dillard's picture of the writer as an empty bell, ready to be rung. But Glenn pushes the image still further in the sequence's last poem, bringing together all its characters and extending their lives—less intent on self-decreation, but no less prone to struggle—as given to song, a chorus in which Weil was just one member. "1943: A prairie ballroom, big band music in the middle of the war, a young woman dancing in spite of what she has destroyed. A blues singer, a factory worker, a writer, a bride. Imagine all these as the chanting of the world" (52). Weil's particular life, and the philosophy it gave rise to, paradoxically emerges in this poem as both just one life among the many "songs of imperfection" *and* the source of the wisdom that helps the poet persona recognize our ephemerality. The tensions in Weil's life and thought paradoxically give rise to *both* the tensions that plague the poet-speaker in this poem and also the concept—*metaxu*—that helps her see how to hold them together. "This is the meantime," the sequence repeats as its final line, before its bookending hymn's repeated four lines about singing through tumult and strife: and the meantime is one more figure, like the bridge, of *metaxu*, the moment that both separates and divides the past from the future. The poem's final sense, then, is that this in-between—temporal, relational, spiritual, conceptual—is the place where we live.

In a way, this in-between is the place where all the poets' Weils live: in between fact and fiction, biography and verse, mysterious absence and overwhelming presence, admiration and critique, solitude and company, life and literature. Again and again, the chorus of poets speak to and of and for Weil, compelled to attend to her, even as they wrestle with the creative possibilities of decreative attention. The poems themselves serve as *metaxu*: they connect readers to Weil, even as they distance us from her. There is no separating the two. This is true of all writing about Weil, but it is amplified by poetry's distinctive features: its condensed scope, its density of allusions and juxtapositions, its gaps, its play with metaphor and the malleability of meaning, its inevitable realization within our bodies' senses of sight and sound and rhythm. Perhaps most of all, poetry through its very form invites a watchful, patient slowing down that embodies Weil's theory of attention.

"What makes biography so curious and endlessly absorbing," writes lauded biographer Hermione Lee, "is that through all the documents and the letters, the context and the witnesses, the conflicting opinions and the evidence of the work, we keep catching sight of a real body, a physical life."[36] Even several layers removed—by virtue of time, of geographical distance, of translation, of source materials already shaped by other editors' and writers' interpretive constructions— Weil's verse biographers insist that Weil wasn't just an anthology of ideas but a real body, a physical life. In this insistence, they may refuse her own efforts at decreation, but they seek to render her in something approaching her real complexity, inviting new communities of readers perhaps unfamiliar with her story to see glimpses of her as she was: flesh and blood and gloriously, perplexingly human, unpindownable in the way of any person and any poem. In this vision, the poets invite us to see her life in its fullness, perhaps for the first time.

CONCLUSION

*The vulnerability of precious things is beautiful, because it is a
sign of existence.*
Blossom of fruit-trees.

        —Simone Weil, *First and Last Notebooks*

For all their differences and particularities, the writers at the
heart of this book turn and return to Weil as an imperfect
source of wisdom. They write of Simone Weil, to Simone
Weil, in the tradition of Simone Weil, compelled by the beauty of
her writing, of her vision for how we might be human together. At
the same time, they resist to varying degrees her myriad extremes:
her self-denials, her self-diminishments, her catastrophically inatten-
tive reading of the Hebrew scriptures, her commitment to an absent
Christian God. Their resistance, though, emerges in the space of
engagement and conversation, of sustained thought and hunger for
something Weil has to offer. The poets in chapter 4 spend full
sequences and even books rendering Weil's life; Rich, Dillard, and
Gordon spend decades in their conversations with her in poetry,
nonfiction, and fiction.

In writing of, to, and in the tradition of Simone Weil, most of these authors attend to her in her affliction—in her chronic headaches, her loneliness, her thwarted desires for justice and connection and the bread and wine of the Eucharist. In attending to Weil, they in some sense create her, over and over again, enfleshing her being in words. And in this creative act of attention, they bring Weil again to life, give birth to her again, perhaps against her own decreative will. They follow Weil's advice in reading Weil: "Creative attention means really giving our attention to that which does not exist."[1] They read and think and write, and behold: a new creation. She lives on, in some sense born again in their self-suspending practice.

As I named at the outset of this book, Adrienne Rich, Annie Dillard, Mary Gordon, Maggie Helwig, Stephanie Strickland, Kate Daniels, Sarah Klassen, Anne Carson, and Lorri Neilsen Glenn, among many others, write of, to, and in the tradition of Simone Weil from various moments and locations both social and geographical, but, again, three intersecting trends emerge when we read them in concert. The first is a fascination—troubled, sympathetic, or both—with Weil's turn toward a Christian God. The second is a fascination, often but not always alarmed, with Weil's self-sacrificial theory and practice. The third is a fascination, typically admiring, with her call to attention, which manifests in an aesthetic, spiritual, and ethico-political tangle that offers a model of artistic and moral seriousness.

These writers read and write Weil in a secular age, which I have been understanding in the postsecular sense of not the end of religion but the cacophonous proliferation of possibilities for belief and unbelief. For some, Weil offers space to grapple with deeply theological questions the contemporary world doesn't always make space for. Annie Dillard finds in Weil a fellow theological traveler, one with whom she can share heady metaphysics and assume God's presence but from there struggle with the question of divine goodness. Dillard's concern isn't with Christian institutions but rather with the problem of evil, a point of both resonance with and departure from Weil's own musings. Sarah Klassen, likewise, treats Weil with an ear for the "breath-taking wingbeat of grace," and Lorri Neilsen Glenn admits to longing with Weil for "belief so deep it will swallow me."[2] Others find in Weil an invitation to imagine a chastened Christianity, a more noncoercive faith that pursues intellectual openness, interfaith dialogue, not power-over but radical love. Mary Gordon, for her part, joins Weil in recognizing places where Christian institutions—especially the Catholic Church—have mapped onto political conflict, in the depiction of Ireland's Troubles in *Pearl* and in the Spanish Civil War in *There Your Heart Lies*: Gordon tirelessly explores both the harm Christian institutions can cause and what is lost when they are wholly abandoned. Like Weil, Gordon models a trenchant critique of the Catholic Church in a way that makes room for both those who would seek to redeem it and those who would seek to reject it altogether. For still others, Weil's religious turn is a step too far. Adrienne Rich is in this camp, calling out the force that Weil "calls God" as precisely the force that harms her. Traveling father than Weil herself managed, Rich did ultimately explore her own Jewish roots, but she did so in a way that never led her to belief. Maggie Helwig's and Kate Daniels's poems seem to join Rich in this space of unbelief, alert to Weil's desperate hunger for God but without a strong sense of joining her in it. Anne Carson, for her part, depicts Weil's spiritual longings as beyond the pale but not without precedent, comparing them not just to a medieval Christian heretic but also to a Greek poet in a sort of postmodern aporia. The very diversity of these approaches to Weil's religious turn exemplifies the secular preponderance of relations to faith and the way Weil's philosophy and life invite fraught reflection on the place of believe in the twentieth and twenty-first centuries.

But even those writers who cannot follow Weil into her belief find in her ethical, political, and aesthetic wisdoms worth the work of sifting out the religious: this, too, Weil herself welcomes in her writings on the purifying possibilities of atheism, the goodness, truth, and beauty available just as fully to those who cannot believe in Christianity or those in other world religions. Yet while her moral seriousness, shining out of her life and writing, may be extricable from Weil's attraction to Christianity, it is maddeningly inextricable from some degree of decreation, that process of giving up "the power to say 'I.'"[3] That is to say, in so much of the literary wrestling with Weil's idea and her person, what concerns is also what compels: what is risky is also what is worthwhile.

Recently, Terry Tempest Williams has addressed this risky integrity in her discussion of Weil in *Erosion: Essays of Undoing* (2019), which includes the poignant sequence "Four Letters to My Father." In these letters, Williams processes her life and seeks her father's wisdom during a residence in Massachusetts, away from her longtime home in Utah, naming her homesickness for the desert, her ecological grief, spiritual seeking, and vocational discernment. The four letters are woven through with quotations from Simone Weil, whose *Waiting for God*, Williams writes, she has been reading and rereading throughout the month of October 2017, when the letters were written.[4] Williams quotes Weil not just on attention's ethical power but on language and communication, affliction, and the love of God. "Simone Weil is writing my mind, my wounded mind," she says. "These words move me."[5] Weil is the only figure whose words Williams copies into her letters, which also include news of family friends, questions about the future, and gratitude for her father's example. She explains in the third letter:

Simone Weil inspires me because she belongs to no one and to everyone. By that I mean she refused to be baptized in the Catholic Church, even though she considered herself Catholic. She refused to join the Communist Party, even though she believed in protecting the rights of the working class and joined them in their factory work and suffering. She was committed to both piety and revolution, embraced God and the God beyond god, engaged in both contemplative prayer and action—all while interrogating justice with her body—well, as you can see, she has become a true heroine of mine. I identify with her because I feel I do not belong to any orthodoxy, nor wish to, and yet, I feel a profound tie and commitment to the life of the Spirit and paying attention to patterns, signs, and synchronicity like cairns in the desert to help us find our way.[6]

Williams's explanation of Weil's appeal replicates the trend Robert Zaretsky notes of introducing Weil by a "series of contradictions," but it contributes to the sense that it is precisely the contradictions that make Weil so compelling.[7] Williams's letter to her father also suggests Weil's importance as a model for longing for something like beauty, truth, goodness, and the divine beyond the bounds our language and institutions have yet allowed. In this vision, Weil offers guidance for those seeking to satiate their postsecular hungers for meaning and for justice.

Within the context of *Erosions*, which draws agonized and rapt attention to the American West, especially its vulnerability to rapacious resource extraction and governmental policy, as well as drawing attention to Indigenous efforts to protect the land and all its creaturely inhabitants, Terry Tempest Williams's interest in Weil highlights another aspect of Weil's importance for a twentieth-century moment. An attitude of humility, attentive love for the world, anti-colonial rootedness, and even self-risking activism is a powerful antidote to the corporate capitalist logic of real estate development and fossil fuel reliance that threatens the land, the animals, the water, and the very sky. Williams embraces Weil as a hero, not of self-immolation, but of the kind of uncommon integrity required to resist the onslaught of ecological disaster. This emphasis aligns with Toril Moi's recent assessment of Weil's hyperbolic life: "Faced with communism, fascism, war, invasion, and concentration camps, Weil's extremism—her asceticism, her saintliness, her thought—was a response to extreme times. If she strikes me as more relevant than ever, it may be because we are beginning to realize that we too live in extreme times. What sacrifices and what heroism will the climate crisis demand of us?"[8]

We who read the writers' renderings of Weil eighty years after her death meet her in an age of unprecedented crises: the planet roils with human-provoked climate emergencies, yes, but we also face long-overdue reckonings with colonial white supremacy and gendered violence. Global flows of power increase disparities, and global disease festers among inequities. As we try to understand these phenomena, much less imagine better futures and enact local and planetary justice, our very attention has become a rapidly traded commodity, held in the sway of attention merchants and technologies engineered to rob us of agency. We live in an era of deep dis-ease with suffering, a profound desire to deny its power even as we are confronted with a dizzying scope of pain and injustice through twenty-four-hour news cycles and social media, scales of information never before known in human history. Living through a twenty-first-century pandemic has shown us the degree to which people will justify prioritizing their own minor comfort over others' safety, yet we also see the power of mutual aid through crowdfunding platforms and donations to far-off victims of war as well as embodied presence in protest marches and education movements. We encounter Weil—or traces of Weil, imaginations of Weil—in this fraught world, all the more hungry for her example of countercultural attention to the world and to suffering in particular, of a radical integrity that *acts* in ways that don't quite make sense within prevailing complacencies.

The risky necessity of self-diminishment in certain contexts is part of what becomes apparent most fully in a gathering of Weil's various literary afterlives: hers is an ethic that demands more of the powerful. Weil calls to those who are not afflicted to attend to affliction, which is almost always the result of some human injustice, in order to ameliorate human suffering. Hers is an asymmetrical ethic: the one who does not suffer attends to the suffering other, substitutes oneself for the suffering other, not for the sake of self-destruction but to create more equitable flourishing. The one who has not been uprooted uproots herself so the other might sink roots deeper into the soil. The one who has bread is obligated to give it to the one who is hungry. One can of course take this too far, as Gordon's *Pearl* especially demonstrates. But the kind of self-giving searching for Suri Feldman Annie Dillard documents in *For the Time Being*, the foundational political significance of hunger that Adrienne Rich versifies and the need to attend to others across social difference in order to forge coalitions that can resist oppression, the openness to "weep for the whole world" while shedding light on economic disparities Sarah Klassen associates with Weil alongside other truth-tellers: taken far enough but not too far, these acts bring goodness into the world. As Weil herself writes, "He who has not been able to become nothing runs the risk of reaching a moment when everything other than himself ceases to exist."[9] Certain acts of self-giving, even giving up, are an antidote to the solipsism that plagues modern industrialized societies.

This helps explain, I think, one reason why so many of Weil's most impassioned literary attendants are white women, like Sigrid Nunez's Weil-modeled Ann Drayton in *The Last of Her Kind*. For those struggling to come to terms with their own power and responsibility within systems that both oppress them and empower them at others' expense, Weil offers a model of the sort of self-suspension justice may require. To be sure, again, as I note at various points in this book, women of color engage with Simone Weil in their writing, though typically with less intense and sustained focus than the writers I've focused on. In fact, M. NourbeSe Philip champions Weil's work in precisely the terms I am discussing here, as both a source of radical political integrity and a kind of secularly inspiring model of belief. In a piece in 2020 on six books that have shaped her work as a poet, Philip lists *Waiting for God*, citing Weil as a "fierce thinker whose work is committed to truth-telling (an increasingly scarce commodity in these times)" and "an engagement with [Christian] spirituality" that "transcends for me belief and non-belief."[10] While she says she no longer practices Christianity, Philip writes that Weil's belief that "the existence of hunger presupposes the existence of bread" seemed to energize the philosopher-mystic's political activism and similarly "continues to sustain" Philip herself in her pursuit of "social justice." She refers to this idea of hunger implying bread—and injustice implying justice—in an interview with Jordan Scott in 2016 as well, citing Weil along with Dietrich Bonhoeffer and Thomas Merton as white Christians whose spirituality pushed them politically.[11] Weil, in particular, both wrote and acted for labor justice and called out European colonization in a way that was inseparable from her faith in the divine, in the presence of grace, in the possibility of a better world. Philip reads this kind of faith mobilization as a radical contrast to the way "religion and politics" are so often a "toxic and explosive mix" in the United States and elsewhere. Even as a nonbeliever herself, Philip sources in Weil a model of a religiously motivated political engagement that is the precise antidote to white Christian Nationalism.

Philip also briefly turns to Weil in "Jammin' Still," which introduces her collection *Bla_k* with a meditation on the uprootings and instabilities of her own location as a "Black, African-descended, female, immigrant (or interloper) and Caribbean" in Canada, a nation built on the injustices of settler colonialism's violence against First Nations. She cites Weil first in an epigraph and later in a short discussion of *The Need for Roots*, drawing on it to describe how European cultures uprooted themselves and others, first through "colonialism later wedded to capitalism, and later still to industrial-ization," which led to "people of colour being made stranger to and winnowed of their own lands, widowed of their own cultures." The results are countless but include both mass migration and planetary unsettling: "climate change, wars, famine, drought, floods"—all while the West says, "never mind."[12] To be clear, Weil is only a minor interlocutor in Philip's expansive oeuvre, but she functions as an exemplar of the kind of integrity that can provoke radical refusals of systemic injustice even among those who benefit from these systems.

Again, I think this example of resistance to white supremacy, col-onization, and even economic privilege helps explain Weil's appeal to white women looking for a model, a firebrand of a foremother, as they struggle with what it means to occupy their fraught social loca-tions. Adrienne Rich was perhaps most explicit about this question, writing from at least the 1980s onward about taking responsibility for her race and class privilege in ways that shifted her out of the pre-sumed center of human experience. In seeking to understand her roots, to acknowledge her own and suffering *and* culpability, as I've argued, Rich was deeply influenced by Weil. Of course, Rich was quick to express concern with Weil's decreative impulses, but she was also increasingly worried at the individualism fostered by the late twentieth century's economic structures and at the way feminism as a collective moment was co-opted into liberal lifestyle choices.[13] As early as the essay "What Does a Woman Need to Know" (1979), Rich writes, "The insistence of the feminist movement, that each woman's selfhood is precious, that the feminine ethic of self-denial and self-sacrifice must give way to a true woman identification, which would affirm our connectedness with all women, is perverted into a com-mercially profitable and politically debilitating narcissism."[14] In contrast to both gendered self-sacrifice and white middle-class self-centering, she called for a rigorous solidarity across difference, a refusal to separate thought and action, an unremitting integrity in the face of degradation: "Liberatory politics is, after all, not simply opposition but an expression of the impulse to create the new, an expanding sense of what's *humanly possible.*"[15] Rich stages personas and characters asking each other, "What are you going through?," across generations, cultures, and nations in several of her later poems, offering Weil's ethic of attention as a mode of interpersonal care that builds activist coalitions.

Even as Rich resists Weil's cruciform self-destruction, she still follows Weil into the risky practice of responsibility, accountability, and self-suspension, not to the point of self-destruction but in ways that refuse comfort and compliance, for the sake of radical liberation. For Rich, this meant using her influence and her pen to champion writers of color, explicitly citing Black, Indigenous, Latinx, working-class, and non-Western literatures in essays and reviews, even while resisting the impulse to appropriate, calling out "white people's tendency to sniff and taste, uninvited, and in most cases to vampirize American Indian, or African, or Asian, or other 'exotic' ways of understanding."[16] It meant refusing awards to make statements against national injustice or insisting on sharing awards with women of color. And it meant openly admitting to past mistakes, a public practice of self-correction—a humility rarely seen in scholarly and literary spaces. For example, in the 1986 edition of *Of Woman Born*, Rich famously included a new introduction and a host of new footnotes taking responsibility for the solipsism her classed, raced, and colonial privilege had produced in the first edition, naming the writers and activists whose work had complicated her understanding of midcentury American motherhood in the ten years since the book's first publication. Years later, introducing *Arts of the Possible* (2001), Rich admits that as she selected earlier essays to include, she had a "rueful sense of how one period's necessary strategies can mutate into the monsters of a later time."[17]

In other words, Rich learned from Weil a way of being in the world that refused to divide the poetic from the material, even to the point of uncomfortable integrity. As Eve Tuck and K. Wayne Yang's influential essay "Decolonization Is Not a Metaphor" insists, the work of doing justice in the wake of colonization is not about pretty words and soft institutional shifts: it's about the costly work of returning the land itself.[18] Antiracist work isn't just about undoing prejudices; it's about material justice, reparations, structural changes that cost something for those who have been used to holding privilege. Addressing the climate emergency requires literal divestment from industries and comforts that characterize so-called First World life and disproportionately harm our global neighbors with less privilege in what the United Nations has called global "sacrifice zones."[19] For all her extremes, and while she did not live to see all these movements, Weil offers something like a model for this kind of seriousness, one that doesn't shy away from the actual cost of doing justice to those who have been afflicted. Attending to an other in this way, she writes, is nearly impossible. It is a miracle. And it's those who have the most privilege who are most in need of Weil's impossible example. The longing for a guide in this risky work is at least partly responsible for Weil's appeal to so very many writers whose work is bound up in questions of beauty, truth, and goodness in the bewildering late modern world.

Strikingly, however, Weil's explicitly political, and especially her doggedly anticolonial, writings have been less influential among her literary interlocutors than the more broadly existential and spiritual writings collected in *Waiting for God* and *Gravity and Grace*. Most of these writers participate in the bifurcation of Weil's reception Deborah Nelson describes, where political commentators focus on one dimension of the writings and those interested in her ethico-religious work focus on other writings. The idea of roots and rooting arises in much of the literary writing, as we have seen, and both Philip and

Strickland draw explicitly on Weil's anticolonial work in *The Need for Roots*, but the anticolonial perspective has not been the most prevalent even among literary writers interested in Weil's politics. This may in part be due to the availability of materials: it was only in 2003 that J. P. Little collected and translated Weil's anticolonial essays into English, publishing them as *Simone Weil on Colonialism: An Ethic of the Other*. These materials, along with Little's introduction constructing a narrative of Weil's awakening to the injustices of France's colonial rule, offer a whole new lens into Weil's impassioned argument against colonization in general, which is predicated on an egalitarian belief in the full humanity of all people and the resulting responsibility that they be treated with respect. Little notes that Weil's extraordinary essay on force in the *Iliad*—and in war more generally—was written during the same period as her most explicitly anticolonial essays, and that Weil conceptualized the uprootings of colonial conquest precisely *as* force, that which turns a human into a thing.[20] In other words, Weil's shame at France's colonial empire, and her suggestions about how to go about ending it, is not a tangential interest but rather a flowering of her most fundamental project. Inese Radzins makes a similar claim in her chapter "Simone Weil's Social Philosophy: Toward a Post-Colonial Ethic," arguing that Weil's suggestion that France give up its colonies would mean risking the nation's economic well-being and global status in a wider-scale literalization of the "risk" of "self-loss" implicated in decreative attention to a suffering other.[21] In other words, as Little notes, Weil's decolonial vision was in many ways nothing more than a scaled-up repetition of her general principle that humans are obligated to help one another, even to the point of their own self-diminishment—an obligation she roots most explicitly in the Christian Gospels.[22] Weil didn't pull punches in her writing on this urgent topic, even during World War II: in *The Need for Roots*, she notes that people need greatness, but "conquest is ersatz greatness." Writing while much of France was occupied by

German forces, she insisted, as Aimé Césaire later did, that France's colonial policy was cut from the same cloth as Hitler's strategy: "It may be that France now has to choose between her attachment to her empire and the need to have a soul of her own again."[23]

Scholars have only begun to unpack the implications of Weil's anticolonialism and the provocative ways it grows out of both her vision of self-giving Christianity and her critical reading of Marx, and given the urgent need to address all manner of imperialist projects, Weil's lesser-known writings offer writers of poetry, fiction, and creative nonfiction a treasure trove of instigation to further thought—an extension of the quest for an example of moral seriousness and politically radical commitment from within the twentieth-century tradition of white women's writing. And I suspect future writers *will* attend to these materials, because there's no sign of an end to literary engagement with Simone Weil. She persists in narratives of discovery, in Patti Smith's *Devotion* (2017), based on her Windham-Campbell Lecture at Yale in 2016, which narrates a trip to France accompanied by Weil's biography and even Weil's imagined person, a pilgrimage of sorts in search of Weil's presence.[24] She persists in Karen Olsson's *The Weil Conjectures* (2019), a lithe book about math and writing that juxtaposes Simone and her brother André.[25] She persists in Maria Popova's popular curatorial website *The Marginalian* (formerly *Brain Pickings*), founded in 2006 and as of 2023 reaching millions of visitors and newsletter subscribers each week: Popova presents Weil's work in nearly a dozen essays devoted to her political, ethical, and relational wisdom, quoting at length from *Waiting for God*, *Gravity and Grace*, *The Need for Roots*, and the *First and Last Notebooks*. "Even for those of us who identify as nonbelievers and disagree with her theological ideas," Popova writes, echoing Philip, "Simone Weil's *Waiting for God* is a masterwork of human thought."[26]

Popova's amplification of Weil for a contemporary literary and popular audience, with its admission that not everyone can follow

Weil in her religious yearnings, showcases several of Weil's other specific attractions for twenty-first-century readers, not least of which is her writing on attention. Aesthetic and ethical practices of attention are key in literary writers' appeals to Weil from at least the 1960s onward, but attention accrues significance in the hectic technological developments that accompany the turn of the twenty-first century, raising urgent questions: How do we *attend* in the ways Weil invites in a market literally driven by competition for our attention, surrounded by objects and software engineered to captivate our attention, a news cycle that demands our attention to the point of robbing our capacity to act? Casey Schwartz looks to Weil for this insight at the end of her popular *Attention: A Love Story* (2020), joining Popova in noting that rather than waning in significance, "Weil's perceptions are profound even now."[27] Schwartz describes reading everything by and about Weil she can find as part of a project to understand modern modes of attention, including the appeal of medications like Aderall to counteract attention deficits and the distractions of contemporary technologies, narrating the familiar tangle of discovery— "Weil, once you know about her, has a way of endearing herself, of seducing, through the sheer force of her words"—and alienation— "often, when reading accounts about Weil, I am left cold and sad."[28] The struggle arises, for Schwartz, from Weil's unrelenting integrity, a sense of never-enoughness that haunts, a pushing even to the point of utmost self-sacrifice that Schwartz joins Rich and others in rejecting. The struggle also arises again in Weil's religious turn: "This, for a hopelessly secular, iPhone-owning city dweller like me is very hard to process, very hard to identify with. I don't know what to do with it. My entire education and culture bias me against such a turn of events."[29] Schwartz paints herself as secular in the sense of nonreligious and connects this lack of religion to her generation, her historical moment, echoing so many of the writers who have gone before her in their fraught approach to Weil.

Still, again like so many writers before her, Casey Schwartz does not turn away from Weil but turns and returns to her as a source of wisdom. Even on the point of belief, she admits, "Strangely, if I look closely at my own reaction, I can see that I'm the tiniest bit jealous: jealous of the capacity to believe as Weil believed."[30] Here Schwartz recalls Lorri Neilsen Glenn: "I realize I am reading you because I am blind, feeling for the walls of belief."[31] Schwartz further admits that Weil is not so unique in her troubling but appealing capacity for faith. The four thinkers on whom she focuses her book about attention— David Foster Wallace, William James, Aldous Huxley, and Simone Weil—were all "irretrievably drawn to the question of belief," wondering whether there might in fact be some connection between the quest for "how to attend and how to believe."[32] Schwartz finds another source in the poet Mary Oliver, whose claims about attention echoed Weil's and who, incidentally, had her own turn to Christianity as beautifully confessed in collections like *Thirst*, but who lived a long and lovely life with her partner Molly Malone Cook, a life thick with both sorrow and joy.[33] The implication, here, is that perhaps the height of Weil's wisdom need not manifest itself in loneliness and early death but can shine in the sometimes minutely self-suspending gifts that lead to love.[34]

It doesn't have to be one or the other. Weil can guide her readers into practices of everyday kindness, the kind that looks up from screens into a neighbor's eyes, the kind that holds a door or an elevator, even as she inspires the countless hours of self-giving it takes to write a book or the steel-spined courage it takes to form a human barricade in front of a pipeline project on Indigenous land. She can lead the way toward a frank refusal of the Church due to its harms even as she gives others room to wrestle with the God for whom they hunger with her, perhaps even the Christ whose presence they have also sensed in the mystery of mystical encounter. Weil can invite versification of her rigorous philosophy and her personal foibles, poetic attention to her throbbing humanity and chronic pain, the woman chain-smoking through a gripping headache, the woman so weak she lies on her back to harvest grapes but refuses to give up harvesting, the woman starting the Our Father again in Greek because she lost focus and wants to say it through just once with perfect attention. She can inspire both poetry and action, provoke both outrage and admiration, invite both pity and self-recognition—and sometimes all at the same time. She has. She does.

And it's never been just Weil's storied life that compels literary writing: it's also her prose, gorgeous even in translation. The books about Weil turn us to her own writing. I still remember the day in my midtwenties when I first read *Waiting for God*, having tracked down a battered used copy after reading about Weil in Rich's *Of Woman Born*. The previous owner or owners had annotated the text in bright yellow highlighter and red ballpoint pen, and so to distinguish my own notes I used purple ink. Sitting in a corner of my dear friend Andrea's Chicago home office while she typed notes for her dissertation in theology, I read the whole book in a day, enraptured and appalled. My notes are all asterisks and question marks and other authors' names. I recognized Annie Dillard in those lines. I wondered fiercely about what Rich found in them. The prose was so readable at points that it was easy to overlook what radically challenging claims Weil was making about the nature of the world, the nature of the divine, the nature of attention. But still I felt some spark of recognition and a strong attraction to the rhythm and vivid simplicity of her language. I was in my own deep struggle with the Christian tradition but not quite willing to give up on it and longing to find a framework to describe the human impulse toward mutual care. *Simone Weil was writing my mind, my wounded mind.*

And still, she was herself wounded. I keep coming back to a page in the New York Notebook, one that reads to me like a found poem:

Compassion is what spans the abyss which creation has opened between
God and the creature.

It is the rainbow.

Compassion should have the same dimension as the act of creation. It
cannot exclude a single creature.

One should love oneself only with a compassionate love.

Every created thing is an object for compassion because it is ephemeral.

Compassion directed to oneself is humility.

Humility is the only permitted form of self-love.

Praise for God, compassion for creatures, humility for the self.

Without humility, all the virtues are finite. Only humility makes them
infinite.[35]

Weil's fraught thoughts, rendered in sparse and lovely sentences,
provoke response: they provoke wondering, resistance, explication.
They provoke creativity: hundreds of pages of prose, of poems, a
dizzying array of imagined lives for Weil. And they provoke compassion: compassion for the brilliant woman, her self-love tangled
in humility, who could not quite find her place within the world and
still somehow guides the way to caring for it and all the creatures who
occupy it, to loving the world no less for its unspeakable pain than its
inestimable beauty. She died too soon, and yet she lives, in her own
words and the words of dozens of writers who attend to her, over and
over again. *If we distort*, I hear them whispering along with Strickland, *we don't abandon.*

ACKNOWLEDGMENTS

I n an excerpt included in *Gravity and Grace*, Simone Weil muses, "Writing is like giving birth: we cannot help making the supreme effort." Writing this book has required some of the same patience, courage, and frankly physical work that was involved in birthing the two children who came into my life during the decade I spent on it. But it was also like giving birth in that I was beautifully and powerfully accompanied. The gratitude I feel for this book's many, many midwives is enormous.

I began thinking about Weil in graduate school, and so I must again thank Pamela Caughie, Suzanne Bost, Micael Clarke, and Hille Haker for their guidance in those earlier conversations. Even before them, I learned the practices of attention from my undergraduate professors Julie Moore, Peggy Wilfong, and especially Don Deardorff, who taught me the joyful discipline of close reading: may his memory be a blessing. Over the years of work on this book, I have benefited from many conversation partners: I am grateful to Jess Klassen-Wright, who worked as a research assistant collating resources on Weil in the project's early stages, and to the students in my graduate seminar "The Ethics of Attention" and my undergraduate honors seminar "Forms of Hunger: The Literary Afterlives of Simone Weil," whose thoughts inevitably sharpened my own. I'm thankful for dialogue about Adrienne Rich with Ed Pavlić, Al and Barbara Gelpi, and Pablo Conrad, whose work at the Adrienne Rich Literary Trust has also supported these projects with immense generosity, including permission to quote from archival materials. For dialogue about Catholic literary imaginations and Weil, I'm grateful to Fr. Mark Bosco, Melissa Bradshaw, Mary Gordon, and Michael Murphy of the Hank Center for the Catholic Intellectual Heritage at Loyola University Chicago, which hosted a conference on Denise Levertov in 2015 that allowed me to present some of these initial ideas on Weil's literary presence. I'm also grateful for the chance to present papers on Weil and literary writers at the American Weil Society and the Modern Language Association annual convention, with special thanks to Sara Judy and Christos Hadjiyiannis for organizing us. I'm also grateful for a Distinctive Area Research Grant, a Seed Grant, a publication subvention, and a sabbatical from St. Thomas More College, all of which supported this work. I also had the chance to think through some of these thoughts in pieces for the *Ploughshares* journal blog, and I'm grateful to managing editor Ellen Duffer for welcoming those essays with such encouragement.

The midwives abound. Thank you, Heidi Epstein, for gloriously expansive conversations. Thank you, Michael O'Connell, for the regular check-ins that kept me going during the most intensive writing phase. Thank you, Joanne Leow and Giuliano Gullotti, for mixing book talk and delicious food and mutual care. Thank you, Matt and Brandi Molby, for your steady, delight-filled presence. Thank you, Terri Lynn Paulson and Thomas Friesen, Emily and Taylor Summach, and Mark Bigland-Pritchard, for sharing life. Thank you, communities of deep friendship near and far, especially the women who *see me* across time and space: Laura and Kristin; Meg and Ruth; Liz (and Peter); Andrea, Annie, Emily, Nicky, Patty, and Susan; Cheryl, Claire, Emily, Susie, and Theresa; Amy, Emily, Kirsten, Ky, Katelyn, and Terri Lynn; Amanda, Jillian, Karen, and

Tanya. In so many ways, you have fed me when I was hungry. May we continue to midwife each other's holy work of creation: may we continue to help each other find rest.

In the publication process, I have been enormously lucky in the support of Wendy Lochner and others at Columbia University Press, including Lowell Frye, Susan Pensak, and Amy Hollywood. I'm also grateful for Anita O'Brien's excellent copyediting and Joel Looper's careful indexing. This book benefited immensely from the comments of two anonymous peer reviewers, to whose insights I hope I have done justice.

I wrote the bulk of this book during the extended isolation of a pandemic that stopped many of us short. I could not have done this without the freedom of a yearlong sabbatical as well as the full partnership of my spouse, who took the lead with remote and home schooling. Josh, your active care has let me bring this work into being—your care for our children and for me, including countless hours of conversation. You're still my favorite person to study with. Michele and Richard Rich were also immensely helpful even from 1,527 miles away, with daily calls to their grandkids (and their parents) that helped us all feel more connected. Thank you, Mom and Dad, for this discipline of love. And finally, Miriam and Pilgram, you are growing up in a time when such courage is asked of you, and I am so very proud of who you are: of your curious minds and caring hearts and stubborn commitment to what is good and fair. Thank you for making room in our family for another book. You two are my greatest gift.

NOTES

INTRODUCTION

1. Simone Weil, *Waiting for God*, trans. Emma Craufurd (New York: Harper and Row, 1951), 113.
2. Peggy Rosenthal, "An Apprenticeship in Affliction: Waiting with Simone Weil," *Image Journal*, no. 77, https://imagejournal.org/article/an-apprenticeship-in-affliction/.
3. Joan Dargan, *Simone Weil: Thinking Poetically* (Albany, N.Y.: SUNY Press, 1999), 16.
4. Simone Weil, *Venice Saved*, trans. Silvia Caprioglio Panizza and Philip Wilson (New York: Bloomsbury Academic, 2019).
5. Robert Zaretsky, *The Subversive Simone Weil: A Life in Five Ideas* (Chicago: University of Chicago Press, 2021), 2.
6. A. Rebecca Rozelle-Stone and Benjamin P. Davis, "Simone Weil," *Stanford Encyclopedia of Philosophy*, ed. Edward N. Zalta, https://plato.stanford.edu/archives/fall2020/entries/simone-weil/.
7. Adrian Grafe's chapter on Weil published in the book *Ecstasy and Understanding Religious Awareness in English Poetry from the Late Victorian to the Modern Period* (New York: Bloomsbury Academic, 2008) reads Weil's presence primarily in poetry by Rowan Williams but also names Elizabeth Jennings, T. S. Eliot, Seamus Heaney, Geoffrey Hill, and Michael Symmons Roberts, noting parenthetically that "there may, of course, be others" (161). Many of these others have lived on the other side of the Atlantic Ocean, a fact scholars are beginning to address.

   Scholarly readings of Weil's presence in North American literature include Brian Teare, "The Apophatic Pilgrim: Simone Weil and Fanny Howe," in *Quo Anima: Spirituality and Innovation in Contemporary Women's Poetry*, ed. Jennifer

Phelps and Elizabeth Robinson (Akron, OH: University of Akron Press, 2019), 6–22; Tanis MacDonald, "'What Is Not Self': Jan Zwicky, Simone Weil, and the Resonance of Decreation," *Philosophy and Literature* 39, no. 1 (2015): 211–18; Tanis MacDonald, "Hunger, History, and the Shape of Awkward Questions: Reading Sarah Klassen's *Simone Weil* as a Mennonite Text," *English and Film Studies Faculty Publications* 8 (2010): 87–102; Kit Fan, "'Between the blank page and the poem': Reading Simone Weil in Contemporary American Poets," *Cambridge Quarterly* 36, no. 2 (2007): 129–54; Romana Huk, "'A single liturgy': Fanny Howe's *The Wedding Dress*," *Christianity and Literature* 58, no. 4 (2009): 657–93; Katy Wright Bushman, "A Poetics of Consenting Attention: Simone Weil's Prayer and the Poetry of Denise Levertov," *Christianity and Literature* 62, no. 3 (2013): 369–92; Cynthia R. Wallace, "'passionate/reverence, active love': Levertov and Weil in the Communion of Struggle," in *This Need to Dance/This Need to Kneel: Denise Levertov and the Poetics of Faith*, ed. Michael P. Murphy and Melissa Bradshaw (Eugene, OR: Wipf and Stock, 2019), 127–39; and Kait Pinder, "Sheila Watson as a Reader of Simone Weil: Decreation, Affliction, and *Metaxu* in *The Double Hook*," *University of Toronto Quarterly* 90, no. 4 (2021): 669–90.

8. Simone Pétrement, *Simone Weil: A Life* (New York: Pantheon, 1976). Some of the influential biographies of Weil written in or translated into English include Joseph Marie Perrin and Gustave Thibon, *Simone Weil as We Knew Her* (New York: Routledge, 1953); Jacques Cabaud, *Simone Weil: A Fellowship in Love* (London: Harvill Press, 1964); Robert Coles, *Simone Weil: A Modern Pilgrimage* (Boston: Addison-Wesley, 1989); Gabriella Fiori, *Simone Weil: An Intellectual History* (Athens: University of Georgia Press, 1989); David McLellan, *Simone Weil: Utopian Pessimist* (London: Palgrave Macmillan, 1990); Thomas R. Nevin, *Simone Weil: Portrait of a Self-Exiled Jew* (Chapel Hill: University of North Carolina Press, 1991); and Francine du Plessix Gray, *Simone Weil: A Penguin Life* (New York: Penguin, 2001).
9. Deborah Nelson, *Tough Enough: Arbus, Arendt, Didion, McCarthy, Sontag, Weil* (Chicago: University of Chicago Press, 2017), 19–20.
10. Rozelle-Stone and Davis, "Simone Weil."
11. E. Jane Doering, *Simone Weil and the Specter of Self-Perpetuating Force* (Notre Dame, IN: University of Notre Dame Press, 2010), 3.
12. Zaretsky, *Subversive*, 3.
13. Weil, *Waiting for God*, 67, 68, 69.
14. Eric O. Springsted, Introduction to Simone Weil, *First and Last Notebooks*, trans. Richard Rees (London: Peters, Fraser, and Dunlop, 1970), ix.
15. Françoise Meltzer, "The Hands of Simone Weil," *Critical Inquiry* 27, no. 4 (2001): 621.
16. Weil, *Waiting for God*, 76.

17. Simone Weil, "Reflections on War," *politics* 2, no. 2 (February 1945): 51–55.

18. Simone Weil, "The *Iliad*; or The Poem of Force," trans. Mary McCarthy, *politics* (November 1945): 321–31; Doering, *Simone Weil*, 218.

19. Elizabeth Hardwick, "Reflections on Simone Weil," *Signs* 1, no. 1 (1975): 163.

20. Nelson, *Tough Enough*, 23, 26, 35.

21. Coles, *Simone Weil*, xv–xvi.

22. Susan Sontag, "Simone Weil," *New York Review of Books* 1, no. 1 (1 February 1963).

23. Each generation since Weil's death seems to have discovered and rediscovered Weil as an answer to what ailed society. Poet Peggy Rosenthal recalls first encountering Weil through the *Simone Weil Reader* (1977), edited by George Panichas, who "was offering her writings as an antidote to the insidious narcissism which had gripped American society in the 1970s" ("An Apprenticeship in Affliction: Waiting with Simone Weil," *Image Journal*, no. 77, https://imagejournal.org/article/an-apprenticeship-in-affliction/). Sandra Gilbert, in a review for *Poetry* magazine, called Weil "that now (alas) all too trendy heroine." Gilbert, Review of *The Lamplit Answer* by Gjertrud Schnackenbergm, *Poetry* 147, no. 3 (1985): 166.

24. Nelson, *Tough Enough*, 17.

25. McLellan, *Simone Weil*; Jerry White, "In Search of Our Roots: Remembering Simone Weil's North American Emergence," *Dalhousie Review* 99, no. 3 (2019): 412.

26. This "saint" language isn't constrained to the more mystically focused approaches to Weil. White notes that even "Gregory D. Sumner's history of the magazine [*politics*] calls Weil the 'patron saint' of Macdonald and his collaborator Nicola Chiaromonte" ("In Search of Our Roots," 413).

27. Leslie Fiedler, Introduction to *Waiting for God* by Simone Weil (New York: Harper and Row, 1951), 3.

28. This sketch of ideas constrains itself to the key concepts taken up by the authors I explicate in this book (which align with popular understandings and celebrations of Weil), but her political and mystical philosophies far exceed these bounds. For an accessible overview of Weil's varied philosophical interventions, see Rozelle-Stone and Davis's excellent entry on Weil in the online *Stanford Encyclopedia of Philosophy*. I should also note that Weil has provoked not just a wide range of literary writing but an extraordinary range of scholarly writing in a wide range of disciplines, including philosophy, religious studies, political studies, and feminist studies. The online Simone Weil Bibliography, housed at the University of Calgary (https://simoneweil.library.ucalgary.ca), included more than 5,200 sources as of June 2023.

29. Adrienne Rich, *Arts of the Possible: Essays and Conversations* (New York: Norton, 2001), 144.

30. Tracy Fessenden, "The Problem of the Postsecular," *American Literary History* 26, no. 1 (2014): 155.

31. Lori Branch, "The Rituals of Our Re-Secularization: Literature Between Faith and Knowledge," *Religion and Literature* 46, no. 2/3 (2014): 9–33.

32. Khaled Furani, "Is There a Postsecular?" *Journal of the American Academy of Religion* 83, no. 1 (2015): 4. Notably, many of these historical phenomena have been documented in literary writing: consider Marjane Satrapi's *Persepolis* (New York: Pantheon, 2004) and Anita Desai's *Clear Light of Day* (New York: HarperCollins, 1980).

33. Talal Asad, *Formations of the Secular: Christianity, Islam, Modernity* (Stanford, CA: Stanford University Press, 2003); Charles Taylor, *A Secular Age* (Cambridge, MA: Belknap, 2007).

34. Peter Coviello and Jared Hickman, "Introduction: After the Postsecular," *American Literature* 86, no. 4 (2014): 645.

35. John A. McClure, *Partial Faiths: Postsecular Fiction in the Age of Pynchon and Morrison* (Athens: University of Georgia Press, 2007), ix.

36. Amy Hungerford, *Postmodern Belief: American Literature and Religion Since 1960* (Princeton, NJ: Princeton University Press, 2010).

37. Fessenden, "The Problem," 165, 161; Branch, "The Rituals," 9.

38. Michael Tomko, "The Seasons of the Secular: Revisiting the Secularization Thesis in Nineteenth-Century Studies," *Religion and Literature* 41, no. 3 (2009): 136. Also see Lori Branch: "The reduction of religion to moralizing is noteworthy, and it's a protestant secularizing spirit that disenchants critique by crying, 'No more hair-splitting, nit-picking, angels-on-the-head-of-a-pin scholasticism!'" Branch, "Postcritical and Postsecular: The Horizon of Belief," *Religion and Literature* 48, no. 2 (2016): 164.

39. Furani, "Is There a Postsecular?" 2.

40. Fessenden, "The Problem," 165.

41. Furani, "Is There a Postsecular?" 20; Coviello and Hickman, "Introduction," 649.

42. Furani, "Is There a Postsecular?" 10, 10, 12, 14, 17.

43. Lissa McCullough, *The Religious Philosophy of Simone Weil: An Introduction* (London: I. B. Tauris, 2014), 11.

44. Claude Gendron, "Moral Attention: A Comparative Philosophical Study," *Journal of Moral Education* 45, no. 4 (2016): 374.

45. Chris Cuomo, *The Philosopher Queen: Feminist Essays on War, Love, and Knowledge* (New York: Rowman & Littlefield, 2002), 139. Murdoch's interest in Weil may have complicated her appeal to feminist philosophers, however. In a review of Sabina Lovibond's *Iris Murdoch, Gender, and Philosophy* (2011), Nora Hämäläinen notes that Lovibond critiques Murdoch for her interest in Weil, blaming Weil for Murdoch's "anti-feminist agenda" due to Weil's "self-denigrating idea of

moral goodness." Lovibond, "Iris Murdoch, Gender, and Philosophy," *Notre Dame Philosophical Reviews*, December 10, 2011, https://ndpr.nd.edu/reviews /iris-murdoch-gender-and-philosophy/.

46. Weil's rejection of the feminine social norms of her day also raises questions few scholars have felt equipped to answer about Weil's own gender identity. Weil famously rejected the trappings of feminine dress and comportment and even signed letters home "Simon" and "your son." Sylvie Courtine-Denamy goes so far as to argue that Weil "hated being a woman, refusing to acknowledge this basic fact of her existence just as she refused to acknowledge her Jewishness." Courtine-Denamy, *Three Women in Dark Times: Edith Stein, Hannah Arendt, Simone Weil* (Ithaca, NY: Cornell University Press, 2001), 2. Commentators tread lightly in this arena; many don't really address it. The difficult—and probably unanswerable—question is whether Weil experienced a deep gender dysphoria we would now associate with transgender experience, or whether her frustration was primarily with the social constraints placed on women in her day. In other words, did Weil wish not to be a woman, or did she wish as a woman to be permitted a wider range of action in early twentieth-century France? Most of the writers I address in this book seem to read Weil as feeling the latter.

    A similar challenge accompanies Weil's sensory and interpersonal quiddities: her avoidance of human touch, limited palate for food, monotonous tone of voice, hyperfocus on topics of interest, and evident oblivion to certain social norms. Is it useful to characterize Weil as neurodivergent in terms only recently available? This is another tenuous question for qualified scholars to address with exceeding care in future work.

47. Consider, for example, Carol Gilligan, *In a Different Voice: Psychological Theory and Women's Development* (Cambridge, MA: Harvard University Press, 1982).

48. Weil, *Waiting for God*, 111–12.

49. Sophie Bourgault, "Beyond the Saint and the Red Virgin: Simone Weil as Feminist Theorist of Care," *Frontiers: A Journal of Women Studies* 35, no. 2 (2014): 1–27.

50. Sara Ruddick, *Maternal Thinking* (Boston: Beacon, 1989), 120.

51. Johannes Zachhuber and Julia Meszaros, Introduction to *Sacrifice and Modern Thought* (Oxford: Oxford University Press, 2013), 1.

52. Elizabeth Cady Stanton, *The Woman's Bible*, 1985 (Boston: Northeastern University Press, 1993), 84, 7.

53. Feminists continue to debate the value of self-sacrifice in both religious and non-religious frames. See, for example, Pamela Sue Anderson, "Sacrifice as Self-destructive 'Love,'" in *Sacrifice and Modern Thought*, ed. Julia Meszaros and Johannes Zachhuber (Oxford: Oxford University Press, 2013), 29–47, for a rejection of self-sacrifice; and Anna Mercedes, *Power For: Feminist and Christ's Self Giving* (Edinburgh: T&T Clark, 2011), for a recuperation of self-sacrifice.

54. Simone Weil, *Simone Weil: An Anthology*, ed. Siân Miles (New York: Grove Press, 1986), 70.

55. Quoted in Cuomo, *Philosopher*, 140.

56. Ann Loades, "Eucharistic Sacrifice: Simone Weil's Use of a Liturgical Metaphor," *Religion and Literature* 17, no. 2 (1985): 51, 53.

57. Francine du Plessix Gray, "At Large and at Small: Loving and Hating Simone Weil," *American Scholar* 70, no. 3 (2001): 11, 8.

58. Cuomo, *Philosopher*, 135, 136, 137.

59. Eric O. Springsted, Introduction to *Simone Weil for the Twenty-First Century* (Notre Dame, IN: University of Notre Dame Press, 2021), viii.

60. Sophie Bourgault, "Hannah Arendt and Simone Weil on the Significance of Love for Politics," in *Thinking About Love: Essays in Contemporary Continental Philosophy*, ed. Diane Enns and Antonio Calcagno (University Park: Pennsylvania State University Press, 2015), 161.

61. Cuomo, *Philosopher*, 139.

62. M. Shawn Copeland, "'Wading Through Many Sorrows': Toward a Theology of Suffering in Womanist Perspective," in *A Troubling in My Soul: Womanist Perspectives on Evil and Suffering*, ed. Emilie M. Townes (Maryknoll, NY: Orbis, 1993), 118.

63. See Michelle Cliff, *If I Could Write This in Fire* (Minneapolis: University of Minnesota Press, 2008), 47; and Cliff, *Into the Interior* (Minneapolis: University of Minnesota Press, 2010), 41, 106. Perhaps tellingly, the narrator in *Into the Interior* states in passing, "The only question in the universe is 'What are you going through?' I think Simone Weil said that, but I cannot remember the citation" (41). This performance of forgetfulness in a sense further decenters Weil.

64. Michelle Cliff, *Free Enterprise: A Novel of Mary Ellen Pleasant* (San Francisco: City Lights, 2004); Cliff, *Abeng* (Berkeley: Crossing Press, 1984); Cliff, *No Telephone to Heaven* (Boston: Dutton, 1987).

65. M. NourbeSe Philip, *Harriet's Daughter* (London: Women's Press, 1988); Philip, *Looking for Livingstone: An Odyssey of Silence* (Toronto: Mercury, 1991).

66. M. NourbeSe Philip, *Zong!* (Toronto: Mercury, 2008); Cliff, *Free Enterprise*, 72.

67. Sigrid Nunez, *The Friend* (New York: Riverhead, 2018), 76, 141; Sigrid Nunez, *What Are You Going Through* (New York: Riverhead, 2020).

68. Sigrid Nunez, *The Last of Her Kind* (New York: Farrar, Straus, and Giroux, 2006). The novel's explicit comparisons between Weil and Ann arise in its very center, on 226–46. The quote is from 215.

69. It also is entirely possible that my own quest for a more diverse range of anglophone literary renderings of Weil has missed important texts—an absence that speaks to the uneven flows of influence and information even within an ostensibly wholly searchable digital age.

1. FORCE

1. Deborah Nelson, *Tough Enough: Arbus, Arendt, Didion, McCarthy, Sontag, Weil* (Chicago: University of Chicago Press, 2017), 17.

2. Adrienne Rich, "Caryatid: A Column," *American Poetry Review* (September/ October 1973): 17.

3. Sontag's *New York Review of Books* essay, "Simone Weil," was later collected in her book *Against Interpretation*, further increasing its circulation and likely introducing more readers to the philosopher.

4. Adrienne Rich, *Collected Poems 1950–2012* (New York: Norton, 2016), 745.

5. A. Rebecca Rozelle-Stone and Benjamin P. Davis, "Simone Weil," *Stanford Encyclopedia of Philosophy*, ed. Edward N. Zalta, https://plato.stanford.edu/archives /fall2020/entries/simone-weil/.

6. Michelle Cliff, "Sister/Outsider: Some Thoughts on Simone Weil," in *Between Women: Biographers, Novelists, Critics, Teachers, and Artists Write About Their Work on Women*, ed. Carol Ascher, Louise DeSalvo, and Sara Ruddick (Boston: Beacon, 1984), 314.

7. Hilary Holladay, *The Power of Adrienne Rich* (New York: Nan A. Talese, 2020), 278.

8. Sigrid Nunez, *Sempre Susan: A Memoir of Susan Sontag* (New York: Riverhead, 2014), 56, 79. Nunez also attended Barnard College, graduating in 1971, as did Mary Gordon, who graduated in 1972, where both studied with Elizabeth Hardwick, and Nunez became part of a circle involved with the *New York Review of Books*.

9. Elizabeth Hardwick, "Reflections on Simone Weil," *Signs* 1, no. 1 (1975): 83, 83, 84, 91, 90, 91.

10. Albert Gelpi, "Powers of Recuperation: Tracking Adrienne Rich," *Women's Studies* 46, no. 7 (2017): 718. Rich's reception history is also complicated by the critical establishment's disapproval of her feminist and explicitly political turn, as various commentators have noted. See, for example, Kathleen Barry, "Reviewing Reviews: *Of Woman Born*," 1977, in *Reading Adrienne Rich: Reviews and Re-Visions 1951–81*, ed. Jane Roberta Cooper (Ann Arbor: University of Michigan Press, 1984), 300–303; and Alice Templeton, "Contradictions: Tracking Adrienne Rich's Poetry," *Tulsa Studies in Women's Literature* 12, no. 2 (1993): 333–40.

11. Quote is from Miriam Marty Clark, "Human Rights and the Work of Lyric in Adrienne Rich," *Cambridge Quarterly* 38, no. 1 (2009): 47.

12. Jeanette Riley, *Understanding Adrienne Rich* (Columbia: University of South Carolina Press, 2016), 84.

13. Maggie Rehm, "'try telling yourself/you are not accountable': Adrienne Rich as Citizen Poet," *Women's Studies*, 46, no. 7 (2017): 685.

14. Indeed, Mark Nowak wrote in 2006 that "few US poets invoke (and critique) the nature and role of capitalism in contemporary poetic practice more consistently and vehemently." Nowack, "Notes Toward an Anticapitalist Poetics," *Virginia Quarterly Review* 82, no. 2 (2006): 236.

15. Ed Pavlić, *Outward: Adrienne Rich's Expanding Solitudes* (Minneapolis: University of Minnesota Press, 2021), 50, 51, 56, 76, 57, 89, 104, 107.

16. Pavlić, 7.

17. Rich, *Collected Poems*, 323.

18. The four poems are, respectively, in Rich, *Collected Poems*, 269, 307, 339, 367.

19. Adrienne Rich, *On Lies, Secrets, and Silence: Selected Prose 1966–1978* (New York: Norton, 1979).

20. Adrienne Rich, "An Interview with Adrienne Rich and Mary Daly," by Valerie Miner, *San Francisco Review of Books* 3, no. 6 (1977): 13.

21. Rich, *Collected Poems*, 443.

22. Rich, "An Interview," 14. Rich goes on to note: "The interesting thing to me is that you have two Simones both in the same class at the Ecole Normale, and one becomes the writer of *The Second Sex* and one becomes the writer of *Waiting for God*. Both come out of middle class French intellectual backgrounds. What are the forces that are playing on these two women? I'd really like to see someone deal with that."

23. Simone Pétrement, *Simone Weil: A Life*, trans. Raymond Rosenthal (New York: Pantheon, 1976).

24. Debound notebook page, undated, carton 4, folder 68, Papers of Adrienne Rich, 1927–1999, Schlesinger Library, Radcliffe Institute.

25. Handwritten notes, 1972, folder 354, Papers of Adrienne Rich.

26. Typewritten and hand-edited manuscript, 1972, folder 354, Papers of Adrienne Rich.

27. The archivists I contacted at Brandeis were unable to locate any recordings or other records of Rich's 1972–1973 lectures. I am grateful for their efforts to track down more information.

28. Rich, *On Lies*, 95.

29. Sophie Bourgault, "Beyond the Saint and the Red Virgin: Simone Weil as Feminist Theorist of Care," *Frontiers: A Journal of Women Studies* 35, no. 2 (2014): 2. Feminist care ethicists who draw on Weil's work include Sara Ruddick, *Maternal Thinking* (Boston: Beacon, 1989); Joan Tronto, *Moral Boundaries* (New York: Routledge, 1993); and Nel Noddings, *The Maternal Factor* (Berkeley: University of California Press, 2010). Bourgault notes that these influential books have inspired "many American and French scholars in sociology, medicine, and nursing" to turn to Weil's "concept of attention" as well (2).

30. Miriam Marty Clark, "Human Rights and the Work of Lyric in Adrienne Rich," *Cambridge Quarterly* 38, no. 1 (2009): 47.

31. Rich, *Collected Poems*, 174; Simone Weil, *Waiting for God*, trans. Emma Craufurd (New York: Harper and Row, 1951), 149.

32. Rich, *Collected Poems*, 176.

33. Rich, 269.

34. Weil, *Waiting for God*, 109, 112.

35. Weil, 114, 115.

36. Weil, 115, 116.

37. Wendy Martin, "From Patriarchy to the Female Principle: A Chronological Reading of Adrienne Rich's Poems," in *Adrienne Rich's Poetry*, ed. Barbara Charlesworth Gelpi and Albert Gelpi (New York: Norton, 1975), 185.

38. Claire Keyes, *The Aesthetics of Power: The Poetry of Adrienne Rich* (Athens: University of Georgia Press, 1986), 101.

39. Rich, *Collected Poems*, 269, 271, 272.

40. Rich, 270, 271.

41. Rich, 273.

42. Rich, 307–8.

43. Pavlić, *Outward*, 36.

44. Rich, *Collected Poems*, 343, 342.

45. Ed Pavlić, "'*how we are with each other*': Adrienne Rich's Radical—Which Is to Say Relational—Legacy," *Women's Studies* 46, no. 7 (2017): 730.

46. Craig Werner, *Adrienne Rich: The Poet and Her Critics* (Chicago: American Library Association, 1988), 33; James McCorkle, *The Still Performance: Writing, Self, and Interconnection in Five Postmodern American Poets* (Charlottesville: University of Virginia Press, 1989), 95, 102; Nick Halpern *Everyday and Prophetic: The Poetry of Lowell, Ammons, Merrill, and Rich* (Madison: University of Wisconsin Press, 2003), 220.

47. Rich, *Collected Poems*, 367.

48. Angela Davis and Andrea Dworkin famously spoke out against the prison, and Sarah Harris, who worked there as a social worker, published the book *Hellhole: The Shocking Story of the Inmates and Life in the New York House of Detention for Women* (New York: Dutton, 1967).

49. Rich, *Collected Poems*, 745, 903.

50. Talia Shalev compellingly explicates Rich's frequent use of apostrophe and its relational implications, arguing that for Rich, apostrophe doesn't only suggest "an unbridgeable distance between a poem's speaker and addressee, . . . it also implies these figures are co-present with others, whoever, wherever, and for Rich, whenever they may be." Shalev, "Adrienne Rich's 'Collaborations': Re-vision as Durational Address," *Women's Studies* 46, no. 7 (2017): 659.

51. Rich, *Collected Poems*, 174, 269, 475.
52. Rich, 507.
53. Rich, 1059, 1060.
54. Rich, 900, 903.
55. Bourgault, "Beyond."
56. Adrienne Rich, *Of Woman Born: Motherhood as Experience and Institution*, 1976, tenth anniversary ed. (New York: Norton, 1986), 158, 159, 280.
57. Rich, *Collected Poems*, 356, 655, 1065.
58. Weil, *Waiting for God*, 118.
59. Rich, *Collected Poems*, 655; Simone Weil, *The Need for Roots*, trans. Arthur Wills, 1952 (New York: Harper Colophon, 1971), 43.
60. Weil, *Waiting for God*, 125.
61. Simone Weil, "The *Iliad*, or the Poem of Force," in *Simone Weil: An Anthology*, ed. Siân Miles (New York: Grove, 1986), 163, 164, 165, 171.
62. Rich, *Collected Poems*, 307, 370, 473.
63. Rachel Blau DuPlessis, "The Critique of Consciousness and Myth in Levertov, Rich, and Rukeyser," *Feminist Studies* 3, no. 1/2 (1975): 211.
64. Rich, *Collected Poems*, 1048, 1049.
65. Weil, "The *Iliad*," 190.
66. Rich, *Collected Poems*, 562, 745, 451.
67. Rich, 451, 453, 454, 453, 452.
68. Rich, 594, 596.
69. Audre Lorde, "An Open Letter to Mary Daly," 1979, in *Sister Outsider: Essays and Speeches* (New York: Crossing Press, 1984), 66–71.
70. Rich, *Collected Poems*, 452.
71. Rich, 452, 453.
72. Weil, *The Need for Roots*, 6, 7.
73. Bourgault, "Beyond the Saint," 6.
74. For example, see Weil, *Waiting for God*, 166.
75. Rich, *Collected Poems*, 453, 454.
76. Adrienne Rich, *Blood, Bread, and Poetry: Selected Prose 1979–1985* (New York: Norton, 1986), 163.
77. Rich, *Collected Poems*, 562, 563.
78. Rich, 367.
79. Weil, *The Need for Roots*, 51.
80. Simone Weil, *Gravity and Grace*, trans. Emma Craufurd, 1952 (New York: Routledge, 1963), 46.
81. Rich was certainly aware of Weil's recourse to Plato's cave allegory. She cites Weil's *First and Last Notebooks* in an epigraph to the first chapter of *Of Woman Born*: ". . . to understand is always an ascending movement; that is why

comprehension ought always to be concrete. (one is never got out of the cave, one comes out of it.)" (21).

82. Weil, *Gravity and Grace*, 52.
83. Rich, *Collected Poems*, 562.
84. Hardwick, "Reflections," 88.
85. Rich, *Collected Poems*, 562.
86. Weil, *Waiting for God*, 113.
87. Rich, *Collected Poems*, 562.
88. Rich, 745.
89. Rich, 745.
90. Rich, 745.
91. Rich, 745, 746.
92. Rich, 746.
93. Rich, *Blood, Bread, and Poetry*, 103; Rich, *Collected Poems*, 576.
94. Rich, *Collected Poems*, 577.
95. Rich, 588.
96. Rich, *Blood, Bread, and Poetry*, 208.
97. Michelle Cliff, "Sister/Outsider: Some Thoughts on Simone Weil," in *Between Women: Biographers, Novelists, Critics, Teachers, and Artists Write About Their Work on Women*, ed. Carol Ascher, Louise DeSalvo, and Sara Ruddick (Boston: Beacon, 1984), 322. I generally follow Weil biographer Francine du Plessix Gray in describing Weil's "troubling views on Jewishness" as "anti-Judaism rather than anti-Semitism," emphasizing Weil's deeply problematic ideological objections to the Jewish religion over a more general internalized racism. (Gray, "At Large and Small: Loving and Hating Simone Weil," *American Scholar* 70, no. 3 [2001]: 6.) In conversation with Mary Gordon's extended fictional grappling with them, I address Weil's anti-Jewish biases at length in chapter 3.
98. Rich, *Blood, Bread, and Poetry*, 123.
99. See Cynthia R. Wallace, *Of Women Borne: A Literary Ethics of Suffering* (New York: Columbia University Press, 2016).
100. Adam Zachary Newton, "Versions of Ethics; or, the SARL of Criticism: Sonority, Arrogation, and Letting-Be," *American Literary History* 13, no. 3 (2001): 606–37.
101. Eric O. Springsted, *Simone Weil for the Twenty-First Century* (Notre Dame, IN: University of Notre Dame Press, 2021), 1–2.
102. Weil, *Waiting for God*, 69, 75, 82, 85.
103. Weil, 181–82, 185.
104. Weil's anticolonialism deserves more attention, a dynamic I take up in my conclusion. For a discussion of this theme, see Inese Radzins, "Simone Weil's Social Philosophy: Toward a Post-Colonial Ethic," *New Topics in Feminist Philosophy of Religion*, ed. P. S. Anderson (New York: Springer, 2010), 69–83. Weil's works

on colonialism are collected in J. P. Little, *Simone Weil on Colonialism: An Ethic of the Other* (Lanham, MD: Rowman & Littlefield, 2003).

105. Rehm, "try telling yourself," 684.

106. Craig Werner, "Trying to Keep Faith: Adrienne Rich's 'Usonian Journals 2000,'" *Virginia Quarterly Review*, 82, no. 2 (2006): 243.

107. E. Jane Doering, *Simone Weil and the Specter of Self-Perpetuating Force* (Notre Dame, IN: University of Notre Dame Press, 2010), 3.

108. Adrienne Rich, *What Is Found There: Notebooks on Poetry and Politics*, 1993 (New York: Norton, 2003), xvii.

2. ATTENTION

1. Philip Yancey, "A Pilgrim's Progress," *Books and Culture*, September/October 1995: 10.

2. Yancey, 11; Leslie Fiedler, Introduction to *Waiting for God*, by Simone Weil (New York: Harper and Row, 1951), 3.

3. Yancey, "A Pilgrim's Progress," 10, 11.

4. George A. Panichas, ed., *The Simone Weil Reader*, by Simone Weil (New York: McKay, 1977), xv.

5. In an email exchange in May 2023, Dillard indicated that she does not remember how she first came across Weil's work. She wondered, though, whether Thomas Merton might have turned her toward Weil. It turns out Merton did in fact write about Weil in the late 1960s, drawing on Jacques Cabaud's biography to discuss Weil's nascent nonviolent resistance in "The Answer of Minerva: Pacifism and Resistance in Simone Weil," in *Faith and Violence* (Notre Dame, IN: University of Notre Dame Press, 1968). Merton also mentions Weil in *Conjectures of a Guilty Bystander* (New York: Doubleday, 1966).

6. Yancey, "A Pilgrim's Progress," 12.

7. Mary Cantwell, "A Pilgrim's Progress," *New York Times*, April 26, 1992.

8. Annie Dillard, "How I Wrote the Moth Essay—and Why," in *The Norton Sampler*, ed. Thomas Cooley (New York: Norton, 1985), 8.

9. Geoff Dyer, "What Kind of Writer Is Annie Dillard?" *Lit Hub*, March 10, 2016, https://lithub.com/geoff-dyer-what-kind-of-writer-is-annie-dillard/.

10. National Endowment for the Humanities, https://www.neh.gov/about/awards/national-humanities-medals/annie-dillard.

11. Michael Joseph Gross, "Apparent Contradictions," *Boston Phoenix*, June 24–July 1, 1999.

12. Annie Dillard, official website, http://www.anniedillard.com/contact.html.

13. Dillard also stands in contrast to the literary marketing ideal of a writer-as-"influencer" in 2023, whereby in order to sell books, the writer must develop a consistent internet presence and "following" via social media.

14. Dillard, "How I Wrote," 8.

15. Yoon Sook Cha, *Decreation and the Ethical Bind: Simone Weil and the Claim of the Other* (New York: Fordham University Press, 2017), xiii.

16. Yancey, "A Pilgrim's Progress," 11.

17. Dyer calls her "pretty much a fruitcake" and cites Eudora Welty's admission in her review of *Pilgrim at Tinker Creek* that at points, "I honestly do not know what she is talking about" ("What Kind of Writer").

18. Pamela A. Smith, "The Ecotheology of Annie Dillard: A Study in Ambivalence," *CrossCurrents* 45, no. 3 (1995): 350.

19. Annie Dillard, *Pilgrim at Tinker Creek* (New York: Harper Perennial, 1974), 30. Subsequent citations occur in the text.

20. Lissa McCullough, *The Religious Philosophy of Simone Weil: An Introduction* (London: Tauris, 2014), 15.

21. James I. McClintock, "'Pray Without Ceasing': Annie Dillard Among the Nature Writers," *Cithara* 30, no. 1 (1990): 69.

22. Both Deborah Nelson in *Tough Enough* and E. Jane Doering in *Simone Weil and the Spectre of Self-Perpetuating Force* situate Weil's later work in the lens of tragedy.

23. Simone Weil, *Waiting for God*, trans. Emma Craufurd (New York: Harper and Row, 1951), 178.

24. E. Jane Doering and Eric O. Springsted, eds. *The Christian Platonism of Simone Weil* (Notre Dame, IN: University of Notre Dame Press, 2004), 4.

25. Weil, *Waiting for God*, 116, 109, 111, 112.

26. Weil, 112, 115.

27. Simone Weil, *Gravity and Grace*, trans. Emma Craufurd, 1952 (New York: Routledge, 1963), 1.

28. Weil, *Waiting for God*, 110.

29. Weil, 137, 160.

30. Weil, 171.

31. Weil, 147, 149, 148.

32. Weil, 146, 145.

33. Deborah Nelson, *Tough Enough: Arbus, Arendt, Didion, McCarthy, Sontag, Weil* (Chicago: University of Chicago Press, 2017), 32, 33.

34. Joan Dargan, *Simone Weil: Thinking Poetically* (Albany, NY: SUNY Press, 1999), 7.

35. Weil, *Gravity and Grace*, 136, 171.

36. A. Rebecca Rozelle-Stone and Lucian Stone, *Simone Weil and Theology* (New York: Bloomsbury T&T Clark, 2013), 137. Here they quote Weil's *On Science, Necessity, and the Love of God*, trans. Richard Rees (Oxford: Oxford University Press, 1968), 133.

37. Suzanne Clark, "Annie Dillard: The Woman in Nature and the Subject of Nonfiction," in *Literary Nonfiction: Theory, Criticism, Pedagogy*, ed. Chris Anderson (Carbondale: Southern Illinois University Press, 1989), 107.

38. Gross, "Apparent Contradictions."

39. Dillard, "To Fashion a Text," in *Inventing the Truth: The Art and Craft of Memoir*, ed. William Zinsser (Boston: Mariner, 1998), 154.

40. Dillard, "How I Wrote," 14.

41. Intriguingly, some commentators link this desire for ego containment to Dillard's choice to enter the Roman Catholic Church. Joseph Michael Gross, for example, links Dillard's self-emptying to her conversion, quoting her response to his question about what motivated it: "One of the main points of Catholicism is anonymity. Nobody looks at you when you go to a Catholic church. You just stand up there and worship and hang out, sort of representing the body of people on earth" ("Apparent Contradictions").

42. Adrienne Rich, *Collected Poems: 1950–2012* (New York: Norton, 2016), 452.

43. Richard Hardack, "'A *Woman* Need Not Be Sincere': Annie Dillard's Fictional Autobiographies and the Gender Politics of American Transcendentalism," *Arizona Quarterly* 64, no. 3 (2008): 79, 76, 79. In a review of *Pilgrim* in 1974, Hayden Carruth accused it of "sentimentalism" (639) and "passivity" (640), lacking the rigorous realism of literal bulldozers. These are, of course, implicitly gendered critiques, but they are not critiques of sacrifice. Carruth, "Attractions and Dangers of Nostalgia," *Virginia Quarterly Review* 50, no. 4 (1974).

44. Hardack, "'A *Woman*,'" 85, 100.

45. Diana Saverin, "The Thoreau of the Suburbs," *Atlantic*, February 5, 2015, https://www.theatlantic.com/culture/archive/2015/02/the-thoreau-of-the-suburbs/385128/.

46. Annie Dillard, radio interview with Melissa Block, NPR, March 12, 2016, https://www.npr.org/2016/03/12/470102363/author-interview-annie-dillard-author-of-the-abundance

47. Sharon Cameron, *Impersonality: Seven Essays* (Chicago: University of Chicago Press, 2007), vii.

48. Annie Dillard, *Holy the Firm* (New York: Perennial, 1977). Page citations for this work appear in the text.

49. Dillard, "How I Wrote," 8, 9, 9.

50. Annie Dillard, *The Writing Life* (New York: Harper Perennial, 1989).

51. For theological readings of *Holy the Firm*, see Linda Smith, *Annie Dillard* (Woodbridge, CT: Twayne, 1991); Susan Felch, "Annie Dillard: Modern Physics in a Contemporary Mystic," *Mosaic: A Journal for the Interdisciplinary Study of Literature* 22, no. 2 (1989): 1–14; Maureen Abood, "Natural Wonders," *U.S. Catholic*, 64, no. 11 (1999); and Kristen Drahos, "Nailed and Aflame: Annie Dillard's Bonaventurian Mysticism," *Religion and Literature* 51, no. 2 (2019): 91–112. All these authors address the book's tripartite structure and mystical approaches to sacrifice.

52. As Dillard implicitly converses throughout *Holy the Firm* with Weil, so both Dillard and Weil implicitly converse with Plato, whose theory posits a realm of Forms or Ideas that is the real, beyond the material realm. One might think Plato would be a clarifying figure to bring into conversation with Dillard and Weil, but Weil's own appeals to Plato are contested. In the words of David Tracy, "What a strange Christian and odd Platonist Simone Weil actually was." Tracy, "Simone Weil and the Impossible," in *The Critical Spirit: Theology at the Crossroads of Faith and Culture*, ed. Andrew Pierce and Geraldine Smyth (Edinburgh: Edinburgh University Press, 2003), 213. See Doering and Springsted's edited collection *The Christian Platonism of Simone Weil* (Notre Dame, IN: University of Notre Dame Press, 2004) for a gathering of perspectives.

53. Louis Dupré argues that Weil's vision of "creation as divine self-emptying" and the "establishment of an extra-divine realm of necessity" is a "Platonic-Gnostic" feature of her thought. Dupré, "Simone Weil and Platonism: An Introductory Reading," in Doering and Springsted, *The Christian Platonism of Simone Weil*, 9. Lissa McCullough, on the other hand, in *Religious Philosophy*, 214–20, challenges the usefulness of Gnosticism as an explanatory frame for Weil's work.

54. Weil, *Waiting for God*, 145.

55. Quoted in E. Jane Doering, *Simone Weil and the Specter of Self-Perpetuating Force* (Notre Dame, IN: University of Notre Dame Press, 2010), 75.

56. McCullough, *Religious Philosophy*, 14; Weil, *Waiting for God*, 135.

57. Dillard, *The Writing Life*, 47.

58. Weil, *Gravity and Grace*, 28.

59. McCullough, *Religious Philosophy*, 5.

60. Tracy, "Simone Weil and the Impossible," 210, 212.

61. Weil, *Waiting for God*, 69.

62. Scholars have struggled to track down Dillard's source material for the concept of "Holy the Firm." The closest anyone comes is Denise N. Baker's helpful contextualization of the substance in terms of spiritual alchemy or theosophy, in conversation with medieval mysticism, in "Julie Norwich and Julian of Norwich: Annie Dillard's Theodicy in *Holy the Firm*," in *Julian of Norwich's Legacy:*

Medieval Mysticism and Post-Medieval Reception, ed. Sarah Salih and Denise N. Baker (New York: Springer, 2009), 87–100.

63. Weil, quoted in McCullough, *Religious Philosophy*, 42.

64. Weil, *Gravity and Grace*, 145.

65. Dillard's choice of masculine pronouns here—much like Weil's—might read as an outdated use of the masculine for the universal or a problematic refusal of femininity, per Hardack's argument. It might also be read as a subversion of the unholy alliance between women and self-sacrifice. Notably, Dillard's moth is female, as is the nun figure, and they are paired with a male Christ, leading to a proliferation of pronouns that might be said to implicitly disrupt gendered assumptions and associations with self-sacrifice.

66. Weil, *Waiting for God*, 133, 134, 135, 135, 136.

67. McCullough, *Religious Philosophy*, 27.

68. Weil, *Waiting for God*, 135.

69. Weil, *Gravity and Grace*, 148.

70. Annie Dillard, personal correspondence, May 2023.

71. Saverin, "The Thoreau."

72. Nelson, *Tough Enough*, 43.

73. Weil, *Waiting for God*, 159.

74. Weil, *Gravity and Grace*, 16.

75. A. Rebecca Rozelle-Stone and Benjamin P. Davis, "Simone Weil," in *Stanford Encyclopedia of Philosophy*, ed. Edward N. Zalta, March 10, 2018, https://plato.stanford.edu/archives/fall2020/entries/simone-weil/.

76. Weil, *Waiting for God*, 132.

77. Annie Dillard, *For the Time Being* (New York: Knopf, 1999), x. Subsequent citations appear in the text.

78. Annie Dillard, "A Face Aflame," interview with Philip Yancey, *Christianity Today*, May 1978: 16.

79. Pamela Smith, "The Ecotheology of Annie Dillard: A Study in Ambivalence." *CrossCurrents* 45, no. 3 (1995): 350, 351.

80. Jack Shindler, "Seeing Through the Trees: Annie Dillard as Writer-Activist," *Journal of the Midwest Modern Language Association* 51, no. 2 (2018). It is tempting to appeal to Dillard's biography: interviewers frequently note her long-standing work in soup kitchens and her generosity with money. Since 2007 Dillard has turned from writing to painting, and prints of her paintings are available for sale on her website, with proceeds going to Partners in Health, the global social justice organization founded by the late Paul Farmer, to whom she has also bequeathed part of her Virginia landholdings.

Of course, appealing to Dillard's biography is just as treacherous as appealing to Weil's, but in both cases, looking to the writers' extratextual behaviors suggests a certain integrity to the selves (however emptied) and ideals represented in their writing. Dillard textually constructs her vocation as an artist and thinker, not a politician or ethicist, and she follows through with that work in the world. To act in consistency with the humility she suggests means refusing to claim expertise in areas beyond her ken, but to use the resources generated by her own work to support those who are experts. This approach satisfies some but certainly not all of her commentators.

81. McCullough, *Religious Philosophy*, 87. Also see Miklos Vetö, *The Religious Metaphysics of Simone Weil*, trans. Joan Dargan (Albany, NY: SUNY Press, 1994).

82. Simone Weil, *First and Last Notebooks*, trans. Richard Rees (Oxford: Oxford University Press, 1970), 70.

83. Weil, *Waiting for God*, 158; Dillard, *Pilgrim at Tinker Creek*, 216.

84. McCullough, *Religious Philosophy*, 86.

85. Weil, *First and Last Notebooks*, 120.

86. McCullough, *Religious Philosophy*, 93.

87. Weil, *Waiting for God*, 72.

88. Weil, *First and Last Notebooks*, 103.

89. Annie Dillard, "Holding on to Holiness," *Christian Century*, June 3, 2020.

90. McCullough, *Religious Philosophy*, 77.

91. Simone Weil, *Simone Weil: An Anthology*, ed. Siân Miles (New York: Grove, 1986), 72.

92. Weil, *First and Last Notebooks*, 112.

3. HUNGER

1. Karen FitzGerald, "The Good Books: Writer's Choices," *Ms.*, December 1985: 80.

2. Mary Gordon, *Not Less than Everything: Catholic Writers on Heroes of Conscience, from Joan of Arc to Oscar Romero*, ed. Catherine Wolff (New York: Harper One, 2013), 126.

3. Mary Gordon, "Talking with Mary Gordon," interview with Edmund White, *Washington Post*, April 9, 1978, https://www.washingtonpost.com/archive/entertainment/books/1978/04/09/talking-with-mary-gordon/d4f40330-645d-4933-b855-6715c3d4f5e6./

4. Mary Gordon, interview with Sean Salai, *America*, July 19, 2014, https://www.americamagazine.org/content/all-things/liars-wife-interview-author-mary-gordon.

5. Mary Gordon, interview with Judy Valentine, *PBS Religion and Ethics Newsweekly*, October 26, 2007. https://www.pbs.org/wnet/religionandethics/2007/10/26/october-26-2007-mary-gordon-extended-interview/3663/.

6. E. Jane Doering and Eric Springsted, eds., *The Christian Platonism of Simone Weil* (Notre Dame, IN: University of Notre Dame Press, 2004), 7.

7. Andrea Hollingsworth, "Simone Weil and the Theo-Poetics of Compassion," *Modern Theology* 29, no. 3 (2013): 205.

8. Mary Gordon, *Pearl* (New York: Pantheon, 2005), 20. Subsequent page references appear in the text.

9. Simone Weil, "The *Iliad*, or the Poem of Force," in *Simone Weil: An Anthology*, ed. Siân Miles (New York: Grove, 1986), 163.

10. Simone Weil, *Waiting for God*, trans. Emma Craufurd (New York: Harper and Row, 1951), 66, 92, 57, 181.

11. Simone Weil, quoted in Simone Pétrement, *Simone Weil: A Life*, trans. Raymond Rosenthal (New York: Pantheon, 1976), 37.

12. Weil, *Simone Weil: An Anthology*, 71.

13. Weil, *Waiting for God*, 118, 122, 125.

14. Weil, *Waiting for God*, 196, 147–48.

15. Consider Pétrement's report in *Simone Weil*, 525, that one individual who saw Weil near the end of her life described her as "a spirit almost completely released from the flesh, a spirit who was the Word." Gordon echoes these Christic overtones in naming Pearl's parent figures Maria and Joseph.

16. See Gordon, *Pearl*, 6, 8, 9, 10, 183, 190, 191, 215, 263, 264, 272, 274, 295, 315.

17. Sissela Bok, "Simone Weil's Unforeseen Legacy," *Common Knowledge*, 12, no. 2 (2006): 253.

18. Robert Coles, *Simone Weil: A Modern Pilgrimage* (Boston: Addison-Wesley, 1987).

19. Weil, *Waiting for God*, 83.

20. Caroline Walker Bynum, *Holy Feast and Holy Fast: The Religious Significance of Food to Medieval Women* (Berkeley: University of California Press, 1987), 194–95, 297.

21. Chris Cuomo, *The Philosopher Queen: Feminist Essays on War, Love, and Knowledge* (New York: Rowman & Littlefield, 2002), 136.

22. As Bynum notes, though the majority of European religious fasts have been performed by women, Ireland in particular has a long tradition of male political fasting: "Medieval Ireland . . . had an actual legal procedure of 'fasting to restrain,' in which a creditor fasted against a debtor to gain repayment or a man fasted against his adversary to gain restitution" (*Holy Feast*, 192).

23. Pétrement, *Simone Weil*, 37.

24. Bynum, *Holy Feast*, 74–75.

25. Richard A. O'Connor and Penny Van Esterik, "De-medicalizing Anorexia," *Anthropology Today* 24, no. 5 (2008): 7–9.

26. O'Connor and Van Esterik, 7.

27. Bynum, *Holy Feast*, 35.

28. Simone Weil, *Gravity and Grace*, trans. Emma Craufurd, 1952 (New York: Routledge, 1963), 121. For more on Weil's approach to reading and interpretation, see Joan Dargan, *Simone Weil: Thinking Poetically* (Albany, NY: SUNY Press, 1999), especially 1–18.

29. The fact that Maria remembers the question word-for-word but misremembers the story seems significant: it is not "magic" in general in Weil's version, but the Grail, "the miraculous vessel that satisfies all hunger by virtue of the consecrated Host" (*Waiting for God*, 115). The de-Christianization of the tale in Maria's memory speaks to her decades-long project of clearing the religious trappings from her imagination. It is likewise significant that while Maria feels the impulse to pose this question to Finbar, she does not in fact do so: knowledge of ethics is not the same as ethical action.

30. Weil, *Simone Weil: An Anthology*, 273.

31. Weil, *Waiting for God*, 205.

32. Weil, *Simone Weil: An Anthology*, 200.

33. Weil, *Gravity and Grace*, 121.

34. Henry Leroy Finch, *Simone Weil and the Intellect of Grace* (New York: Continuum, 1999), 125.

35. Simone Weil, *The Need for Roots*, 1952, trans. Arthur Wills (New York: Harper Colophon, 1971), 89.

36. Simone Weil, *First and Last Notebooks*, trans. Richard Rees (Oxford: Oxford University Press, 1970), 285, emphasis added.

37. Ann Loades, "Eucharistic Sacrifice: Simone Weil's Use of a Liturgical Metaphor," *Religion and Literature* 17, no. 2 (1985): 53.

38. Susan Sontag, "Simone Weil," *New York Review of Books*, February 1, 1963: 51.

39. Numerous commentators have noted that Weil's self-starvation and ultimate death may have resulted from her frustration that she was barred by her gender from the political participation she longed for. Many have also noted the gendering of the hagiography that has followed her life: as Miles claims in *Simone Weil*, 44, rendering Weil saintly, absurd, or stereotypically feminine risks marginalizing her in a way that "kills the very thing it purports to celebrate."
At the same time, one also wonders whether Weil's writings (and life-text) would have been so popular, so widely disseminated and admired, if not for the extremism of her early death and the move to saint such a figure that inevitably occurs *after* her death. If Weil, like Pearl, had chosen life, would her words have been as legible?

40. Mary Gordon, *Simone Weil in New York*, in *The Liar's Wife: Four Novellas* (New York: Pantheon, 2014), 69. Subsequent page references appear in the text.

41. E. Jane Doering, *Simone Weil and the Specter of Self-Perpetuating Force* (Notre Dame, IN: University of Notre Dame Press, 2010), 15.

42. Valerie Miner, "An Interview with Adrienne Rich and Mary Daly," *San Francisco Review of Books* 3, no. 6 (1977): 14.

43. Robert Zaretsky, *The Subversive Simone Weil: A Life in Five Ideas* (Chicago: University of Chicago Press, 2021), 158.

44. Jacques Cabaud, *Simone Weil: A Fellowship in Love* (Fredericton, NB: Channel Press, 1964), 127–28.

45. Doering, *Simone Weil and the Specter*, 71.

46. See Thomas R. Nevin, *Simone Weil: Portrait of a Self-Exiled Jew* (Chapel Hill: University of North Carolina Press, 1991), 242–43.

47. Emmanuel Levinas, "Simone Weil Against the Bible," in *Difficult Freedom: Essays on Judaism*, trans. Seán Hand (Baltimore: John Hopkins University Press, 1990), 133, 134.

48. Gillian Rose's "Angry Angels—Simone Weil and Emmanuel Levinas," collected in *Judaism and Modernity: Philosophical Essays*, offers a compelling reading of the two philosophers' ethical similarities: "Their thought converges at the deepest level: where it exposes the intrinsic violence of the sovereign individual towards herself, her others, and towards God" (212). Rose by no means excuses Weil's bad reading of the Hebrew scriptures and tradition, but she does show how Levinas falls into some of the same interpretive traps as Weil by failing to recognize the nuance of her thought.

49. Martin Buber, *On Judaism* (New York: Schocken, 1996), 206, 207.

50. David Tracy, "Simone Weil and the Impossible," in *The Critical Spirit: Theology at the Crossroads of Faith and Culture: Essays in Honour of Gabriel Daly OSA*, ed. Andrew Pierce and Geraldine Smyth (Edinburgh: Edinburgh University Press, 2003), 210, 213, 215.

51. Doering, *Simone Weil and the Specter*, 77, 80.

52. Doering, 83.

53. Sylvie Courtine-Denamy, *Three Women in Dark Times: Edith Stein, Hannah Arendt, Simone Weil*, trans. G. M. Goshgarian (Ithaca, NY: Cornell University Press, 2001), 142.

54. Michelle Cliff, "Sister/Outsider: Some Thoughts on Simone Weil," in *Between Women: Biographers, Novelists, Critics, Teachers, and Artists Write About Their Work on Women*, ed. Carol Ascher, Louise DeSalvo, and Sara Ruddick (Boston: Beacon, 1984), 322, 323.

55. Nevin, *Simone Weil*, xi. There is, of course, a particular risk in attributing a Jewishness to Weil that she herself did not embrace, whether it's positive, as in Nevin's case, or negative, as in the opinion of the priest who visited Weil in

hospital and, according to Jacques Cabaud (*Simone Weil*, 340), considered her both too "feminine" and too "Judaic."

56. Nevin, *Simone Weil*, 236–38, 247, 256.
57. Mary Gordon, *There Your Heart Lies* (New York: Pantheon, 2017), 5–6, 72. Subsequent page references appear in the text.
58. Simone Weil, *Seventy Letters*, trans. Richard Rees, 1965 (Eugene, OR: Wipf and Stock, 2015), 105.
59. Weil, 109.
60. Weil, 108.
61. Weil, *Waiting for God*, 82.
62. Weil, *Waiting for God*, 148, 146.
63. Weil, *Waiting for God*, 52–53, 75, 77.
64. Weil, *Waiting for God*, 82, 181.
65. Weil, *Waiting for God*, 67, 70, 76, 95, 55.
66. Weil, *Waiting for God*, 76.
67. Weil, *Waiting for God*, 66–67.
68. Weil, *Waiting for God*, 182.
69. Weil, *First and Last Notebooks*, 207.

4. (DE)CREATION

1. Yoon Sook Cha, *Decreation and the Ethical Bind: Simone Weil and the Claim of the Other* (New York: Fordham University Press, 2017), xii; Anne Carson, *Decreation: Poetry, Essays, Opera* (New York: Vintage Contemporaries, 2005), 171. Subsequent page references to Carson appear in the text.
2. M. NourbeSe Philip, *She Tries Her Tongue, Her Silence Softly Breaks* (Middletown, CT: Wesleyan University Press, 1989).
3. Fanny Howe, *Meditations on Word and Life* (Berkeley: University of California Press, 2003); Gjertrud Schnackenberg, "The Heavenly Feast," in *Supernatural Love: Poems 1976–2000* (Hexam, UK: Bloodaxe, 2001), 99–102; Edward Hirsch, *Earthly Measures* (New York: Knopf, 1994).
4. Mary Karr, "Waiting for God: Self-Portrait as Skeleton," in *Sinners Welcome: Poems* (New York: Harper Collins, 2009), 18; Jorie Graham, "Praying (Attempt of June 6 '03)," in *Overlord* (Manchester, UK: Carcanet, 2005), 16–19.
5. Christian Wiman, *Survival Is a Style* (New York: Farrar, Straus and Giroux, 2020); Christian Wiman, ed., *Joy: 100 Poems* (New Haven, CT: Yale University Press, 2017).
6. Jan Zwicky, *Wisdom and Metaphor* (Edmonton: Brush Education, 2014); Nathalie Stephens, *Touch to Affliction* (Toronto: Coach House, 2006); Rita Mae Reese, *The*

Book of Hulga (Madison: University of Wisconsin Press, 2016). For an overview of scholarly essays about Weil among the poets, see the introduction to the present book, note 7.

7. Anna Jackson, "The Verse Biography: Introduction," *Biography* 39, no. 1 (2016): iv, vi, vii.

8. Jessica Wilkinson, "Experiments in Poetic Biography: Feminist Threads in Contemporary Long Form Poetry," *Biography* 39, no. 1 (2016): 2.

9. Carolyn G. Heilbrun, *Writing a Woman's Life* (New York: Ballantine, 1988), 12.

10. Helen Rickerby, "Articulating Artemisia: Revisioning the Lives of Women from History in Biographical Poetry," *Biography* 39, no. 1 (2016): 24.

11. Maggie Helwig, *Talking Prophet Blues* (Kingston, ON: Quarry Press, 1989), 10. Subsequent page references appear in the text.

12. Simone Weil, *First and Last Notebooks*, trans. Richard Rees (Oxford: Oxford University Press, 1970), 146.

13. Simone Weil, *Œuvres Complètes* 6:2:298, quoted in Joan Dargan, *Simone Weil: Thinking Poetically* (Albany, NY: SUNY Press, 1999), 141.

14. Christina Rossetti, *Goblin Market*, 1861 (Chicago: Blue Sky, 1905).

15. Franz Kafka, "A Hunger Artist," in *A Hunger Artist and Other Stories*, trans. Joyce Crick (Oxford: Oxford University Press, 2012).

16. Simone Weil, *Waiting for God*, trans. Emma Craufurd (New York: Harper and Row, 1951), 149.

17. Stephanie Strickland, interview with Devin Becker, *CTRL+SHIFT*, May 20, 2014, https://ctrl-shift.org/interviews/transcripts/strickland.html.

18. Stephanie Strickland, *The Red Virgin: A Poem of Simone Weil* (Madison: University of Wisconsin Press, 1993), 3. Subsequent page references appear in the text.

19. Here are the actual quotations from *The Notebooks of Simone Weil*, translated by Arthur Wills and first published in English in 1956: "Poetry: pain and joy that are *impossible*. A poignant touch, a nostalgia—such is Provençal and English poetry. A joy which, just because it is so pure and unmixed, hurts. (A pain which, just because it is so pure and unmixed, soothes—that is something Greek)" (447).
    "For him who performs it, the act is as inseparable from love as are the inward words which express a thought from the mind. As soon as the mind, becoming relaxed, descends a little below the maximum degree of concentration, it spreads itself out in words; and genuine love does exactly the same in acts" (448).

20. Jacques Cabaud, *Simone Weil: A Fellowship in Love* (Fredericton, NB: Channel Press, 1964), 340.

21. Cabaud, *Simone Weil*, 74.

22. Kate Daniels, *Four Testimonies: Poems* (Baton Rouge: Louisiana State University Press, 1998), 3. Subsequent page references appear in the text.

23. Kate Daniels, "Kate Daniels," in *Southbound: Interviews with Southern Poets*, ed. Ernest Suarez, T. W. Stanford, and Amy Verner (Minneapolis: University of Minnesota Press, 1999), 214.

24. "The Red Virgin: A Poem of Simone Weil," *Publishers Weekly* 240, no. 46 (November 15, 1993): 76.

25. Sarah Klassen, *Simone Weil: Songs of Hunger and Love* (Hamilton, ON: Wolsak and Wynn, 1999), 7. Subsequent page references appear in the text.

26. The "Terrible Prayer" is referenced in Weil, *First and Last Notebooks*, 243–44.

27. Weil, *Gravity and Grace*, 71, quoted in Carson, *Decreation*, 167.

28. Weil quotes from Porete's text in her notebooks (e.g., *First and Last Notebooks*, 205) but does not appear to have known the author's name or gender due to the fact that Porete was not discovered as the author of the *Mirror of Simple Souls* until 1946.

29. Consider, for example, John D. Caputo, *What Would Jesus Deconstruct? The Good News of Postmodernism for the Church* (Grand Rapids, MI: Baker Academic, 2007).

30. Carson asserts Weil was "never a Christian herself" (177), a claim most Protestant commentators would dispute. Weil was not a baptized Catholic, but many Christian traditions do not require such an initiatory rite to claim the label Christian.

31. A performance of "Decreation: Fight Cherries" from 2001 can be viewed at https://vimeo.com/67009433. (Note that the staging does not fully align with the print version of 2005.)

32. Joan Dargan, *Simone Weil: Thinking Poetically* (Albany, NY: SUNY Press, 1999), 86–87.

33. Lorri Neilsen Glenn, *Lost Gospels* (Kingston, ON: Brick, 2010), 45, 52. Subsequent page references appear in the text.

34. Glenn here quotes from Weil, *Gravity and Grace*, 134.

35. Glenn likely borrows this gathering from the work of Jan Zwicky, whose *Wisdom and Metaphor* she cites in the collection's notes.

36. Hermione Lee, *Body Parts: Essays on Life-Writing* (London: Pimlico, 2008), 3.

CONCLUSION

1. Simone Weil, *Waiting for God*, trans. Emma Craufurd (New York: Harper and Row, 1951), 149.

2. Sarah Klassen, *Simone Weil: Songs of Hunger and Love* (Hamilton, ON: Wolsak and Wynn, 1999), 80; Lorri Neilsen Glenn, *Lost Gospels* (Kingston, ON: Brick, 2010), 50.

3. Simone Weil, *Gravity and Grace*, trans. Emma Craufurd, 1952 (New York: Routledge, 1963), 23.

4. Perhaps not incidentally, Williams encounters Weil's work during a residence at Harvard Divinity School, echoing Robert Coles's introduction to Weil at Harvard some seventy years prior.

5. Terry Tempest Williams, *Erosion: Essays of Undoing* (New York: Sarah Crichton, 2019), 217.

6. Williams, 226–27.

7. Robert Zaretsky, *The Subversive Simone Weil: A Life in Five Ideas* (Chicago: University of Chicago Press, 2021), 2.

8. Toril Moi, "I Came with a Sword," *London Review of Books* 43, no. 1 (2021), https://www.lrb.co.uk/the-paper/v43/n13/toril-moi/i-came-with-a-sword.

9. Weil, *Gravity and Grace*, 128.

10. M. NourbeSe Philip, "M. NourbeSe Philip Shares 6 Titles That Helped Hone Her Writing Craft," *CBC Books*, April 29, 2020, https://www.cbc.ca/books/m -nourbese-philip-shares-6-titles-that-helped-hone-her-writing-craft-1.5482347

11. M. NourbeSe Philip, "Sycorax, Spirit, and *Zong!*" Interview with Jordan Scott. *Jacket2*, May 14, 2019, https://jacket2.org/interviews/sycorax-spirit-and-zong.

12. M. NourbeSe Philip, *Bla_k: Essays and Interviews*, 2d ed. (Toronto: Book Hug, 2017), 13, 20.

13. Adrienne Rich, *Arts of the Possible: Essays and Conversations* (New York: Norton, 2001), 2–3.

14. Adrienne Rich, *Blood, Bread, and Poetry: Selected Prose 1979–1985* (New York: Norton, 1986), 8–9.

15. Rich, *Arts*, 84, 154.

16. Adrienne Rich, *What Is Found There: Notebooks on Poetry and Politics* (New York: Norton, 1993), 7.

17. Rich, *Arts*, 2.

18. Eve Tuck and K. Wayne Yang, "Decolonization Is Not a Metaphor," *Decolonization: Indigeneity, Education & Society* 1, no. 1 (2012): 1–40.

19. Damien Gayle, "Millions Suffering in Deadly Pollution 'Sacrifice Zones,' Warns UN Expert," *Guardian*, March 10, 2022, https://www.theguardian.com /environment/2022/mar/10/millions-suffering-in-deadly-pollution-sacrifice -zones-warns-un-expert.

20. J. P. Little, *Simone Weil on Colonialism: An Ethic of the Other* (Lanham, MD: Rowman & Littlefield, 2003), 15.

21. Inese Radzins, "Simone Weil's Social Philosophy: Toward a Post-Colonial Ethic," in *New Topics in Feminist Philosophy of Religion*, ed. P. S. Anderson (New York: Springer, 2010), 82.

22. Little, *Simone Weil on Colonialism*, 22.

23. Simone Weil, *The Need for Roots*, trans. Arthur Wills, 1952 (New York: Harper Colophon, 1971), 97, 170, 169. Also consider Césaire's claims in "Discourse on

Colonialism" that Hitler "applied to Europe colonialist procedures which until then had been reserved exclusively for the Arabs of Algeria, the coolies of India, and the blacks of Africa." In the same essay, Césaire similarly parallels Weil's claim that colonization proceeds through the force that "turns x into a thing" by arguing that "colonization = 'thing-ification.'" Little notes that there is no evidence Weil was familiar with Césaire's work (15), but there are powerful affinities in their stances on the causes and consequences of colonial domination. Aimé Césaire, "Discourse on Colonialism," 1955, trans. Joan Pinkham (New York: Monthly Review Press: 1972), https://medium.com/religion-bites/discourse-on-colonialism-by-aimé-césaire-793b291a0987.

24. Patti Smith, *Devotion* (New Haven, CT: Yale University Press, 2017).

25. Karen Olsson, *The Weil Conjectures: On Math and the Pursuit of the Unknown* (New York: Farrar, Straus and Giroux, 2019).

26. Maria Popova, "The Mountain View of the Mind: Simone Weil on the Purest and Most Fertile Form of Thought," https://www.themarginalian.org/2015/09/28/simone-weil-waiting-for-god-thought/. Weil also persists in smaller-scale literary endeavors, like Clark McCann's self-published novel *The Red Virgin: A Novel Inspired by the Life of Simone Weil* (N.p.: Solesmes Press, 2019), which reads as a kind of fan-fiction mystery thriller fantasizing about Weil being the narrator's mother. Weil is also flourishing among beautiful small press offerings, like Susan M. Schulz, *Memory Cards: Simone Weil Series* (Cambridge, UK: Equipage Press, n.d.); and Lisa Robertson, *Anemones: A Simone Weil Project* (Amsterdam: If I Can't Dance, 2021).

27. Casey Schwartz, *Attention: A Love Story* (New York: Pantheon, 2020), 210. Schwartz's book is one of a number to explicitly address the attention crisis of contemporary Western life, but, as Robert Zaretsky notes, a surprising number of these projects fully overlook Weil. Naming Jenny Odell's oversight of Weil in the popular *How to Do Nothing* and Matthew Crawford's in *Shop Class as Soul Craft*, Zaretsky drily comments, "Neither makes mention of Weil. This is no more a shortcoming than making the case for skepticism but omitting all mention, say, of David Hume" (*The Subversive Simone Weil*, 13). To Zaretsky's list of personal nonfiction I would add the more scholarly texts *The Ecology of Attention* by Yves Citton (2014 French, 2017 trans.) and *Attention: Beyond Mindfulness* by Gay Watson (2017), which reference Weil only briefly in passing. As Zaretsky notes, writers who overlook Weil as the most insightful twentieth-century philosopher of attention risk "reinventing arguments—and doing so less compellingly" (13).

28. Schwartz, *Attention*, 207, 213.

29. Schwartz, 210.

30. Schwartz, 210.

31. Glenn, *Lost Gospels*, 50.

32. Schwartz, *Attention*, 214.

33. Mary Oliver, *Thirst: Poems* (Boston: Beacon, 2007).

34. Schwartz, *Attention*, 216.

35. Simone Weil, *First and Last Notebooks*, trans. Richard Rees (London: Peters, Fraser, and Dunlop, 1970), 103–4.

WORKS CITED

Abood, Maureen. "Natural Wonders." *U.S. Catholic*, 64, no. 11 (1999).

Anderson, Pamela Sue. "Sacrifice as Self-destructive 'Love.'" In *Sacrifice and Modern Thought*, ed. Julia Meszaros and Johannes Zachhuber, 29–47. Oxford: Oxford University Press, 2013.

Asad, Talal. *Formations of the Secular: Christianity, Islam, Modernity*. Stanford, CA: Stanford University Press, 2003.

Baker, Denise N. "Julie Norwich and Julian of Norwich: Annie Dillard's Theodicy in *Holy the Firm*." In *Julian of Norwich's Legacy: Medieval Mysticism and Post-Medieval Reception*, ed. Sarah Salih and Denise N. Baker, 87–100. New York: Springer, 2009.

Barry, Kathleen. "Reviewing Reviews: *Of Woman Born*." 1977. In *Reading Adrienne Rich: Reviews and Re-Visions 1951–81*, ed. Jane Roberta Cooper, 300–303. Ann Arbor: University of Michigan Press, 1984.

Bok, Sissela. "Simone Weil's Unforeseen Legacy." *Common Knowledge*, 12, no. 2 (2006): 252–60.

Bordo, Susan. *Unbearable Weight: Feminism, Western Culture, and the Body*. Berkeley: University of California Press, 1993.

Bourgault, Sophie. "Beyond the Saint and the Red Virgin: Simone Weil as Feminist Theorist of Care." *Frontiers: A Journal of Women Studies* 35, no. 2 (2014): 1–27.

——. "Hannah Arendt and Simone Weil on the Significance of Love for Politics." In *Thinking about Love: Essays in Contemporary Continental Philosophy*, ed. Diane Enns and Antonio Calcagno, 151–166. University Park: Pennsylvania State University Press, 2015.

Branch, Lori. "Postcritical and Postsecular: The Horizon of Belief." *Religion and Literature* 48, no. 2 (2016): 160–67.

——. "The Rituals of Our Re-Secularization: Literature Between Faith and Knowledge." *Religion and Literature* 46, no. 2/3 (2014): 9–33.

Buber, Martin. *On Judaism*. New York: Schocken, 1996.

Bynum, Caroline Walker. *Holy Feast and Holy Fast: The Religious Significance of Food to Medieval Women*. Berkeley: University of California Press, 1987.

Cabaud, Jacques. *Simone Weil: A Fellowship in Love*. Fredericton, NB: Channel Press, 1964.

Cantwell, Mary. "A Pilgrim's Progress." *New York Times*, April 26, 1992.

Caputo, John D. *What Would Jesus Deconstruct? The Good News of Postmodernism for the Church*. Grand Rapids, MI: Baker Academic, 2007.

Carruth, Hayden. "Attractions and Dangers of Nostalgia." *Virginia Quarterly Review* 50, no. 4 (1974): 637–40.

Carson, Anne. *Decreation: Poetry, Essays, Opera*. New York: Vintage Contemporaries, 2005.

Cha, Yoon Sook. *Decreation and the Ethical Bind: Simone Weil and the Claim of the Other*. New York: Fordham University Press, 2017.

Clark, Miriam Marty. "Human Rights and the Work of Lyric in Adrienne Rich." *Cambridge Quarterly* 38, no. 1 (2009): 45–65.

Clark, Suzanne. "Annie Dillard: The Woman in Nature and the Subject of Nonfiction." In *Literary Nonfiction: Theory, Criticism, Pedagogy*, ed. Chris Anderson, 107–24. Carbondale: Southern Illinois University Press, 1989.

Cliff, Michelle. *Abeng*. Berkeley: Crossing Press, 1984.

——. *Free Enterprise: A Novel of Mary Ellen Pleasant*. San Francisco: City Lights, 2004.

——. *No Telephone to Heaven*. Boston: Dutton, 1987.

——. "Sister/Outsider: Some Thoughts on Simone Weil." In *Between Women: Biographers, Novelists, Critics, Teachers, and Artists Write About Their Work on Women*, ed. Carol Ascher, Louise DeSalvo, Sara Ruddick, 311–25. Boston: Beacon, 1984.

Coles, Robert. *Simone Weil: A Modern Pilgrimage*. Boston: Addison-Wesley, 1987.

Copeland, M. Shawn. "'Wading Through Many Sorrows': Toward a Theology of Suffering in Womanist Perspective." In *A Troubling in My Soul: Womanist Perspectives on Evil and Suffering*, ed. Emilie M. Townes, 109–29. Maryknoll, NY: Orbis, 1993.

Courtine-Denamy, Sylvie. *Three Women in Dark Times: Edith Stein, Hannah Arendt, Simone Weil*, trans. G. M. Goshgarian. Ithaca, NY: Cornell University Press, 2001.

Coviello, Peter, and Jared Hickman. "Introduction: After the Postsecular." *American Literature* 86, no. 4 (2014): 645–54.

Cuomo, Chris. *The Philosopher Queen: Feminist Essays on War, Love, and Knowledge*. New York: Rowman & Littlefield, 2002.

Daly, Mary. *Gyn/Ecology: The Metaethics of Radical Feminism*. 1978. Boston: Beacon, 1990.

Daniels, Kate. *Four Testimonies: Poems*. Baton Rouge: Louisiana State University Press, 1998.

——. "Kate Daniels." In *Southbound: Interviews with Southern Poets*, ed. Ernest Suarez, T. W. Stanford, and Amy Verner, 200–222. Minneapolis: University of Minnesota Press, 1999.

Dargan, Joan. *Simone Weil: Thinking Poetically*. Albany, NY: SUNY Press, 1999.

Desai, Anita. *Clear Light of Day*. New York: HarperCollins, 1980.

Dillard, Annie. *An American Childhood*. New York: Harper & Row, 1987.

——. "A Face Aflame." Interview with Philip Yancey. *Christianity Today*, May 1978: 14–19.

———. *For the Time Being*. New York: Knopf, 1999.

——. "Holding on to Holiness." *Christian Century*, June 3, 2020.

——. *Holy the Firm*. New York: Perennial, 1977.

——. "How I Wrote the Moth Essay—and Why." In *The Norton Sampler*, ed. Thomas Cooley, 8–15. New York: Norton, 1985.

——. *The Maytrees*. New York: Harper Collins, 2007.

——. *Pilgrim at Tinker Creek*. New York: Harper Perennial, 1974.

——. Radio interview with Melissa Block. NPR, March 12, 2016. https://www.npr.org/2016/03/12/470102363/author-interview-annie-dillard-author-of-the-abundance.

——. "To Fashion a Text." In *Inventing the Truth: The Art and Craft of Memoir*, ed. William Zinsser, 39–60. Boston: Mariner, 1998.

——. *The Writing Life*. New York: Harper Perennial, 1989.

Doering, E. Jane. *Simone Weil and the Specter of Self-Perpetuating Force*. Notre Dame, IN: University of Notre Dame Press, 2010.

Doering, E. Jane, and Eric O. Springsted, eds. *The Christian Platonism of Simone Weil*. Notre Dame, IN: University of Notre Dame Press, 2004

Drahos, Kristen. "Nailed and Aflame: Annie Dillard's Bonaventurian Mysticism." *Religion and Literature* 51, no. 2 (2019): 91–112.

DuPlessis, Rachel Blau. "The Critique of Consciousness and Myth in Levertov, Rich, and Rukeyser." *Feminist Studies* 3, no.1/2 (1975): 199–221.

Dupré, Louis. "Simone Weil and Platonism: An Introductory Reading." In *The Christian Platonism of Simone Weil*, ed. E. Jane Doering and Eric O. Springsted, 9–22. Notre Dame, IN: University of Notre Dame Press, 2004.

Dyer, Geoff. "What Kind of Writer Is Annie Dillard?" *Lit Hub*, March 10, 2016. https://lithub.com/geoff-dyer-what-kind-of-writer-is-annie-dillard/.

Fan, Kit. "'Between the blank page and the poem': Reading Simone Weil in Contemporary American Poets." *Cambridge Quarterly* 36, no. 2 (2007): 129–54.

Fessenden, Tracy. "The Problem of the Postsecular." *American Literary History* 26, no. 1 (2014): 154–67.

Felch, Susan M. "Annie Dillard: Modern Physics in a Contemporary Mystic." *Mosaic: A Journal for the Interdisciplinary Study of Literature* 22, no. 2 (1989): 1–14.

Fiedler, Leslie. Introduction to *Waiting for God*, by Simone Weil. New York: Harper and Row, 1951.

Finch, Henry Leroy. *Simone Weil and the Intellect of Grace*. New York: Continuum, 1999.

Fiori, Gabriella. *Simone Weil: An Intellectual Biography*, trans. Joseph R. Berrigan. Athens: University of Georgia Press, 1989.

FitzGerald, Karen. "The Good Books: Writer's Choices." *Ms.*, December 1985, 80–81.

Furani, Khaled. "Is There a Postsecular?" *Journal of the American Academy of Religion* 83, no. 1 (2015): 1–26.

Gayle, Damien, "Millions Suffering in Deadly Pollution 'Sacrifice Zones,' Warns UN Expert." *Guardian*, March 10, 2022. https://www.theguardian.com/environment /2022/mar/10/millions-suffering-in-deadly-pollution-sacrifice-zones-warns-un -expert.

Gelpi, Albert. "Powers of Recuperation: Tracking Adrienne Rich." *Women's Studies* 46, no. 7 (2017): 718–19.

Gendron, Claude. "Moral Attention: A Comparative Philosophical Study." *Journal of Moral Education* 45, no. 4 (2016): 1–14.

Gilbert, Sandra. Review of *The Lamplit Answer* by Gjertrud Schnackenberg. *Poetry* 147, no. 3 (1985): 165–67.

Gilligan, Carol. *In a Different Voice*. Cambridge, MA: Harvard University Press, 1982.

Glenn, Lorri Neilsen. *Lost Gospels*. Kingston, ON: Brick, 2010.

Gordon, Mary. Interview with Judy Valentine. *PBS Religion and Ethics Newsweekly*, October 26, 2007. https://www.pbs.org/wnet/religionandethics/2007/10/26/october -26-2007-mary-gordon-extended-interview/3663/.

——. Interview with Sean Salai. *America*, July 19, 2014. https://www.americamagazine .org/content/all-things/liars-wife-interview-author-mary-gordon

——. *Not Less than Everything: Catholic Writers on Heroes of Conscience, from Joan of Arc to Oscar Romero*, ed. Catherine Wolff, 126–33. New York: Harper One, 2013.

——. *Payback*. New York: Pantheon, 2020.

——. *Pearl*. New York: Pantheon, 2005.

——. *Simone Weil in New York*. In *The Liar's Wife: Four Novellas*, 65–136. New York: Pantheon, 2014.

——. "Talking with Mary Gordon." Interview with Edmund White. *Washington Post*, April 9, 1978. https://www.washingtonpost.com/archive/entertainment/books/1978 /04/09/talking-with-mary-gordon/d4f40330-645d-4933-b855-6715c3d4f5e6/.

——. *There Your Heart Lies*. New York: Pantheon, 2017.

Grafe, Adrian. "Simone Weil Among the Poets." In *Ecstasy and Understanding Religious Awareness in English Poetry from the Late Victorian to the Modern Period*, ed. Adrian Grafe, 161–71. New York: Bloomsbury Academic, 2008.

Graham, Jorie. *Overlord*. Manchester, UK: Carcanet, 2005.

Gray, Francine Du Plessix. "At Large and at Small: Loving and Hating Simone Weil." *American Scholar* 70, no. 3 (2001): 5–11.

——. *Simone Weil: A Penguin Life*. New York: Viking, 2001.

Gross, Michael Joseph. "Apparent Contradictions." *Boston Phoenix*, June 24–July 1, 1999.

Halpern, Nick. *Everyday and Prophetic: The Poetry of Lowell, Ammons, Merrill, and Rich*. Madison: University of Wisconsin Press, 2003.

Hämäläinen, Nora. "Iris Murdoch, Gender, and Philosophy." *Notre Dame Philosophical Reviews*, December 10, 2011. https://ndpr.nd.edu/reviews/iris-murdoch-gender-and-philosophy/.

Hardack, Richard. "'A *Woman* Need Not Be Sincere': Annie Dillard's Fictional Autobiographies and the Gender Politics of American Transcendentalism." *Arizona Quarterly* 64, no. 3 (2008): 75–108.

Hardwick, Elizabeth. "Reflections on Simone Weil." *Signs* 1, no. 1 (1975): 83–91.

Harris, Sarah. *Hellhole: The Shocking Story of the Inmates and Life in the New York House of Detention for Women*. New York: Dutton, 1967.

Heilbrun, Carolyn G. *Writing a Woman's Life*. New York: Ballantine, 1988.

Helwig, Maggie. *Talking Prophet Blues*. Kingston, ON: Quarry Press, 1989.

Hermans, Cor. "Simone Weil and Franz Kafka: A Forceful Parallel." In *Interbellum Literature: Writing in a Season of Nihilism*, 400–36. Leiden: Brill, 2017.

Hirsch, Edward. *Earthly Measures*. New York: Knopf, 1994.

Holladay, Hilary. *The Power of Adrienne Rich*. New York: Nan A. Talese, 2020.

Hollingsworth, Andrea. "Simone Weil and the Theo-Poetics of Compassion." *Modern Theology* 29, no. 3 (2013): 203–29.

Howe, Fanny. *The Wedding Dress: Meditations on Word and Life*. Berkeley: University of California Press, 2003.

——. *The Winter Sun: Notes on a Vocation*. Minneapolis: Graywolf Press, 2009.

Huk, Romana. "'A single liturgy': Fanny Howe's *The Wedding Dress*." *Christianity and Literature* 58, no. 4 (2009): 657–93.

Hungerford, Amy. *Postmodern Belief: American Literature and Religion since 1960*. Princeton, NJ: Princeton University Press, 2010.

Jackson, Anna. "The Verse Biography: Introduction." *Biography* 39, no. 1 (2016): iii–xvi.

Kafka, Franz. *A Hunger Artist and Other Stories*, trans. Joyce Crick. Oxford: Oxford University Press, 2012.

Karr, Mary. *Sinners Welcome: Poems*. New York: Harper Collins, 2009.

Kauffman, Michael. "Locating the Postsecular." *Religion and Literature* 41, no. 3 (2009): 68–73.

Keyes, Claire. *The Aesthetics of Power: The Poetry of Adrienne Rich*. Athens: University of Georgia Press, 1986.

Klassen, Sarah. *Simone Weil: Songs of Hunger and Love*. Hamilton, ON: Wolsak and Wynn, 1999.

Levinas, Emmanuel. "Simone Weil Against the Bible." *Difficult Freedom: Essays on Judaism*, trans. Seán Hand, 133–41. Baltimore: John Hopkins University Press, 1990.

Little, J. P. *Simone Weil on Colonialism: An Ethic of the Other*. Lanham, MD: Rowman & Littlefield, 2003.

Loades, Ann. "Eucharistic Sacrifice: Simone Weil's Use of a Liturgical Metaphor." *Religion and Literature* 17, no. 2 (1985): 43–54.

Lorde, Audre. "An Open Letter to Mary Daly." 1979. In *Sister Outsider: Essays and Speeches*, 66–71. Trumansburg, NY: Crossing Press, 1984.

MacDonald, Tanis. "Hunger, History, and the Shape of Awkward Questions: Reading Sarah Klassen's *Simone Weil* as a Mennonite Text." *English and Film Studies Faculty Publications* 8 (2010): 87–102.

——. "'What Is Not Self': Jan Zwicky, Simone Weil, and the Resonance of Decreation." *Philosophy and Literature* 39, no. 1 (2015): 211–18.

Martin, Wendy. "From Patriarchy to the Female Principle: A Chronological Reading of Adrienne Rich's Poems." In *Adrienne Rich's Poetry*, ed. Barbara Charlesworth Gelpi and Albert Gelpi, 175–89. New York: Norton, 1975.

McCann, Clark. *The Red Virgin: A Novel Inspired by the Life of Simone Weil*. N.p.: Solesmes Press, 2019.

McClintock, James I. "'Pray Without Ceasing': Annie Dillard Among the Nature Writers." *Cithara* 30, no. 1 (1990): 44–57.

McClure, John A. *Partial Faiths: Postsecular Fiction in the Age of Pynchon and Morrison*. Athens: University of Georgia Press, 2007.

McCorkle, James. *The Still Performance: Writing, Self, and Interconnection in Five Postmodern American Poets*. Charlottesville: University of Virginia Press, 1989.

McCullough, Lissa. *The Religious Philosophy of Simone Weil: An Introduction*. London: Tauris, 2014.

McLellan, David. *Simone Weil: Utopian Pessimist*. New York: Palgrave Macmillan, 1989.

Meltzer, Françoise. "The Hands of Simone Weil." *Critical Inquiry* 27, no. 4 (2001): 611–28.

Mercedes, Anna. *Power for: Feminism and Christ's Self-Giving*. Edinburgh: T&T Clark, 2011.

Merton, Thomas. "The Answer of Minerva: Pacifism and Resistance in Simone Weil." In *Faith and Violence*. Notre Dame, IN: University of Notre Dame Press, 1968.

Miles, Siân. Introduction to *Simone Weil: An Anthology*, by Simone Weil, 1–47. New York: Grove Press, 1986.

Miner, Valerie. "An Interview with Adrienne Rich and Mary Daly." *San Francisco Review of Books* 3, no. 6 (1977): 8–14.

Moi, Toril. "I Came with a Sword." *London Review of Books* 43, no. 1 (2021). https://www.lrb.co.uk/the-paper/v43/n13/toril-moi/i-came-with-a-sword.

Nelson, Deborah. *Tough Enough: Arbus, Arendt, Didion, McCarthy, Sontag, Weil.* Chicago: University of Chicago Press, 2017.

Nevin, Thomas R. *Simone Weil: Portrait of a Self-Exiled Jew.* Chapel Hill: University of North Carolina Press, 1991.

Newton, Adam Zachary. "Versions of Ethics; Or, the SARL of Criticism: Sonority, Arrogation, and Letting-Be." *American Literary History* 13, no. 3 (2001): 606–37.

Noddings, Nel. *The Maternal Factor.* Berkeley: University of California Press, 2010.

Nowak, Mark. "Notes Toward an Anticapitalist Poetics." *Virginia Quarterly Review* 82, no. 2 (2006): 236–40.

Nunez, Sigrid. *The Friend.* New York: Riverhead, 2018.

——. *The Last of Her Kind.* New York: Farrar, Straus, and Giroux, 2006.

——. *Sempre Susan: A Memoir of Susan Sontag.* New York: Riverhead, 2014.

——. *What Are You Going Through.* New York: Riverhead, 2020.

O'Connor, Richard A., and Penny Van Esterik. "De-medicalizing Anorexia." *Anthropology Today* 24, no. 5 (2008): 6–9.

Oliver, Mary. *Thirst: Poems.* Boston: Beacon, 2007.

Olsson, Karen. *The Weil Conjectures: On Math and the Pursuit of the Unknown.* New York: Farrar, Straus and Giroux, 2019.

Pavlić, Ed. *"how we are with each other"*: Adrienne Rich's Radical—Which Is to Say, Relational—Legacy." *Women's Studies* 46, no. 7 (2017): 730–31.

——. *Outward: Adrienne Rich's Expanding Solitudes.* Minneapolis: University of Minnesota Press, 2021.

Perrin, Joseph-Marie, and Jacques Cabaud. *Simone Weil as We Knew Her.* 1953. New York: Routledge, 2003.

Pétrement, Simone. *Simone Weil: A Life,* trans. Raymond Rosenthal. New York: Pantheon, 1976.

Philip, M. NourbeSe. *Bla_k: Essays and Interviews.* 2d ed. Toronto: Book Hug, 2017.

——. *Harriet's Daughter.* London: Women's Press, 1988.

——. *Looking for Livingstone: An Odyssey of Silence.* Toronto: Mercury Press, 1991.

——. "M. NourbeSe Philip Shares 6 Titles That Helped Hone Her Writing Craft." *CBC Books,* April 29, 2020. https://www.cbc.ca/books/m-nourbese-philip-shares-6-titles-that-helped-hone-her-writing-craft-1.5482347.

——. *She Tries Her Tongue, Her Silence Softly Breaks.* Middletown, CT: Wesleyan University Press, 1989.

——. "Sycorax, Spirit, and *Zong!*" Interview with Jordan Scott. *Jacket2,* May 14, 2019. https://jacket2.org/interviews/sycorax-spirit-and-zong.

——. *Zong!* Toronto: Mercury Press, 2008.

Pinder, Kait. "Sheila Watson as a Reader of Simone Weil: Decreation, Affliction, and *Metaxu* in *The Double Hook.*" *University of Toronto Quarterly* 90, no. 4 (2021): 669–90.

Popova, Maria. *The Marginalian.* https://www.themarginalian.org.

Radzins, Inese. "Simone Weil's Social Philosophy: Toward a Post-Colonial Ethic." *New Topics in Feminist Philosophy of Religion,* ed. P. S. Anderson, 69–83. New York: Springer, 2010.

"The Red Virgin: A Poem of Simone Weil." *Publishers Weekly* 240, no. 46 (November 15, 1993): 76.

Rees, Rita Mae. *The Book of Hulga.* Madison: University of Wisconsin Press, 2016.

Rehm, Maggie. "'try telling yourself / you are not accountable': Adrienne Rich as Citizen Poet." *Women's Studies* 46, no. 7 (2017): 684–703.

Rich, Adrienne. *Arts of the Possible: Essays and Conversations.* New York: Norton, 2001.

——. *Blood, Bread, and Poetry: Selected Prose 1979–1985.* New York: Norton, 1986.

——. "Caryatid: A Column." *American Poetry Review,* September/October 1973.

——. *A Change of World.* New Haven, CT: Yale University Press, 1951.

——. *Collected Poems: 1950–2012.* New York: Norton, 2016.

——. *Of Woman Born: Motherhood as Experience and Institution.* 1976. Tenth anniversary ed. New York: Norton, 1986.

——. *On Lies, Secrets, and Silence: Selected Prose 1966–1978.* New York: Norton, 1979.

——. *What Is Found There: Notebooks on Poetry and Politics.* New York: Norton, 1993.

Rickerby, Helen. "Articulating Artemisia: Revisioning the Lives of Women from History in Biographical Poetry." *Biography* 39, no. 1 (2016): 23–33.

Riley, Jeanette E. *Understanding Adrienne Rich.* Columbia: University of South Carolina Press, 2016.

Robertson, Lisa. *Anemones: A Simone Weil Project.* Amsterdam: If I Can't Dance, 2021.

Rose, Gillian. *Judaism and Modernity: Philosophical Essays.* Hoboken, NJ: Blackwell, 1993.

Rossetti, Christina. *Goblin Market.* 1861. Chicago: Blue Sky, 1905.

Rozelle-Stone, A. Rebecca, and Benjamin P. Davis. "Simone Weil." *Stanford Encyclopedia of Philosophy,* ed. Edward N. Zalta. March 10, 2018. https://plato.stanford.edu/archives/fall2020/entries/simone-weil/.

Rozelle-Stone, A. Rebecca, and Lucian Stone. *Simone Weil and Theology.* New York: Bloomsbury T&T Clark, 2013.

Ruddick, Sara. *Maternal Thinking: Toward a Politics of Peace.* Boston: Beacon, 1989.

Satrapi, Marjane. *Persepolis.* New York: Pantheon, 2004.

Saverin, Diana. "The Thoreau of the Suburbs." *Atlantic,* February 5, 2015. https://www.theatlantic.com/culture/archive/2015/02/the-thoreau-of-the-suburbs/385128/

Schnackenberg, Gjertrud. *Supernatural Love: Poems 1976–2000.* Hexam, UK: Bloodaxe, 2001.

Schulz, Susan M. *Memory Cards: Simone Weil Series.* Cambridge, UK: Equipage Press, n.d.

Schwartz, Casey. *Attention: A Love Story*. New York: Pantheon, 2020.

Shalev, Talia. "Adrienne Rich's 'Collaborations': Re-vision as Durational Address." *Women's Studies* 46, no. 7 (2017): 646–62.

Sheridan, Susan. "Adrienne Rich and the Women's Liberation Movement: A Politics of Reception." *Women's Studies* 35 (2006): 17–45.

Shindler, Jack. "Seeing Through the Trees: Annie Dillard as Writer-Activist." *Journal of the Midwest Modern Language Association* 51, no. 2 (2018): 169–82.

Smith, Linda L. *Annie Dillard*. Woodbridge, CT: Twayne, 1991.

Smith, Pamela A. "The Ecotheology of Annie Dillard: A Study in Ambivalence." *CrossCurrents* 45, no. 3 (1995): 341–58.

Smith, Patti. *Devotion*. New Haven, CT: Yale University Press, 2017.

Sontag, Susan. "Simone Weil." *New York Review of Books*, February 1, 1963.

Springsted, Eric O. *Simone Weil for the Twenty-First Century*. Notre Dame, IN: University of Notre Dame Press, 2021.

Stanton, Elizabeth Cady. *The Woman's Bible*. 1985. Boston: Northeastern University Press, 1993.

Stephens, Nathalie. *Touch to Affliction*. Toronto: Coach House, 2006.

Strickland, Stephanie. Interview with Devin Becker. *CTRL+SHIFT*, May 20, 2014. https://ctrl-shift.org/interviews/transcripts/strickland.html.

——. *The Red Virgin: A Poem of Simone Weil*. Madison: University of Wisconsin Press, 1993.

Taylor, Charles. *A Secular Age*. Cambridge, MA: Belknap, 2007.

Teare, Brian. "The Apophatic Pilgrim: Simone Weil and Fanny Howe." In *Quo Anima: Spirituality and Innovation in Contemporary Women's Poetry*, ed. Jennifer Phelps and Elizabeth Robinson, 6–22. Akron, OH: University of Akron Press, 2019.

Templeton, Alice. "Contradictions: Tracking Adrienne Rich's Poetry." *Tulsa Studies in Women's Literature* 12, no. 2 (1993): 333–40.

Tomko, Michael. Review: "The Seasons of the Secular: Revisiting the Secularization Thesis in Nineteenth-Century Studies." *Religion and Literature* 41, no. 3 (2009): 127–37.

Tracy, David. "Simone Weil and the Impossible." In *The Critical Spirit: Theology at the Crossroads of Faith and Culture: Essays in Honour of Gabriel Daly OSA*, ed. Andrew Pierce and Geraldine Smyth, 208–22. Edinburgh: Edinburgh University Press, 2003.

Tronto, Joan. *Moral Boundaries*. New York: Routledge, 1993.

Tuck, Eve, and K. Wayne Yang. "Decolonization Is Not a Metaphor." *Decolonization: Indigeneity, Education & Society* 1, no. 1, (2012): 1–40.

Vetleson, Johan Arne. *A Philosophy of Pain*. 2004, trans. John Irons. London: Reaktion, 2009.

Vetö, Miklos. *The Religious Metaphysics of Simone Weil*, trans. Joan Dargan. Albany, NY: SUNY Press, 1994.

Wallace, Cynthia R. *Of Women Borne: A Literary Ethics of Suffering*. New York: Columbia University Press, 2016.

———. "'passionate/reverence, active love': Levertov and Weil in the Communion of Struggle." In *This Need to Dance/This Need to Kneel: Denise Levertov and the Poetics of Faith*, ed. Michael P. Murphy and Melissa Bradshaw, 127–39. Eugene, OR: Wipf and Stock, 2019.

———. "'Whatever Else We Call It': The Great Price of Secular Sainthood in Mary Gordon's *Pearl*." *Religion and Literature* 48, no. 3 (2016): 1–25.

Weil, Simone. *First and Last Notebooks*, trans. Richard Rees. Oxford: Oxford University Press, 1970.

———. *Gravity and Grace*, trans. Emma Craufurd. 1952. New York: Routledge, 1963.

———. "Human Personality." In *Simone Weil: An Anthology*, ed. Siân Miles, 49–78. New York: Grove, 1986.

———. "The *Iliad*, or the Poem of Force." In *Simone Weil: An Anthology*, ed. Siân Miles, 162–95. New York: Grove, 1986.

———. *The Need for Roots*, trans. Arthur Wills. 1952. New York: Harper Colophon, 1971.

———. *On Science, Necessity, and the Love of God*, trans. Richard Rees. Oxford: Oxford University Press, 1968.

———. *Oppression and Liberty*. Amherst: University of Massachusetts Press, 1973.

———. "Reflections on War." *Politics* 2, no. 2 (1945): 51–55.

———. *Selected Essays, 1934–43*, trans. Richard Rees. 1962. Eugene, OR: Wipf and Stock, 2015.

———. *Seventy Letters*, trans. Richard Rees. 1965. Eugene, OR: Wipf and Stock, 2015.

———. *Simone Weil on Colonialism: An Ethic of the Other*, ed. and trans. J. P. Little. Lanham, MD: Rowman and Littlefield, 2003.

———. *The Simone Weil Reader*, ed. George A. Panichas. New York: McKay, 1977.

———. *Venice Saved*, trans. Silvia Caprioglio Panizza and Philip Wilson. New York: Bloomsbury Academic, 2019.

———. *Waiting for God*, trans. Emma Craufurd. New York: Harper and Row, 1951.

Werner, Craig. *Adrienne Rich: The Poet and Her Critics*. Chicago: American Library Association, 1988.

———. "Trying to Keep Faith: Adrienne Rich's 'Usonian Journals 2000.'" *Virginia Quarterly Review* 82, no. 2 (2006).

White, Jerry. "In Search of Our Roots: Remembering Simone Weil's North American Emergence." *Dalhousie Review* 99, no. 3 (2019): 411–20.

Wilkinson, Jessica. "Experiments in Poetic Biography: Feminist Threads in Contemporary Long Form Poetry." *Biography* 39, no. 1 (2016): 1–22.

Williams, Terry Tempest. *Erosion: Essays of Undoing*. New York: Sarah Crichton, 2019.

Wiman, Christian, ed. *Joy: 100 Poems*. New Haven, CT: Yale University Press, 2017.

———. *Survival Is a Style*. New York: Farrar, Straus and Giroux, 2020.

Wolfteich, Claire. "Attention or Destruction: Simone Weil and the Paradox of the Eucharist." *Journal of Religion* 81, no. 3 (2001): 359–76.

Wright-Bushman, Katy. "A Poetics of Consenting Attention: Simone Wei's Prayer and the Poetry of Denise Levertov." *Christianity and Literature* 62, no. 3 (2013): 369–92.

Yancey, Philip. "A Face Aflame." *Christianity Today*, May 5, 1978.

——. "A Pilgrim's Progress." *Books and Culture*, September/October 1995.

Young, Iris Marion. "Throwing like a Girl: A Phenomenology of Feminine Body Comportment Motility and Spatiality." *Human Studies* 3, no. 2 (1980): 137–56.

Zachhuber, Johannes, and Julia Meszaros. Introduction to *Sacrifice and Modern Thought*, 1–11. Oxford: Oxford University Press, 2013.

Zaretsky, Robert. *The Subversive Simone Weil: A Life in Five Ideas*. Chicago: University of Chicago Press, 2021.

Zwicky, Jan. *Wisdom and Metaphor*. Edmonton: Brush Education, 2014.

LIST OF CREDITS

INDEX

Printed in the USA
CPSIA information can be obtained
at www.ICGtesting.com
JSHW081436020524
62398JS00001B/2

9 780231 214193